SCOTS IN JAMAICA
1655-1855

SCOTS
IN
JAMAICA
1655-1855

By
David Dobson

CLEARFIELD

Copyright © 2011
by David Dobson
All Rights Reserved

Printed for Clearfield Company by
Genealogical Publishing Company
Baltimore, Maryland
2011

ISBN 978-0-8063-5540-5

Made in the United States of America

INTRODUCTION

During the seventeenth and eighteenth centuries Jamaica was a major destination for Scottish emigrants. Initially many of them were transported in chains deported by Oliver Cromwell in the 1650s, or as Covenanters banished as rebels in the 1660s and 1680s, and later as Jacobite prisoners in 1716 and 1746. The first 'voluntary' emigrants landed in Jamaica during 1700 as refugees from the failed Scots colony at Darien on the Isthmus of Panama. Among them were men Highlanders from Argyll such as Colonel John Campbell. He encouraged subsequent immigration from Argyll forming a network of Highland Scots in Jamaica. The success of these men encouraged subsequent emigration from Scotland to Jamaica and elsewhere in the New World, notably the Argyll Colony in North Carolina in the 1730s with which there were links. By the mid eighteenth century it is reckoned that approximately one third of the white population was Scottish or of Scots origin. Jamaica was considered as a place where fortunes could be made and consequently attracted planters, merchants, and professional workers such as physicians, colonial administrators, clergymen, book-keepers, and skilled tradesmen, men such as Archibald McLean from Mull, who worked as a surgeon in New York before settling in Jamaica. Landed families in Scotland, such as the Malcolms of Poltalloch, would invest capital in Jamaica hoping the restore the families' fortunes. While some settled permanently in Jamaica others returned home having acquired wealth, some of which was used to acquire property or to invest in companies engaged in transatlantic-trade, while a number having served out their period of indenture or seeing opportunities in the Thirteen Colonies moved there. After 1783 a number of American Loyalists especially from the South, including Scots, settled in Jamaica as planters, merchants, professionals or tradesmen, for example John Chisholm, a Loyalist merchant from South Carolina, or Alexander Aikman, a printer from Charleston. Jamaica continued to attract Scots immigrants during the late eighteenth and nineteenth centuries – Robert Burns, the National Poet, was about to board ship in Greenock bound for a post of book-keeper on a Jamaican plantation in 1786 when he heard of the great success of his first book of poetry he abandoned his plan to emigrate and become a leading figure in Scottish literature.

This book identifies many of the early Scottish settlers in early Jamaica and is based on sources, both manuscript and published, in Scotland, England, and Jamaica.

David Dobson

Dundee, Scotland, 2011.

SCOTS IN JAMAICA, 1655-1855

REFERENCES

ACA	=	Aberdeen Council Archives
APB	=	Aberdeen Proprinquity Books, ms
AJ	=	Aberdeen Journal, series
AUL	=	Aberdeen University Library
AUPC	=	Annals of the United Presbyterian Church, Edinburgh, 1873
AyrBR	=	Ayr Burgess Roll
BBR	=	Banff Burgess Roll
BL	=	British Library
BM	=	Blackwood's Magazine, series
CCGA	=	Cornwall Chronicle and General Advertiser, series
CFR	=	Cockburn Family Records
CM	=	Caledonian Mercury, series
CMR	=	Canongate Marriage Register
CRP	=	Cheape of Rossie Papers, University of St Andrews
DBR	=	Dundee Burgess Roll
DC	=	Dundee Courier, series
DCA	=	Dundee City Archives
DD	=	Darien Disaster, J. Prebble, London, 1970
DP	=	Darien Papers, J H Burton, Edinburgh, 1849
DPCA	=	Dundee, Perth, and Cupar Advertiser, series
EAR	=	Edinburgh Academy Register
EBR	=	Edinburgh Burgess Roll
EC	=	Edinburgh Courant, series
EEC	=	Edinburgh Evening Courant, series
EMA	=	Emigrant Ministers to America
EMG	=	Edinburgh Medical Graduates
EMR	=	Edinburgh Marriage Register
ETR	=	Edinburgh Tolbooth Records
EUL	=	Edinburgh University Library
F	=	Fastii Ecclesiae Scoticanae
FA	=	Fife Advertiser, series
FH	=	Fife Herald, series
FJ	=	Fife Journal, series
FPA	=	Fulham Papers, American
GA	=	Glasgow Archives
GBR	=	Glasgow Burgess Roll
GCr	=	Glasgow Courier, series
GM	=	Glasgow Mercury, series
GM.NS	=	Gentleman's Magazine, New Series

SCOTS IN JAMAICA, 1655-1855

GrAd	=	Greenock Advertiser, series
GSP	=	Glasgow Sunday Post, series
HSP	=	Historical Society of Pennsylvania
IBR	=	Inveraray Burgess Roll
IJ	=	Inverness Journal, series
IRO	=	Island Record Office, Jamaica
JC	=	Jamaica Courant, series
JCTP	=	Journal of the Committee for Trade and the Plantations
JRG	=	Jamaica Royal Gazette, series
KCA	=	King's College, Aberdeen
LJ	=	Letters and Journals, 1663-1887, J G Dunlop, London, 1953
MAGU	=	Matriculation Albums, Glasgow University
MCA	=	Marischal College, Aberdeen
MI	=	Monumental Inscription
MIBWI	=	Monumental Inscriptions, British West Indies
NA	=	National Archives, Kew
NAS	=	National Archives of Scotland, Edinburgh
NLJ	=	National Library of Jamaica
NLS	=	National Library of Scotland
NNQ	=	Northern Notes and Queries, series
PA	=	Perth Advertiser, series
Rawl.	=	Rawlinson Manuscripts
REA	=	Register of Edinburgh Apprentices
RGD	=	Registrar General's Department
RPCS	=	Register of the Privy Council of Scotland
S	=	The Scotsman, series
SG	=	Scottish Guardian, series
SM	=	Scots Magazine, series
SNQ	=	Scottish Notes and Queries, series
SP	=	The Scots Peerage
SPAWI	=	State Papers, America and the West Indies, series
W	=	Witness, series

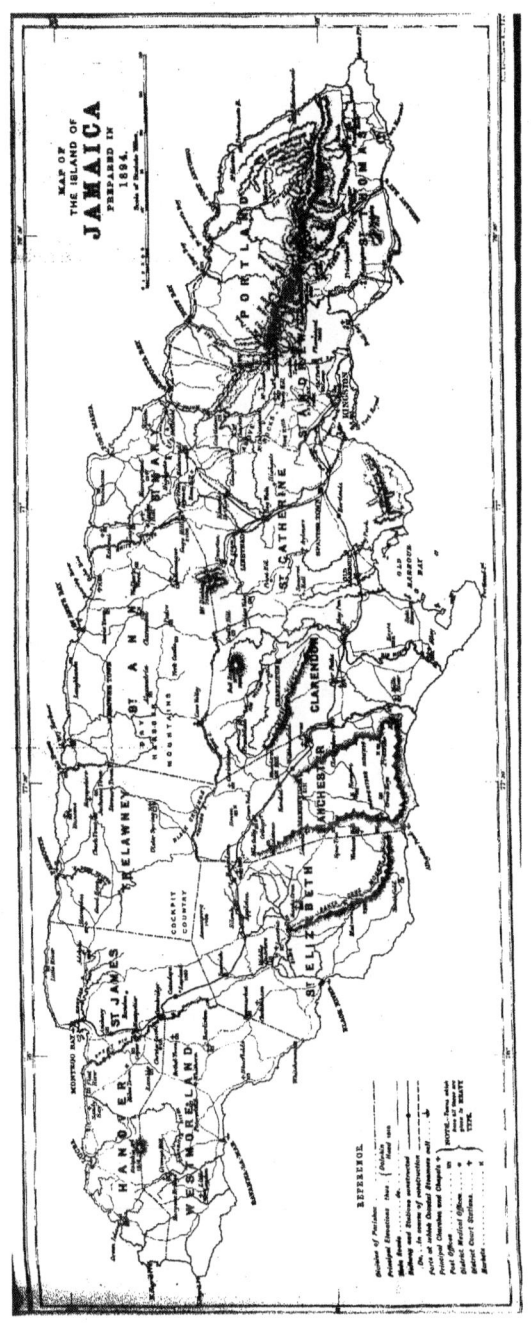

SCOTS IN JAMAICA, 1655-1855

ABERCROMBIE, JOHN, at Montego Bay, 6 Nov1798. [NAS.SC20.33.13]
ABERCROMBIE, WILLIAM, to Jamaica, 1789. [NAS.GD171.362]
ABERDEEN, CHARLES, born 1753, a clerk, emigrated via London to Jamaica on the Reward in Dec 1773. [NA.T47.9/11]
ABERNETHY, GEORGE, in Aberdeen and in Jamaica, 1751. [NAS.RD4.177.309]
ABERNETHY, JAMES, a ships carpenter in Jamaica, husband of Elizabeth Power, 1778. [NAS.CS16.1.173/126]
ABERNETHIE, MARGARET, daughter of the late Dr Abernethie, a physician in Jamaica, married Colquhoun Grant, from Jamaica, in London on 28 Jan 1798. [SM.60.148][GM.68.168]
ABERNETHY, PATRICK, died in Jamaica, 1791. [GM.61.186]
ADAM, JOHN, a rebel from Ormidale, Argyll, who was transported from Leith to Jamaica on 7 Aug 1685. [RPCS.XI.329]
ADAM, PATRICK, from Arbroath, Angus, in Kingston, Jamaica, testament, 16 June 1761. [NAS.CC8.8.118]
ADAMS, Mr., from Glasgow aboard the Betsy and Brothers bound for Jamaica, arrived in Kingston in May 1793. [JRG:25.5.1794]
ADAMSON, ALEXANDER, in Jamaica, 1780. [NAS.CS16.1.179]
ADAMSON, DAVID, born 1661, emigrated via London as an indentured servant aboard the Providence in Mar 1684. [CLRO/AIA]
ADAMSON, GEORGE, born 1825, second son of Mr Adamson, an accountant, died on Golden Grove Estate, Jamaica, on 29 Sep 1850. [AJ#5364]
ADAMSON, ROBERT KEY, youngest son of Reverend Adamson in Cupar, Fife, died in Kingston, Jamaica, on 28 Dec 1827. [AJ#4180]
ADDISON, Rev. George Augus, Manchester, married Anna, 2nd dau of the late Charles Farquharson, Clarendon, Jamaica, 4 Feb 1851. [GM.NS35.545]
ADISON, ..., from Leith to Jamaica on the Roselle, arrived in Kingston in Apr 1793. [JRG:27.4.1793]
AFFLECK, JAMES, born 1739, a carpenter who emigrated via London to Jamaica on the Dawes in Nov 1774. [NA.T47.9/11]
AFFLECK, JAMES MCVICAR, a barrister in Jamaica, 1803, 1805. [NAS.RD4.273.457; CS313.888]
AFFLECK, Miss, dau of the late Dr Affleck, sister of J. Affleck barrister in Spanish Town, Jamaica, died there 8 Nov 1802. [GM.73.83]
AGNEW, ANDREW, a minister who settled in Jamaica in 1706, later moved to Virginia, [EMA#10]
AGNEW, FRANCIS, probate 1743, Jamaica. [RGO/Spanish Town, liber 24]
AGNEW, WILLIAM, probate 1743, Jamaica.

SCOTS IN JAMAICA, 1655-1855

AIKEN, JOHN, a wright in Carncarron Estate, Jamaica, 1799, son of John Aiken at Bridge of Johnstone, Renfrewshire. [NAS.CS18.712.13]

AIKIN, ALEXANDER, born 1755, died in Kingston, Jamaica, in 1838. [St Andrew's MI, Jamaica]

AIKIN, ROGER, died 1790 in Jamaica. [GM.60.1053]

AIKMAN, ALEXANDER, born 23 June 1755 in Bo'ness, 2nd son of Andrew Aikman and Anne Hunter, to S.C. in 1771, a Loyalist, to Jamaica 1778, printer and publisher, died Prospect Pen, St Andrews, Jamaica, on 6 July 1838. [GM.NS10.556]

AIKMAN, ALEXANDER, jr, HM Printer in Jamaica, md Charlotte, 2nd dau of Robert Cory, attorney in Great Yarmouth, at Mount Hybla, Jamaica, 7 Apr 1805. [GM.75.582]

AIKMAN, LOUISA SUSANNA, born Charleston, SC, 2ND dau of Alexander Aikman, late printer in Jamaica, died West Cowes, 29 Nov 1831. [GM.101.571]

AIKMAN, WILLIAM, died in Jamaica 1784, brother of Reverend John Aikman, papers, 1790-1834. [NAS.GD1.1429.3.3]; probate 1785 PCC.

AIRD, GEORGE, a gentleman in Westmoreland, inventory, 1802, Jamaica. [RGD.1B.11.3.96/193]

AIRD, JAMES, in Jamaica, probate 1798, PCC

AIRD, WILLIAM, born 1783, died on 10 Jan 1823. [Kingston MI, Jamaica]

AITCHISON, PETER, a physician and surgeon in St Elizabeth's, Jamaica, died 1752, testament, 3 Apr 1758. [NAS.CC8.8.117]

AITKEN, DAVID, born 1827, son of William Aitken, a smith, and Margaret Anderson in Carnwath, died in Goodwell, Jamaica, 8 Mar 1847. [Carnwath MI]

AITKEN, JAMES, a millwright, eldest son of Archibald Aitken in the Canongate, Edinburgh, died at Mount Lebanus, St Thomas in the East, Jamaica, on 8 Nov 1799. [AJ#2719]

AITKEN, JOHN, late of Jamaica, now in Aberdeen, 1790. [NAS.CS228.A.6.9.1]

AITKEN, PETER, a mariner in St Ann's, Middlesex County, Jamaica, and his wife Ann Elizabeth, a conveyance, 1787. [NAS.B56.16.132]

AITKEN, ROBERT, a surgeon, second son of Robert Aitken a writer in Cupar, Fife, died in Jamaica on 12 Aug 1841. [FJ: 14.10.1841]

AITKEN, WALTER, born 1809, youngest son of Robert Aitken, 107 Canongate, Edinburgh, died in Kingston, Jamaica, on 20 Apr 1825. [EEC:17752]

AITKENHEAD, ELIZABETH, born 1760, emigrated via London to Jamaica on the Fanny in Dec 1773. [NA.T47.9/11]

AITKENHEAD, WILLIAM, in St Thomas in the Vale, Jamaica, bond, 1752, testament, 30 June 1768. [NAS.RD178/1.582; CC8.8.121]

ALEXANDER, DUNCAN, a rebel from Argyll, who was transported from Leith to Jamaica on 7 Aug 1685. [RPCS.XI.329]

SCOTS IN JAMAICA, 1655-1855

ALEXANDER, ELIZABETH, in Aberdeen, relict of Patrick Alexander sometime in Jamaica, testament, 2 Aug 1821, Comm. Aberdeen. [NAS]
ALEXANDER, GEORGE BOYLE, born in Dalry on 4 Aug 1828, graduated MA from Glasgow University in 1853, a United Presbyterian minister at Ebenezer, Jamaica, died in Glasgow on 15 Mar 1895. [GG#10]
ALEXANDER, HUGH, born 1777, eldest son of John Alexander a merchant in Glasgow, died at Eden Hill, St Mary's, Jamaica, in 1802. [AJ#2867][GkAd#100]
ALEXANDER, QUENTIN, a planter in Portland, Jamaica, dead by 1803. [NAS.RD3.302.346]
ALEXANDER, ROBERT, a mason in St Mary's, Jamaica, a deed, 1803. [NAS.RD3.302.346]
ALEXANDER, ROBERT FULTON, in Jamaica, 1811. [NAS.CS42.4.2]
ALEXANDER, THOMAS, a mariner in Jamaica, 1803. [NAS.RD3.302.346]
ALLAN, ALEXANDER, at Montego Bay, died Sep1791, brother of William Alan a skipper in Greenock. [NAS.CS26/906.18][GM.60.1148]
ALLAN, CATHERINE, daughter of George Allan a banker in Kingston, Jamaica, died in St Andrews, Fife, on 5 June 1841. [FH]
ALLAN, DAVID, a jobber, St James, Jamaica, 1774. [BL.Add.MS22676/8]
ALLAN, DAVID, mason and bricklayer in St Catherine's, Jamaica, will, 1783. [NAS.RD2.235/2.215]
ALLAN, GEORGE, a banker in Kingston, Jamaica, died before 5 June 1841. [St Andrews Cathedral, Fife, MI]
ALLAN, JOHN, a Covenanter in Cumnock, Ayrshire, who was transported from Leith to Jamaica on 7 Aug 1685. [RPCS.XI.330]
ALLAN, JOHN, an attorney at law in Kingston, Jamaica, 25 Nov 1770. [NAS.RS10.315.510]
ALLAN, ..., from Glasgow aboard the Mary bound for Jamaica, arrived in Kingston in May 1793. [JRG:18.5.1793]
ALLAN, Mrs, of Orangehill, died in Jamaica in 1804. [AJ#2980]
ALLARDYCE, ALEXANDER, a merchant in Kingston, 1780, was granted Dunottar in 1782, late of Jamaica, 1788. [NAS.RGS.121.149; RS7.11].
ALLARDYCE, JAMES, son of James Allardyce the Customs Collector in Aberdeen, died in Jamaica on 10 Nov 1808.[NAS.GD171.844] [EA#4706][SM#71.237]
ALSTON, Major JAMES, Deputy Quartermaster General of Jamaica, 1795. [NAS.GD1.394.37]
ALSTON, JAMES, in Spanish Town, Jamaica, letters, 1801. [NAS.GD1.394.51/52/53/54]
ALVES, ALEXANDER, 2nd son of Dr John Alves in Inverness, died in Jamaica, 1797. [GM.67.1797]

SCOTS IN JAMAICA, 1655-1855

ALVES, JOHN, from Edinburgh, died in Kingston, Jamaica, on 14 Dec 1825. [FH#206][EEC#17853]

ALVES, THOMAS, in Spanish Town, 1786, 1789; at Montego Bay, St James, Jamaica, 1792. [NAS.GD23.6.441; RD3.290.92; RS38.400]

AMOS, JAMES, in Jamaica, later in Moffat, Dumfries-shire, testament, 26 Feb 1828. [NAS.SC15.41.4.485]

ANDERSON, ADAM, son of Adam Anderson MD in Jamaica, educated at King's College, Aberdeen, 1794. [KCA.2.377]

ANDERSON, ADAM, Jamaica, married Ann, eldest daughter of the late James Fraser, in Greenock on 17 Jan 1815. [GrAd: 20.1.1815]

ANDERSON, ALEXANDER, of Udall, late of Hanover, Jamaica, 1775; 1814. [NAS.RD38.13.375; RS38.223]

ANDERSON, CHARLES, in Jamaica, died Jan 1715, testament, 27 Oct 1815, Comm. Edinburgh, [NAS.CC8.8.141/407; SC70.1.14]

ANDERSON, CHARLES, in Riverhead, Jamaica, died 19 May 1853 in Edinburgh, inventory, 1853. [NAS.SC70.1.53; E3489]

ANDERSON, DUNCAN, born 7 May 1751, in Stenton, East Lothian, embarked in Jamaica for New York on the Sally of New York, master Robert Latimer, 'never heard of again'. [Montego Bay MI, Jamaica]

ANDERSON, JAMES, a laborer from Lanarkshire, an indentured servant who was shipped from London to Jamaica in Nov 1684. [CLRO/AIA]

ANDERSON, Dr JAMES, at Marischal College, Aberdeen, 1737, in Kingston, Jamaica, May 1744; graduated MD 1755 and M.Corp.S 1761 from Marischal College. [Caribbeana.6.23][AUL]

ANDERSON, JAMES, married Fanny Taylor Vick, daughter of Thomas Dick of St Thomas in the East, Jamaica, in Kingston, Jamaica, on 2 Aug 1851. [W#1261]

ANDERSON, JOHN, St James, Jamaica, 1774. [BL.Add.MS22676/8]

ANDERSON, JOHN, a surgeon in Jamaica, dead by 1783. [NAS.C17.1.2/245]

ANDERSON, Dr PATRICK, born 1806 in Fife, died in Trelawney, Jamaica, on 1 Aug 1846. [Falmouth MI, Jamaica]

ANDERSON, REBECCA, in St James, Jamaica, 1774. [BL.Add.MS22676/8]

ANDERSON, ROBERT, a surgeon in Jamaica, later in Newmilns, Ayrshire, husband of Margaret Arrot, testament, 1768, Comm. Glasgow. [NAS]

ANDERSON, ROBERT, a jobber, St James, Jamaica, 1774. [BL.Add.MS22676/8]

ANDERSON, ROBERT, born in Tranent, East Lothian, 1747, emigrated to Jamaica in May 1778, died at Flower Hill, St James, Jamaica, 9 Aug 1796. [Montego Bay MI, Jamaica]

ANDERSON, ROBERT, born 1818, son of John Anderson and Janet Lawson, died in Colleygrove, St Thomas in the East, Jamaica, 14 Apr 1852. [Abernethy, Strathspey, MI]

SCOTS IN JAMAICA, 1655-1855

ANDERSON, ROBERT BRUNTON, MD, born 1820, died in Jamaica, 5 Dec 1842. [Dean MI, Edinburgh]
ANDERSON, Mrs SUSANNAH, wife of Thomas Anderson, died in Vere, Jamaica, Nov 1801. [GM.72.181]
ANDERSON, THOMAS, born 1738, son of John Anderson and Jean Hastie, settled in Westmoreland, Jamaica, died 12 Feb 1796. [Kirkliston MI]
ANDERSON, WILLIAM, a merchant in Jamaica, a decreet, 1774. [NAS.CS16.1]
ANDERSON, WILLIAM, a Presbyterian missionary in Jamaica during the 1840s. [NLS.Melville ms2981/2]
ANDERSON, ..., son of Izett W. Anderson, MD, was born in Kingston, Jamaica, 10 Sep 1873. [EC#27790]
ANDREWS, JOHN, son of John Andrews a merchant in Edinburgh, died in Jamaica, 1817. [S.I.31]
ANGUS, THOMAS MCQUISTIN, in Jamaica, died 25 Aug 1825, inventory, 1831, Comm. Edinburgh. [NAS.SC70.1.44; C349]
ANGUS, WILLIAM, born 10 Feb 1771, son of William Angus and Elspeth Mortimer in Aberdeen, educated at King's College, Aberdeen, 1784-1788, a surgeon in Jamaica. [KCA.2.362]
ANGUS, WILLIAM JOHN, son of William Angus at Montego Bay, St James, Jamaica, educated at King's College, Aberdeen, 1799-1803, graduated MA. [KCA.2.385]
ANGUS, WILLIAM, at Montego Bay, St James, Jamaica, son of Alexander Angus a book-seller in Aberdeen, died off Port Antonio in 1807.[AJ#3112][DPCA#267]
ARBUCKLE, GEORGE, probate, 1697, Jamaica. [RGO/Spanish Town, liber 9]
ARBUCKLE, WILLIAM, probate, 1729, Jamaica. [RGO/SpanishTown, liber 18]
ARBUCKLE, WILLIAM, probate, 1738, Jamaica. [RGO/SpanishTown, liber 22]
ARCHER, Dr GEORGE, from Jamaica, was educated at Edinburgh University and graduated MD from King's College, Aberdeen, on 23 Sep. 1786. [KCA#136]
ARCHER, JAMES, second son of George Archer a physician in Jamaica, at Glasgow University, 1812. [MAGU#266]
ARCHER, Mrs MARY, wife of Dr James King Archer, third daughter of Alexander Edgar late of Wedderly, Jamaica, died at Springmount, Jamaica, on 9 Oct 1831. [EEC#18746]
ARCHER, MARY, from Ascog, Bute, died 2 Feb 1853 in Jamaica, inventory, 1857. [NAS.SC70.1.93; G407]
ARIS, DOUGLAS, died at Montego Bay 12 Apr 1825, inventory, 1827, Comm. Edinburgh. [NAS]
ARMOUR, JAMES, born 1821, a laborer, arrived at Bluefields, Westmoreland, on 23 Jan 1841 aboard the William Pirie, from Stranraer. [NA.CO.140/33]

SCOTS IN JAMAICA, 1655-1855

ARMOUR. JOHN, eldest son of John Armour a merchant in Edinburgh, died at Heywood Hall, St Mary's, Jamaica, 16 Mar 1805. [GM.75.677]
ARMOUR, WILLIAM, an engineer in Jamaica, inventory, 1894. [NAS.SC70.1.326]
ARMSTRONG, JAMES, born 1821, a carpenter, arrived at Bluefields, Westmoreland, on 23 Jan 1841 aboard the William Pirie, from Stranraer. [NA.CO.140/33]
ARMSTRONG, JOHN, in Jamaica, probate 1752 PCC.
ARMSTRONG, SARAH, born 1822, arrived at Bluefields, Westmoreland, on 23 Jan 1841 aboard the William Pirie, from Stranraer. [NA.CO.140/33]
ARMSTRONG, THOMAS, youngest son of William Armstrong in Niddry Street, Edinburgh, died in St Ann's, Jamaica, on 14 Apr 1821. [EEC#172421]
ARMSTRONG, WILLIAM, son of William Armstrong in Niddry Street, Edinburgh, died at Winders Hill, Jamaica, on 14 Mar 1821. [S.5.226]
ARNOT, JAMES, cabin passenger from Greenock to Jamaica aboard the Mary of Glasgow in Nov 1773. [NAS.CE60]
ARRIS, DOUGLAS, at Montego Bay, 18 Apr 1827. [NAS.CC8.8.151/243]
ARTHUR, JAMES, from Glasgow, died in St Mary's, Jamaica, on 6 Mar 1819. [S.3.122]
ARTHUR, MARY, born during 1806 in Bonhill, Dunbartonshire, daughter of Robert Arthur and Marion Turnbull, died in Jamaica in 1853. [Bonhill MI]
AUCHINLECK, THOMAS, probate, 1708, Jamaica. [RGO/SpanishTown,12/116]
AUCHTERLONY, JOHN, a silk dyer in Kingston, Jamaica, 10 Jan 1827. [NAS.RS27.29.243]
AULD, Rev. J. M., from Glasgow, died in Kingston, Jamaica, 8 Feb 1851. [W#1202]
AUSTIN, ADAM, a witness in Kingston, Jamaica, 1783. [NAS.RD2.237.825]
AYER, THOMAS, born 1826, a labourer, arrived at Bluefields, Westmoreland, on 23 Jan 1841 aboard the William Pirie, from Stranraer. [NA.CO.140/33]
AYTON, PATRICK, a merchant in Kingston, Jamaica, second son of William Ayton, WS, a deed, 1789. [NAS.RD4.250.160]
AYTON, ..., from Kingston, Jamaica,aboard the Roselle bound for Leith in June 1793. [JRG:29.6.1793]
BAILLIE, GRANT, born 1812, 2nd son of John Baillie in Roehampton, Jamaica, died on Carawina Estate, Westmoreland, Jamaica, 18 Mar 1854.[EEC#22572]
BAILLIE, JAMES, a merchant in Jamaica, son of Robert Baillie a merchant in Edinburgh, letters, 1740-1758. [In 1753 he moved to the Begbie Plantation on the Newport River, Georgia] [NAS.GD1.1155.64/65]
BAILLIE, JAMES, born 1724, died at Morant Bay, Jamaica, on 3 Oct 1785. [Morant Bay MI]

SCOTS IN JAMAICA, 1655-1855

BAILLIE, JAMES, a surveyor, died in Clarendon, Jamaica, 12 Oct 1789. [GM.60.179]

BAILLIE, JOHN, surgeon of the Hope, died in Jamaica during Sep 1700. [DD#325]

BAILLIE, ROBERT, a merchant in Jamaica, late planter in Georgia, son of George Baillie of Hardington, 1750. [NAS.GD1.1155.65]

BAILLIE, SAMUEL CRUICKSHANK, born 1743, died at Morant Bay, Jamaica, in 1790. [Morant Bay MI][GM.60.476]

BAILLIE, WILLIAM, born 1712, '50 years in Jamaica', died at Morant Bay, Jamaica, on 19 Jan 1786. [Morant Bay MI]

BAIN, ALEXANDER, died at Wynter's Prospect Pen, Jamaica, in 1798. [AJ#2649]

BAIN, DONALD, born Thurso, Caithness, in 1774, a surgeon, died in St Jago Savanna, Clarendon, Jamaica, June 1801. [GM.72.83]

BAIN, ROBERT, a planter, Clarendon, Jamaica, a witness, 1776. [NAS.RD2.220.656]

BAIRD, ADAM, died in Jamaica, 1790. [GM.60.1214]

BAIRD, GEORGE, a merchant in Kingston, Jamaica, 1760, 1778.[AUL.ms3175/668/3/bundle 4]

BAIRD, JAMES, a Covenanter in Calderwood, Lanarkshire, transported from Leith to Jamaica on 7 Aug 1685. [RPCS.XI.330]

BAIRD, JOHN, a witness in Kingston, Jamaica, 1783. [NAS.RD4.237.901]

BAIRD, ROBERT, first son of Robert Baird a lawyer in Glasgow, matriculated at Glasgow University in 1853, Judge of the District of Port Antonio, Jamaica, died in Kingston, Jamaica, on 11 Oct 1888. [MAGU]

BAIRNSFATHER, WILLIAM, a baker, died in Jamaica before 1791, son of Peter Bairnsfather a tenant farmer in Harperdean, testament, 20 Feb 1794. [NAS.GD1.570.44; CC8.8.129]

BALCANQUELL, ROBERT GEORGE, a planter in St John's, Middlesex, Jamaica, son of James Balcanquell of Balcanquell, Fife, a deed, 1793. [NAS.RD4.254.934]

BALDERSTON, THOMAS, fourth son of the late David Balderston of HM Customs at Port Glasgow, died in Jamaica on 20 Nov 1821. [GrAd: 27.6.1822]

BALDIE, ..., cabin passenger from Greenock to Jamaica aboard the Mary of Glasgow in Nov 1773. [NAS.CE60]

BALDIE, JOHN, in Jamaica, dead by 1798. [NAS.SC20.33.13]

BALFOUR, CATHERINE, daughter of Charles Balfour in Jamaica, and wife of Dr John Tennant in Virginia, a deed, 1805. [NAS.RD3.312.185]

BALFOUR, CHARLES, late in Jamaica, died at Cardona, 29 Oct 1786. [GM.IX.462][NAS.RD2.235/2.215]

BALFOUR, JOHN, a merchant at Black River, Jamaica, testament, 9 Nov 1750. [NAS.CC8.8.113]

SCOTS IN JAMAICA, 1655-1855

BALFOUR, JOHN, a merchant in Glasgow, husband of Janet Corbett, late of Jamaica, was granted Kenmuir, 2 June 1813; May 1814. [NAS.RGS.148.55] [NAS.CS17.1.34/401]

BALFOUR, WILLIAM, at Montego Bay, St James's, Jamaica, 1788, 1792; died there on 20 Dec 1820. [NAS.RS38.101/224][S.5.225]

BALFOUR, WILLIAM, in Martha Brae, Jamaica, died 9 Jan 1804. [CM#121875]

BALLANTYNE, DAVID, born 1753, son of David Ballantyne and Elisabeth Mitchell, died in Kingston, Jamaica, on 4 June 1777. [Burntisland, Fife, MI]

BALLANTYNE, PATRICK, a merchant in Kingston, Jamaica, a witness, 1816; co-owner of the <u>Mercury of Glasgow</u>, 1795. [NAS.RD5.97.266; CE60.11.4/21]

BALLANTYNE, JAMES, late a writer in Edinburgh, then in Jamaica, 1783. [NAS.CS17.1.2/256]

BALLENTINE, ..., from Greenock to Jamaica on the <u>Bell</u>, arrived in Kingston in Jan 1793. [JRG:19.1.1793]

BALLOCH, JOHN, book-keeper to Stirling, Gordon and Company in Jamaica, died 1835, inventory, 1844, Comm. Edinburgh. [NAS.SC70.1.66; F118]

BARCLAY, ALEXANDER, a witness in Hanover, Jamaica, 1739. [seeRGD.Jamaica.LOS.22/100]

BARCLAY, ALEXANDER, born 1784 son of Charles Barclay in Knockleith, Auchterless, Aberdeenshire, Assemblyman for St Thomas in the East, Jamaica, Receiver General of Jamaica, died at Chariton Cottage, St Andrew's, Jamaica, on 30 Oct 1864. [St Andrew's, Jamaica, MI][GM.NS2/18.114]

BARCLAY, ALEXANDER, born 1829, Collector of Customs, died in Falmouth, Jamaica, on 29 Nov 1874. [Falmouth, Jamaica, MI]

BARCLAY, BATHIA, 2nd dau of Charles Barclay in Inchbroom, Moray, married Thomas McNeel, Custos of Westmoreland, Jamaica, 25 Jan 1842. [GM.NS17.429]

BARCLAY, CHARLES, died in Jamaica 4 Aug 1818. [AJ#3700]

BARCLAY, CHARLES, born 1785, Receiver General of Jamaica, died in 1864. [AJ:7 Dec 1864]

BARCLAY, DAVID, in Jamaica, probate 1750, PCC.

BARCLAY, DUNCAN, died in Jamaica, 1735. [NAS.GD170.3089]

BARCLAY, GEORGE, from Cairnes, Peterhead, settled in Jamaica pre-1727. [AUL.ms1160.5.2/11]

BARCLAY, GEORGE, a burgess and guilds-brother of Aberdeen, a merchant in Jamaica, 1741. [NAS.GD67.93]

BARCLAY, HENRY, from Dunbar, died at the Hermitage, Jamaica, 3 May 1860. [DC#23505]

SCOTS IN JAMAICA, 1655-1855

BARCLAY, JAMES, emigrated in 1727, a book-keeper in Kingston, Jamaica, 1729, a merchant there in 1748, by 1762 he was Auditor Receiver General there. [AUL.ms1160/5,2,3] [NAS.RD3.211/1.521; GD67.34.35.37]
BARCLAY, JAMES, a planter in St Andrew's, Jamaica, 1754. [NA.CO137/28/191]
BARCLAY, JAMES, in Kingston, Jamaica, 1750, pro 1765 PCC [NAS.RD3.211.521]
BARCLAY, JAMES, born 1694, Chief Judge of the Court of Common Pleas in Westmoreland, Jamaica, died 22 Aug 1764. [Llandilo MI, Jamaica]
BARCLAY, or TURNBULL, ROBINA, in Jamaica, 21 Aug1810. [NAS.RS27.2.95]
BARDNER, ELIZABETH, second daughter of John Bardner a warehouseman in Dunfermline, Fife, married Sergeant Thomas Hart an inspector of musketry, at Craigton, Jamaica, on 8 Jan 1869. [FA]
BARKER, JOHN, a merchant in Kingston, Jamaica, 1778.[NAS.CS16.1.173/159]
BARR, JOHN RITCHIE, in Jamaica, 1813. [NAS.RS54.PR146/75]
BATHGATE, WILLIAM, a writer in Edinburgh, indented with John McLeod a merchant in Edinburgh, to serve in Jamaica or another of His Majesty's Plantations for 4 years, on 13 Sep 1736. [NAS.RH9.17.316]
BAYNE, Rev. JAMES, of Mount Zion Church, Jamaica, married Agnes, youngest daughter of Alexander Grant of Spot Valley Estate, on 31 Jan 1878. [EC#29151]
BEAN, JAMES, in Jamaica, probate 1767 PCC.
BEAN, THOMAS, a witness in Kingston, Jamaica, 1791. [NAS.RD2.252.108]
BEATTIE, ALEXANDER, born 1815, with Christina, born 1817, and John, born 1840, emigrated from Aberdeen aboard the Rob Roy bound for Jamaica, arrived at Kingston on 11 May 1841. [NA.CO140/33]
BEGBIE, JAMES, a shipbuilder in Charleston, South Carolina, a Loyalist who settled in Kingston, Jamaica, by 1783. [NA.AO12.51.184]
BEGG, JOHN, Jamaica, graduated MD at Edinburgh University, 1793. [EMG#24]
BELL. ALEXANDER, in Jamaica, was admitted as a burgess and guilds-brother of Ayr, 27 July 1776. [AyrBR]
BELL, Dr ALLAN, second son of Hugh Bell, Half Merkland, Dalrymple, died in Jamaica, 18 June 1845. [ASG#14/1424]
BELL, ELIZABETH, from Glasgow, married John Campbell at Lanethall, Jamaica, 1790. [GM.60.1213]
BELL, FRANCIS, of Carruthers, eldest son of John Bell a writer in Lockerbie, Dumfries-shire, died in Falmouth, Jamaica, on 27 Jan 1823. [DPCA#1081]
BELL, JAMES, MD, from Kelso, died in Bluecastle, Westmoreland, Jamaica, on 15 Jan 1801. [GM.71.372]
BELL, JAMES, born 1776, son of James Bell and Mary Haugh in Dalton, Dumfries-shire, died at Morant Bay, Jamaica, on 10 Nov 1814. [Dalton MI]
BELL, JOHN, from Glasgow, in Jamaica, testament, 30 Dec 1773. [NAS.CC8.8.122]

SCOTS IN JAMAICA, 1655-1855

BELL, JOHN, in Woodstock, Jamaica, a bond, 1786. [NAS.RD2.244/2.530]
BELL, JOHN, only son of James Bell in Jamaica, matriculated at Glasgow University in 1817. [MAGU]
BELL, JOHN, of St Mary's, Jamaica, died in Edinburgh, 8 Sep 1843, inventory, 1844, Comm. Edinburgh. [NAS.SC70.1.65; E75]
BELL, MARGARET, born 1815, with Margaret born 1832, and Helen born 1834, arrived at Bluefields, Westmoreland, on 23 Jan 1841 aboard the William Pirie, from Stranraer. [NA.CO.140/33]
BELL, SAMUEL, in Westmoreland, Cornwall, Jamaica, a deed, 1794. [NAS.RD2.272.38]
BENNET, ISAAC, son of Robert Bennet in Fort George, died in Jamaica during 1800. [AJ#2720]
BENNETT, MAXWELL, a writer from Edinburgh, in Jamaica, 1780. [NAS.CS16.1.179]
BERRY, A.G., son of William Berry in Jamaica, married Catherine, youngest daughter of the late James Peter in Gourock, at Glasgow, 11 July 1861.
BERRY, JAMES, a merchant from Jamaica, died in Glasgow, testament, 22 Aug 1817. [NAS.CC9.9.83]
BETHUNE, Reverend JOSEPH, a missionary, from Leith to Jamaica in 1800, died in Kingston, Jamaica, on 5 June 1800. [AJ#2750][F.7.669][GM.70.905]
BIGGAR, JAMES, born 1779 in Dumfries son of John Biggar in Fourmerkland, a merchant who died in Greenwich, Kingston, Jamaica, on 25 June 1804. [Kingston MI][AJ#2957]
BIGGAR, JAMES, born 1783, died 17 Feb 1825. [Kingston, Jamaica, MI]
BIGGAR, JOHN, died 13 July 1829. [Kingston, Jamaica, MI]
BIGGS, ADAM, late in Jamaica, died in Glasgow on 21 June 1798. [AJ#2633]
BINNIE, JOHN, eldest son of John Binnie a flesher in Edinburgh, died in Clarendon, Kingston, Jamaica, on 7 Dec 1830. [FH#467]
BISHOP, Mr., from Greenock aboard the Friends, Captain Dunlop, bound for Jamaica, arrived there in Oct 1794. [JRG:25.10.1794]
BISSETT, JOSEPH, in Jamaica, 1804. [NAS.CS228.R.7.4.2]
BISSLAND, JOHN, from Port Glasgow, died in Kingston, Jamaica, 10 Oct 1817, a passenger on the Surprise of Glasgow which was wrecked on the coast of Mogadore. [S.I.49][GrAd: 26.12.1817]
BIZZET, WILLIAM W., second son of Alexander Bizzet a planter in Jamaica, matriculated at Glasgow University in 1847. [MAGU]
BLACK, GEORGE, born 1789, a surgeon in the Royal Navy, son of Alexander Black in Pitsligo, died in Port Royal, Jamaica, on 15 Oct 1825. [AJ#4073]
BLACK, JAMES, a surgeon in Jamaica, later in Glasgow before 1835. [GA.O623.T-MJ.386/2]

SCOTS IN JAMAICA, 1655-1855

BLACK, JOHN, a merchant in Falmouth, Trelawney, Jamaica, a witness, 1797; in Jamaica, sasine, 1818; testament, 26 Aug 1826. [NAS.RD3.278.840; RS10.2991; CC8.8.151/118; SC70.1.35]

BLACK, MARY ANN, born 1819, a laborer, arrived at Bluefields, Westmoreland, on 23 Jan 1841 aboard the William Pirie, from Stranraer. [NA.CO.140/33]

BLACK, PETER, born 1823, son of Peter Black and Ann Skeen, died on Fonte Bella Estate, Port Maria, St Mary's, Jamaica, on 23 Nov 1845. [Inveraven MI]

BLACK, ROBERT, a surgeon in Jamaica, son of James Black a leather cutter and merchant in Glasgow, 1799. [NAS.CS26.908.13]

BLACK, Mrs SUSANNA, Union St., Edinburgh, died 9 Jan 1831, inventory, 1833, widow of Andrew Black in Jamaica, Comm. Edinburgh. [NAS]

BLACK, ..., from Glasgow aboard the Nancy bound for Jamaica, arrived in Kingston in June 1793.[JRG:22.6.1793]

BLACKBURNE, Mr., from Greenock aboard the brig Jane bound for Jamaica, arrived there in July 1794. [JRG:2.8.1794]

BLACKBURN, JOHN, a planter in St Thomas in the Vale, Jamaica, 1803; was granted the lands of Killearn, 5 July 1813; died 29 Apr 1840, inventory, 1840. [NAS.RH15.76.23; RGS.148.17; Comm. Edinburgh, NAS]

BLACKWELL, CHARLES, in Jamaica, son of Principal Blackwell, graduated MD from Marischal College, Aberdeen, on 1 Nov 1743. [MCA]

BLAIR, DAVID, a prisoner in Newgate, London, sentenced to be transported to Jamaica on 15 Dec 1716. [NA.C66.3519.10]

BLAIR, HOMER, son of Reverend David Blair in Brechin, Angus, died in Savanna-la-Mar, Westmoreland, Jamaica, in 1817. [S.2.60]

BLAIR, HOMER, a planter in Jamaica, died Feb 1832, inventory, 1854. [NAS.SC70.1.85; E4037]

BLAIR, JAMES, a merchant in Vere, Jamaica, probate 25 Apr 1677, Jamaica.

BLAIR, JOB, from Perthshire, in Jamaica, died July 1736, testament, 27 June 1738. [NAS.CC8.8.101]

BLAIR, JOHN, a physician from Angus, settled in Port Royal, Jamaica, before 1700, agent there for the Darien Company. [DP#313][DD#326]

BLAIR, JOHN, born 1668, emigrated to Darien in 1699, settled in St Catherine's, Jamaica, in 1700. Husband of (1) Nadime ...., (2) Elizabeth, father of John, Thomas, Christian, and Mary, died 27 June 1728, probate 1728, PCC. [Spanish Town Cathedral Monumental Inscription, Jamaica]

BLAIR, JOHN, a planter in St Thomas in the Vale, father of Elizabeth, Anne, Frances, and John, probate, 1728, PCC.[Brook, Q.283][NA.Prob.11/624]

BLAIR, JOHN, of Inchira, MD, in Clarendon, Jamaica, died around 1740, father of Marjory, Ann, Isabel and Jacobina Blair, testament, 1746, Comm. St Andrews. [NAS.GD1.545.19/22/23/25/26] [RGO/SpanishTown, liber 21]

SCOTS IN JAMAICA, 1655-1855

BLAIR, JOHN, born 1734, a planter in St Andrew's, Jamaica, 1754, died 3 July 1764. [NA.CO137/28/191-196][St Andrew's MI, Kingston]

BLAIR, JOHN, in Jamaica, probate 1763, PCC.

BLAIR, JOHN, late of Worthy Park, Jamaica, died in London 15 Dec 1846. [GM.NS27.213]

BLAIR, ROBERT, fourth son of John Blair a merchant in Glasgow, died in Jamaica during 1817. [S.2.67]

BLAW, JAMES, possibly from Kirkwall, Orkney, in Jamaica 1780, then in Kelso, testament, 1801. [NAS.CS16.1.177; CC8.8.132/59]

BLOUNT, ROBERT, a surgeon, died on New Pera Estate, St Thomas, Jamaica, 11 June 1833. [Bath MI, Jamaica]

BLOUNT, SAMUEL, born in Dumfries 1796, died in St Thomas in the East, Jamaica, on 19 Sep 1828; inventory, 1833. Comm. Edinburgh. [NAS.SC70.1.49; C960] [Bath MI, Jamaica]

BLYTH, HENRY, youngest son of John Blyth a planter in Jamaica, matriculated at Glasgow University in 1847. [MAGU]

BLYTH, JOHN, born in Old Meldrum 1774, son of John Blyth a merchant, a merchant who died in Trelawney, Jamaica, on 18 Nov 1809. [Falmouth MI, Jamaica][PC#61]

BLYTH, JOHN, late of Kendall, Jamaica, died 1 June 1835, inventory, 1838, Comm. Edinburgh. [NAS.SC70.1.56; C1908]

BLYTH, JOHN, first son of John Blyth a merchant in Jamaica, at Glasgow University in 1830, graduated MD from Edinburgh University in 1839. [MAGU]

BOAG, ROBERT, in Jamaica, died in Edinburgh, inventory, 1813. [NAS.SC70.1.8]

BOGLE, ALLAN JAMES, of Bogle & Co in Jamaica, drowned 1814.[GM.84/508]

BOGLE, ANDREW, a merchant in Jamaica, co-owner of the Magnet of Glasgow, 1800; in Kingston, Jamaica, 1809; was granted land in Provan, 2 June 1817; a deed, 1820. [NAS.CE60.11.6/18; NRAS#0063; RGS.155.74; RD5.193.513]

BOGLE, JOHN, born 1823, arrived at Bluefields, Westmoreland, on 23 Jan 1841 aboard the William Pirie, from Stranraer. [NA.CO.140/33]

BOGLE, LAUCHLAN, a merchant in Kingston, Jamaica, a witness, 1800; died there on 9 Nov 1808. [NAS.RD4.289.454][SM.71.158]

BOGLE, MARY ANN, born 1818, a servant, arrived at Bluefields, Westmoreland, on 23 Jan 1841 aboard the William Pirie, from Stranraer. [NA.CO.140/33]

BOGLE, ROBERT, passenger from Greenock to Jamaica aboard the Ross in Nov 1773. [NAS.CE60]

BOGLE, ROBERT, third son of Robert Bogle of Gilmorehill, died in Kingston, Jamaica, on 21 Dec 1819. [S.4.161]

BOGUE, GEORGE, born 1795, son of William Bogue and Elizabeth Murray in Coldingham, a surgeon who died in Jamaica on 5 Sep 1817. [Coldingham MI]

SCOTS IN JAMAICA, 1655-1855

BONNIMAN, ..., son of Rev. John Bonniman [1743-1785] and Susan Grant in Premnay, Aberdeenshire, emigrated to Jamaica. [Premnay MI]
BONTEIN, ARCHIBALD, H.M.Engineer in Jamaica, a deed, 1751. [NAS.RD2.169.88]; probate, 1756, PCC.
BONTEIN, THOMAS, a gentleman in Kingston and in Port Royal, Jamaica, 1749, 1750. [NAS.RD2.168.145:RD2.169.499]; a burgess of Edinburgh, 1750. [EBR]
BONTEIN, THOMAS, Jamaica, married the daughter of Thomas Cudden the Master of Chancery, 12 Sep 1777. [GM.47.459]
BONTEIN, Mrs, wife of Thomas Bontein, died in Jamaica 10 June 1806. [GM.76.678]
BORTHWICK, GEORGE, a smith late of Jamaica now in Fountainbridge, Edinburgh, 1799. [NAS.CS22.776.8]
BORELAND, JOHN, a store-keeper in Jamaica, died Sep 1728, testament, 13 May 1789. [NAS.CC8.8.128]
BOSWELL, DAVID, died at Montego Bay, Jamaica, 18 Jan 1790. [GM.60/372]
BOWIE, ROBERT, born 1813, eldest son of Alexander Bowie a builder in Stirling, died in Kingston, Jamaica, on 17 Apr 1833. [SG#149]
BOYACK, DAVID, born 1784, died in Kingston, Jamaica, on 25 June 1820. [Dundee, Howff, MI]
BOYD, HUGH, born 1821, arrived at Bluefields, Westmoreland, on 23 Jan 1841 aboard the William Pirie, from Stranraer. [NA.CO.140/33]
BOYD, JAMES W., son of Thomas Boyd in Dumfries, died in St Mary's, Jamaica, on 15 Oct 1817. [AJ#3653]
BOYD, MARY, from Jamaica, married Robert Kalley a merchant in Glasgow on 3 Aug 1795. [GM.65.702]
BRANDER, ADAM, a planter in Portland, Surrey, Jamaica, a deed, 1783. [NAS.RD2.236/2.612]
BRANDER, MICHAEL, a gentleman in Trelawney, Cornwall, Jamaica, a deed, 1794. [NAS.RD4.255.660]
BRANDS, JAMES, son of James Brands and Ann Stewart in Aberdeen, died at Montego Bay, St James, Jamaica, in 1794. [St Nicholas MI, Aberdeen]
BRANDS, ROBERT, MD in Jamaica, 5 July 1786. [NAS.RS8.482]; of Caledonia Estate, Jamaica, youngest son of James Brands of Ferry Hill, Aberdeen, and Anne Stewart, died in Hanover, Jamaica, 1788. [St Nicholas MI, Aberdeen]
BRASS, ..., son of Robert S. Brass, was born 4 Mar1869 at 26 High Holburn St., Kingston, Jamaica. [S#8013]
BREARCLIFFE, DONALD, born 1788, son of Matthew Brearcliffe [1748-1824] and Catherine ...... [1750-1829], died in Jamaica, 24 Oct1867. [Wigtown MI]
BREBNER, Dr WILLIAM, born in Boharm, Banffshire, died in Pedro, Lucca, Hanover, Jamaica, on 3 Oct 1842. [AJ#4954]

SCOTS IN JAMAICA, 1655-1855

BREMNER, P.W.G., born 1824, youngest son of P. Bremner a merchant in Huntly, died at Montego Bay, Jamaica, on 9 June 1844. [AJ#5034]

BREMNER, ROBERT, in Jamaica, later in Huntly, Aberdeenshire, testament, 14 Dec 1808, Comm. Moray. [NAS.CC16.5.9.428]

BREMNER, WILLIAM, in Jamaica, MD Edinburgh University, 1818. [EMG#55]

BRENNAN, JAMES, born 1817, with Margaret, born 1822, and Margaret, aged 2 months, emigrated from Aberdeen aboard the Rob Roy bound for Jamaica, arrived at Kingston on 11 May 1841. [NA.CO140/33]

BRENNER, JOHN, born 1805, with Isabella, born 1807, John, born 1835, Elspeth, born 1837, and Jane, born 1839, from Aberdeen aboard the Rob Roy bound for Jamaica, arrived at Kingston on 11 May 1841. [NA.CO140/33]

BRENNER, JOSEPH, born 1823, a clerk, from Aberdeen aboard the Rob Roy bound for Jamaica, arrived at Kingston on 11 May 1841. [NA.CO140/33]

BREWSTER, GEORGE, MD, Royal Navy, son of George Brewster DD, minister of Scoonie, Fife, died at Port Royal, Jamaica, on 5 Apr 1850. [W#1108]

BREWSTER, JAMES, sometime in Jamaica, later an attorney in London, 1778. [NAS.RS10.352]

BRODIE, JAMES, born 1769, youngest son of James Brodie of Muiresk, the Customs Collector at Lucca, Jamaica, died there 30 July 1831. [AJ#4370]

BRODIE, HUGH, in Jamaica, probate 1748, PCC

BRODIE, OSWALD, of Flamstead Estate, died in St Ann's, Jamaica, on 9 Aug 1818. [GM.88.469]

BROWN, AGNES, born 1841, daughter of John Brown and Isabella Duncan, wife of Rev. Andrew Baillie, died in Lucca, Jamaica, on 25 Nov 1872.[St Andrews MI]

BROWN, ALEXANDER, a surgeon, late of Jamaica, 1752. [NAS.RS8.342/3]; husband of Ann Boyd in Glasgow, testament, 1749, Comm. Glasgow. [NAS]

BROWN, ALEXANDER, son of Alexander Brown a surgeon in Jamaica, at Glasgow University in 1743. [MAGU]

BROWN, ALEXANDER, Receiver General of Jamaica, died 10 Oct 1770, testament, 17 Dec 1779. [NAS.CC8.8.124]

BROWN, ALEXANDER, a surgeon on York Estate, Falmouth, Jamaica, 1822. [NAS.CS228.B.16.3]

BROWN, ALEXANDER, second son of Robert Brown a Writer to the Signet, died in Jamaica on 29 Apr 1826. [EEC#17913]

BROWN, CHARLES, in Jamaica, graduated MD from Edinburgh University, 1797. [EMG#28]

BROWN, DAVID, sometime of Glasgow, thereafter in Jamaica, died Aug 1822, inventory, 1835, Comm. Edinburgh. [NAS.SC70.1.52]

BROWN, DAVID, born 1785, son of David Brown and Helen Oswald, died in Jamaica on 2 Jan 1830. [Kingsbarns, Fife, MI]

BROWN, EBENEZER JOHN, third son of Charles Brown a merchant in Jamaica, matriculated at Glasgow University in 1828. [MAGU]
BROWN, JAMES, captain of a privateer in the West Indies, found guilty of piracy and sentenced to death in Jamaica on 5 Aug 1677. [SPAWI.1677#243]
BROWN, JAMES, born 1787, son of Samuel Brown and Mary Thomson, died in Jamaica, on 12 July 1824. [Senwick MI]
BROWN, JAMES, in Manchester, Jamaica, a deed, 1816. [NAS.RD5.109.235]
BROWN, JAMES, son of Alexander Brown in Chapel of Garioch, Aberdeenshire, died at Montego Bay, 12 Aug 1848. [AJ.4.10.1848]
BROWN, JEANNIE, dau of the late William Brown a glover, married John Smith of Hanover, Jamaica, in Glasgow, 1792. [GM.62.181]
BROWN, JOHN, born 17 June 1783, possibly second son of Andrew Brown in Stewarton, Ayrshire, educated at Glasgow University, by 1819 a minister in Kingston, Jamaica, died 17 Mar 1820. [F.7.669][St Andrew's MI, Jamaica]
BROWN, JOHN, born 1807, son of Rev. William Brown [1774-1829] and Christine Whyte [1775-1862], died at Montego Bay, St James, Jamaica, on 24 Jan 1845. [Greyfriars MI, Perth]
BROWN, JOHN, born 1847, elder son of Mathew Brown of Braehead, Saltcoats, Ayrshire, died at Montego Bay on 25 June 1865. [Montego Bay MI]
BROWN, JONATHAN, born 1783, died in Jamaica, 13 Nov 1843. [Wigtown MI]
BROWN, PRICE CARFRAE, fourth son of Charles Brown a merchant in Jamaica, graduated MD, died 1 Nov 1835. [MAGU]
BROWN, ROBERT, in Jamaica, then in Arran, testament, 4 July 1820. [NAS.SC15.41.3.80]
BROWN, ROBERT, in Low Layton, Jamaica, inventory, 1837. [NAS.C2322]
BROWN, WILLIAM, from Greenock to Jamaica aboard the Ross in Nov 1773. [NAS.CE60]
BROWN, WILLIAM, in Jamaica, 1773, eldest son of the late Alexander Brown a writer in Airdrie, Lanarkshire. [NAS.CS16.1]
BROWN, WILLIAM, a planter in Jamaica, son of James Brown a skipper in Dundee, 1781. [DCA.H4511]
BROWN, WILLIAM, born in Lanarkshire, thirrd son of Laurence Brown of Edmundston, at Glasgow University in 1774, died in Jamaica on 30 June 1811. [MAGU#111][Car.4.5]
BROWN, ……, brother of William Brown in Falkirk, Stirlingshire, in Jamaica 1823. [NAS.CS44.1824]
BRUCE, ALEXANDER, in Jamaica, dead by 1768. [NAS.GD237.21.51/11]
BRUCE, ALEXANDER, late of Polmont Bank, Falkirk, Stirlingshire, died at Hopewall, St Mary's, Jamaica, on 24 July 1841. [EEC#20267]

SCOTS IN JAMAICA, 1655-1855

BRUCE, ALEXANDER, born 1836, son of James Bruce [1792-1864] and Janet McDonald [1805-1876], died in Jamaica during Aug 1864. [Tomnacross MI]
BRUCE, CHARLES, from Musselburgh, East Lothian, died at Rio Bueno, Trelawney, Jamaica, on 18 July 1819. [S.3.144][AJ#3746]
BRUCE, ELIZABETH MARY, born 14 Apr 1821, Countess of Elgin and Kincardine, daughter of Charles Bruce of Kinnaird, wife of Governor Basil Keith, died in Craigton, Blue Mountains, Jamaica, on 7 June 1843. [Spanish Town Cathedral MI]
BRUCE, GEORGE ABERCROMBY, born 1798, 2nd son of Alexander Bruce of Kennet, died in Tulloch, Jamaica, on 14 Nov 1817. [AJ#3658][S.2.56]
BRUCE, JAMES, Lt. Gov. of Jamaica, married Margaret, daughter of John Thomson of Spring Garden, in Edinburgh, 1798. [GM#68.1147]
BRUCE, JESSIE, daughter of John Bruce of Brucefield, Jamaica, married Charles Hay of Laxfirth, at Canonmills House, Edinburgh, on 1 Oct 1839. [SG#808]
BRUCE, STEWART, '32 years resident', died in Kingston, Jamaica, 26 Jan 1807. [GM.77.376]
BRYCE, JOHN, at Montego Bay, Jamaica, married Jane, eldest daughter of James Mitchell an engineer, at York Place, Glasgow, 31 Oct 1839. [SG#8/817]
BRYCE, RICHARD, a planter, St Thomas in the East, Surry, Jamaica, a witness, 1792. [NAS.RD3.256.777]
BRYDIE, WILLIAM, a merchant in Jamaica, 1796. [NAS.CS17.1.15/216]
BUCHANAN, CUNNINGHAM, in Fellowship Hall, Jamaica, father of John Buchanan in Glasgow, 1821. [NAS.CS228.B.15.52]
BUCHANAN, GEORGE, late from Jamaica, died in Glasgow on 14 Jan 1801. [GM.71.185]
BUCHANAN, GEORGE, only son of George Buchanan a merchant in Jamaica, at Glasgow University in 1813. [MAGU]
BUCHANAN, JAMES, a planter in Jamaica, later in America, 1801. [NAS.CS17.1.20/14]
BUCHANAN, JAMES, Glasgow, married Mary Anne, eldest dau of the late William Finlayson, St Elizabeth, Jamaica, 7 Aug 1819. [GM.89.178]
BUCHANAN, JEAN, in Newport, St Mary's, Jamaica, died in Glasgow, testament, 13 Dec 1823. [NAS.CC9.7.81]
BUCHANAN, JOHN, died in Jamaica, 1790. [GM.60.476]
BUCHANAN, WALTER, eldest son of William Buchanan, late of the 1st Royal Veteran Battalion, died in Spanish Town, Jamaica, 22 Oct 1838. [SG#8/735]
BUCHANAN, W., died in St Anne's, Jamaica, 1810. [GM.80.498]
BUCHANAN, ..., an overseer, St James's, Jamaica, 1774. [BL.Add.MS22676/8]
BUNTEIN, THOMAS, sometime in Port Royal, Jamaica, son of Robert Bontein of Mildowan, 1754. [NAS.CS16.1.92/266]

SCOTS IN JAMAICA, 1655-1855

BUNTINE, JAMES, passenger from Greenock to Jamaica aboard the Ross in Nov 1773. [NAS.CE60]

BURD, JOHN, in Clarendon, Middlesex, Jamaica, then in Edinburgh, 1801. [NAS.RD2.282.787]

BURDON, JAMES GRAHAM, fourth son of Robert Burdon of Feddal, Perthshire, at Glasgow University in 1788, died in Jamaica on 16 Jan 1806. [MAGU]

BURGESS, COLIN, born 23 July 1749, son of John Burgess in Dingwall, Easter Ross, a clergyman in St Ann's, Jamaica, 1795. [FPA#316]

BURNET, JOHN, in Kingston, Jamaica, 30 Nov1716. [BM.Sloane#4044/250]

BURNETT, THOMAS, in Jamaica, probate 1751, PCC.

BURNET, ..., daughter of George Burnet in Jamaica, buried in St Nicholas churchyard, Aberdeen, 25 Nov 1755. [ACA]

BURNETT, ..., a planter in St Andrew's, Jamaica, 1754. [NA.CO137/28]

BURNS, JOHN, in Jamaica, son of the late James Burns of Glenfuir one of the Principal Clerks of the Bills, 1768. [NAS.CS97.11.57]

BURNS, JOHN, born 1817, a nailer, arrived at Bluefields, Westmoreland, on 23 Jan 1841 aboard the William Pirie, from Stranraer. [NA.CO.140/33]

BURNSIDE, ANDREW, a victualler in Port Royal, probate 21 Apr 1676, Jamaica.

BURNSIDE, JOHN, born 1821, arrived at Bluefields, Westmoreland, on 23 Jan 1841 aboard the William Pirie, from Stranraer. [NA.CO.140/33]

BURNSIDE, ROBERT, born 1805, with Amy born 1803, and Robert born 1837, arrived at Bluefields, Westmoreland, on 23 Jan 1841 aboard the William Pirie, from Stranraer. [NA.CO.140/33]

BURNSIDE, THOMAS, a planter in St Andrew's, Jamaica, 1754. [NA.CO137/28/191-196]

BYGRAVE, ANN, wife of Rev. J. M. Frew, rector of St Thomas in the East, Jamaica, died 29 Mar 1842. [GSP#718]

BYRNE, PETER, from Creetown, Kirkcudbright, aboard the Countess of Galloway on 15 Mar 1793 bound for Jamaica, arrived in Kingston in May 1793. [RJG:1.6.1793]

CAIRNS, MARGARET, born 1822, arrived at Bluefields, Westmoreland, on 23 Jan 1841 aboard the William Pirie, from Stranraer. [NA.CO.140/33]

CALDER, GEORGE, only son of George Calder a merchant in Jamaica, matriculated at Glasgow University in 1806. [MAGU#222]

CALDER, Mr., from Glasgow aboard the Betsy and Brothers bound for Jamaica, arrived in Kingston in May 1793. [JRG:25.5.1794]

CALLENDAR, GEORGE, probate 17 May 1694, Jamaica.

CALLENDAR, JAMES, a surgeon in Jamaica, dead by 1746. [see NA.PROB 11/753]

CALLENDAR, THOMAS P., minister of St Andrew's, Kingston, Jamaica, 1847, died 22 Jan 1849. [F.7.669]
CALLUM, ALEXANDER, formerly a clerk to Campbell, Ruthven and Lindsay merchants in Greenock, later a merchant in Jamaica, 1804. [NAS.AC7/77]
CALVERT, JOHN, born 1772, son of James Calvert in Braehead, Hoddam, Dumfries-shire, died in Jamaica on 5 Sep 1805. [St Kentigern's MI]
CAMERON, ALEXANDER, in Port Royal, Jamaica, 1736. [NAS.GD170.735]
CAMERON, ALEXANDER, son of Donald Cameron (1772-1836) a farmer in Carnoch and Helen Ross (1753-1823), settled in Corrimony, Jamaica. [Corrimony MI]
CAMERON, ALEXANDER, in Jamaica, natural son of John Cameron. [no date]. [NAS.PS3.13/103]
CAMERON, ALLAN, in Jamaica, eldest son of Angus Cameron in Camqheron, Rannoch, Perthshire, and Christian Menzies, a deed, 1771. [NAS.RD2.218.744]
CAMERON, ALLAN, died in Kingston, Jamaica, on 27 May 1796. [GM.66.615]
CAMERON, Mrs ANNE, spouse of Dr Donald Cameron a physician in St Thomas, Jamaica, testament, 17 Dec 1792, Comm. Aberdeen. [NAS]
CAMERON, ARCHIBALD, from Lochaber, to Jamaica 10 Oct 1764, arrived there 21 Dec1764. [AUL.BDpp/H1766/01]
CAMERON, Dr DONALD, a physician in St Thomas, Jamaica, husband of Anne Cameron testament, 1792, Comm. Aberdeen. [NAS]
CAMERON, DONALD, born 1808, a sawyer, emigrated from Aberdeen aboard the Rob Roy bound for Jamaica, arrived at Kingston on 11 May 1841. [NA.CO140/33]
CAMERON, HUGH, son of John Cameron of Carntyne, Glasgow, died in Westmoreland, Jamaica, 1804. [AJ#2970]
CAMERON, JAMES, in Kingston, Jamaica, May 1744. [Carribeana.6.23]
CAMERON, JAMES, second son of Allan Cameron of Inverscadie, Argyll, died at Montego Bay, Jamaica, 29 Apr 1836. [S#1724]
CAMERON, JOHN, second son of John Cameron of Carntyne, Barony, Glasgow, matriculated at Glasgow University in 1767, died in Jamaica in 1794. [MAGU]
CAMERON, JOHN, born in Inverness 1796, died in Farm, Jamaica, on 13 Sep 1835. [AJ#4596]
CAMERON, ROBERT, born in the Mains of Orton 1816, died in Kingston, Jamaica, on 8 Feb 1843. [Dondurcas MI][AJ#4969]
CAMERON, Dr, died in Kingston, Jamaica, on 23 Aug 1800. [GM.70.1214]
CAMPBELL, ALEXANDER, in Jamaica, probate 1750, PCC.
CAMPBELL, ALEXANDER, a physician in Jamaica, died 1751, testament, 17 Nov 1753. [NAS.CC8.8.114]
CAMPBELL, ALEXANDER, from Islay, Argyll, in Jamaica 1780. [NAS.CS16.1.179]

SCOTS IN JAMAICA, 1655-1855

CAMPBELL, ALEXANDER, at Green River, Jamaica, 1780. [NAS.CS16.1.179]
CAMPBELL, ALEXANDER, a surgeon late of Kingston, Jamaica, second son of the late Alexander Campbell, 1782. [NAS.CS17.1.1/20]
CAMPBELL, ALEXANDER, eldest son of Alexander Campbell a merchant in Jamaica, matriculated at Glasgow University in 1783. [MAGU]
CAMPBELL, Dr ALEXANDER, of Lancet Hall, late of St Ann's, Jamaica, died in Edinburgh, 15 Feb 1792. [EEC:18.2.1792][GCr#75]
CAMPBELL, ALEXANDER, born 1766, died in Westmoreland, Jamaica, on 27 July 1839. [Thornhill MI, Jamaica]
CAMPBELL, ALEXANDER, born 12 Apr 1778 in Creich, educated at Edinburgh and Glasgow universities, a minister in St Andrew's, Jamaica, from 1803, died 8 Dec 1858. [EMA#18][FPA#316][St Andrew's MI]
CAMPBELL, ALEXANDER, only son of Rev. Colin Campbell rector of St Andrews, Jamaica, at Glasgow University, 1792. [MAGU#168]
CAMPBELL, ALEXANDER BOWERBANK, MD, son of Rev. John Campbell in Jamaica, died at Stoney Hill, Jamaica, 12 Sep 1879. [EC#29653]
CAMPBELL, ANDREW, a merchant in Jamaica, 1744. [NAS.RD2.169.74]
CAMPBELL, ANN, relict of William McDonald a planter in Jamaica, 1768. [NAS.RS27.179.206/211]
CAMPBELL, ARCHIBALD, a planter in Jamaica, a witness, 1770. [NAS.RD2.215.143]
CAMPBELL, Major General ARCHIBALD, Lieutenant Governor of Jamaica, 1780, a burgess of Glasgow 23 Sep 1784. [EUL.Campbell of Inverneil pp][GBR]
CAMPBELL, ARCHIBALD, a merchant in Kingston, Jamaica, 1788. [NAS.RS54.1045/1050]
CAMPBELL, ARCHIBALD, of Minard, and family, arrived in Falmouth, Jamaica, on the Elizabeth in June 1793. [JRG:29.6.1793]
CAMPBELL, ARCHIBALD, of Providence Estate, Macheneill, Jamaica, 31 Dec 1793, only son of John Campbell a merchant in Greenock later tacksman of Larkfield, Innerkip, and his wife Jean Campbell. [NAS.SC58.58.7]
CAMPBELL, ARCHIBALD, of Knockbuy, died in Minard, Jamaica, on 8 July 1798. [SM.60.652][AJ#2647][GM.68.811]
CAMPBELL, ARCHIBALD, a merchant, late of Jamaica, died in Glasgow on 17 Jan 1820. [S.4.158]
CAMPBELL, ARCHIBALD, from Askinish, born 1752, died in Hanover, Jamaica, on 18 June 1830. [Hanover MI]
CAMPBELL, ARCHIBALD, born 1781, third son of John Campbell of New Hope, Westmoreland, Jamaica, died there 21 Apr 1833. [Auchendour MI, Jamaica]
CAMPBELL, CHARLES, a physician in Kingston, Jamaica, inventory, 1873.[NAS.SC70.1.164/729]

SCOTS IN JAMAICA, 1655-1855

CAMPBELL, CHARLES, born 1853, fourth son of Archibald Campbell a feuar and shipowner in Lochgilphead, Argyll, died in Clarksonville, Jamaica, 5 Nov 1878. [EC#29391]

CAMPBELL, COLIN, son of Rev. Patrick Campbell in Kenmore, Perthshire, a soldier shipped to Darien, died in Jamaica during 1699, testament, 1707, Comm. Edinburgh. [NAS.CC8.8.83; NRAS#2177/1416]

CAMPBELL, COLIN, son of John Campbell in Jamaica, at Glasgow University, 1720. [MAGU#219]

CAMPBELL, COLIN, born 1704, died in Jamaica on 16 June 1760. [New Hope Estate MI, Jamaica]

CAMPBELL, COLIN, an Anglican minister sent to Jamaica on 22 Sep 1751. [FPA]

CAMPBELL , COLIN, a land-owner in Jamaica, son of John Campbell of Black River, St Elizabeth, husband of Margaret Campbell, parents of Colin, John, Elizabeth, and Margaret Jane, probate 1752, PCC. [NA.Prob.11/793; CO142/31]

CAMPBELL, COLIN, deceased, formerly a merchant in Jamaica, son of Archibald Campbell of Barnacraig, 1789. [Argyll Sheriff Court Book XIX]

CAMPBELL, COLIN, late merchant in Greenock, then in Holland Estate, St Elizabeth's, Jamaica, husband of Henrietta, daughter of Duncan Campbell, who were married in Glasgow, Aug 1776, Process of Divorce, 1790. [NAS.Comm.Edinburgh]

CAMPBELL, COLIN, jr., arrived in Kingston. Jamaica, in Jan 1794 and settled in Hanover, Jamaica. [NAS.GD1.512.26]

CAMPBELL, COLIN, jr., a merchant in Glasgow now in Jamaica, 1785. [NAS.CS17.1.4/344]

CAMPBELL, COLIN, of Campbell & O'Hara, died at Tandragee Castle, Kingston, Jamaica, in Sept 1808. [GM.78.952]

CAMPBELL, Dr COLIN, born 4 July 1777, son of Rev. Peter Campbell and Margaret Scott in Glassary, Argyll, a physician educated at Glasgow University 1791, formerly of Greenock, died in Jamaica on 9 May 1824. [GrAd:6.7.1824][F.4.7] [MAGU#163][GM.94.574]

CAMPBELL, COLIN, in St Ann's, Middlesex, Jamaica, a deed, 1797. [NAS.RD4.263.273]

CAMPBELL, COLIN, born 1788, possibly graduated MD from Edinburgh University, 1812, of Waterhouse, St Andrew's, Jamaica, died 8 Aug 1849. [EMG#45][St Andrew's MI]

CAMPBELL, COLIN, second son of Lauchlin Campbell an agent in Jamaica, matriculated at Glasgow University in 1846. [MAGU]

CAMPBELL, DANIEL, a planter in St Andrew's, Jamaica, 1754. [NA.CO137/28/191]

SCOTS IN JAMAICA, 1655-1855

CAMPBELL, DANIEL, a planter in St Elizabeth's, Cornwall, Jamaica, an indenture, 1772. [NAS.RD2.215.143]

CAMPBELL, DAVID, a planter in St Thomas in the Vale, Jamaica, 1762, and executor of John Balneavis a planter in Claredon, Jamaica, who died 1770. [NAS.NRAS.0319][Argyll Sheriff Court Book XVI]

CAMPBELL, Dr DAVID, a physician in Jamaica, brother of John Campbell of Glen Lyon, Perthshire, 1781. [NAS.GD155/287]

CAMPBELL, DONALD, a Covenanter who was transported from Leith to Jamaica on 7 Aug 1685. [RPCS.XI.330]

CAMPBELL, DONALD, a planter, St Mary's, Jamaica, 1777. [Argyll Sheriff Court Deeds, 9 July 1781]; 1780. [NAS.CS16.1.179]

CAMPBELL, DONALD, Secretary to the Governor, Spanish Town, Jamaica, 1784. [NAS.GD461.56]

CAMPBELL, DONALD, second son of Archibald Campbell of Lerags, Argyll, died at Lucea, Jamaica, 21 June 1812. [SM.74.727]

CAMPBELL, DONALD, born 1801, died in Jamaica on 29 Oct 1859. [St Andrew's MI, Jamaica]

CAMPBELL, Captain DOUGAL, died in Jamaica, 1791. [GM.61.187]

CAMPBELL, DOUGALD, of Glen Carradale, Argyll, formerly in St Andrew's, Jamaica, 1745. [NAS.RD2.169.250]

CAMPBELL, DOUGALD, son of the late George Campbell, a surgeon in Landay, St Ann's, Jamaica, a deed, 1774. [NAS.RD4.217.5]

CAMPBELL, DUGALD, born 1697, son of Colin Campbell of Attichuan, settled in Salt Spring, Hanover by 1739, died 27 June 1744. [Winchester MI, Jamaica]

CAMPBELL, DUGALD, a merchant in Kingston, Jamaica, son of Colin Campbell the Customs Controller in Campbeltown, Argyll, edict of executry, 1801. [NAS.CC2.105.9]

CAMPBELL, DUGALD, fourth son of Archibald Campbell of Jerags, a planter of Saltspring Estate, Hanover, Jamaica, letters, 1813; died in Jamaica, 1817; probate, 1818, London. [NA.J90.536; Prob.11/1600][S.1.15][GM.87.87]

CAMPBELL, DUNCAN, gentleman, St Thomas, Jamaica, probate July 1693, Jamaica.

CAMPBELL, DUNCAN, a merchant in Jamaica, eldest son of Rev. James Campbell in Kilbrandon, Argyll, a deed, 1770. [NAS.RD2.215.143]

CAMPBELL, DUNCAN, a partner in the merchant house of McDuffie and Campbell in Kingston, Jamaica, 1771, 1774. [NAS.CS16.1.143/128; CS16.1.287]

CAMPBELL, DUNCAN, in St Anne's, Jamaica, died 1791. [GM.61.1065]

CAMPBELL, DUNCAN, of Knapdale, Jamaica, died at Aux Cayes, St Domingo, 1795. [EEC: 21.12.1795][SM.57.818][GM.65.1057]

CAMPBELL, DUNCAN, born 12 May 1770, son of Rev. Peter Campbell and Margaret Scott in Glassary, Argyll, died in Jamaica in Jan 1797. [F.4.7]

CAMPBELL, DUNCAN, son of Dr Neil Campbell in Glasgow, a planter at Saltspring estate, Hanover, Jamaica, probate, 1803, London. [NA.Prob.11.1388]

CAMPBELL, DUNCAN, a planter, a deed, 1770; of Morven Estate, Hanover, Jamaica, died 9 Sep 1810, probate, 1810, London. [NA.Prob.11.1515][EEC] [NAS.RD4.275.233][SM.72.720]

CAMPBELL, DUNCAN, from Culchenna, died in Campbeltown, Jamaica, 1817. [S.1.15]

CAMPBELL, DUNCAN, first son of Alexander Campbell a minister in St Andrew's, Jamaica, matriculated at Glasgow University in 1835. [MAGU]

CAMPBELL, Dr D. MCEACHERN, died in Lucca, Jamaica, 24 June 1814. [EEC]

CAMPBELL, ELIZABETH, a prisoner in Newgate, to be shipped to Jamaica on 15 Dec 1716. [NA.C66.3519.10]

CAMPBELL, ELIZABETH, dau of Alexander Campbell in Jamaica, widow of D. Davies in London, married Rev H W Marychurch, London, 5 Sep 1849. [GM.NS32.529]

CAMPBELL, ELIZABETH, born 1766, dau of Angus Campbell in Jamaica, died in Bristol, 18 Sep 1850. [GM.NS34.560]

CAMPBELL, GEORGE, eldest son of Rev. Dr Campbell in Ancrum, died in Jamaica during 1817. [S.1.42]

CAMPBELL, GEORGE, fourth son of John Campbell of Prospect, Argyll, died in Lucca, Jamaica, on 11 Feb 1822. [EEC#17350]

CAMPBELL, GEORGE JAMES, born 12 Oct 1814 in Ardchattan, son of Rev. George Campbell and Jane McDiarmid, in HEICS and later Vice Consul in Jamaica, died 3 June 1841. [F.4.82]

CAMPBELL, GRACE BUCHANAN, daughter of Colin Campbell in Jamaica, and wife of Robert Stevens a solicitor in Edinburgh, was granted part of the lands of Lumloch, on 3 Feb 1818. [NAS.RGS.157.23.52]

CAMPBELL, HENRY RIDDALL, son of the late Archibald Campbell of Minard, St Ann's, Jamaica, a Lieutenant of the 1st Battalion, 60th Foot, husband of Elizabeth Stewart, died at Fort Dundas, Rio Bueno, Jamaica, 26 Mar 1807, probate 1808, London. [NA.PROB.11/1485]

CAMPBELL, HEW, a merchant in Jamaica, 1744. [NAS.RD2.169.74]

CAMPBELL, IVER, a planter in Hanover, Cornwall, Jamaica, son of Dugald Campbell of Ardlaroch, Argyll, a deed, 1788. [NAS.RD4.248.68]

CAMPBELL, J., youngest son of Dugald Campbell of Carradale, Ayrshire, died on Georgia Estate, Blue Mountain Valley, Jamaica, in 1804. [AJ#2958]

CAMPBELL, Colonel JAMES, born 1697, son of Dugald Campbell of Torbhlaren, husband of Henrietta Campbell, parents of Elizabeth and John, died 13 July

1744, probate, 1744, Jamaica; buried at Orange Bay, Hanover, Jamaica. [RGD.Jamaica.LOS.24/330][MIBWI][Orange Bay Estate MI]
CAMPBELL, JAMES, in Jamaica, a burgess of Glasgow, 8 Mar 1717. [GBR]
CAMPBELL, Sir JAMES, in Jamaica, died in Houston, Renfrewshire, before 1744. [NAS.RD2.169.74]
CAMPBELL, JAMES, a Jacobite transported via Liverpool to Jamaica on the Elizabeth, on 7 Feb 1748, landed 21 Mar1748. [NA.T53/44]
CAMPBELL, JAMES, of St James, Jamaica, father of John and James, administration, 1766, PCC. [NA.Prob.11/917]
CAMPBELL, JAMES, of Kames in Cowal, (brother of Duncan Campbell of Kilduskland), formerly a merchant in Glasgow, sometime of Hanover, Jamaica, died 1758, husband of Margaret Lamont, testament, 23 July 1761, Comm. of the Isles. [NAS]; administration, 1776, PCC. [NAS.CC12.3.6][NA.Prob.11/1025] [NAS.GD64.1.279/4]
CAMPBELL, JAMES, born 1723, of Passagefort, Jamaica, died in Glasgow, 1761. [SM.23.55]
CAMPBELL, JAMES, in Snowhill, Kingston, Jamaica, 1768. [NAS.GD236.21.51/11]
CAMPBELL, JAMES, late a merchant in Kingston, Jamaica, then in Crieff, Perthshire, 1771. [NAS.CS16.1.143/128]
CAMPBELL, JAMES, from Dowan Vale, Jamaica, a burgess of Banff, 1783.[BBR]
CAMPBELL, JANE, in Jamaica, probate 1763, PCC.
CAMPBELL, JANE, born 1820, arrived at Bluefields, Westmoreland, on 23 Jan 1841 aboard the William Pirie, from Stranraer. [NA.CO.140/33]
CAMPBELL, JANET, from Argyll, in Kingston, Jamaica, died 1790, testament, 30 July 1799. [NAS.CC8.8.131]
CAMPBELL, JEAN, spouse of ..Turner a silversmith in Jamaica, sister of the late James Campbell a goldsmith in Edinburgh, a decreet, 1773. [NAS.CS16.1.75]
CAMPBELL, JOHN, a rebel from Dunalter, Kintyre, Argyll, who was transported from Leith to Jamaica on 7 Aug 1685, son of Walter Campbell. [RPCS.XI.329]
CAMPBELL, JOHN, a rebel from Auchenchrydie, Cowal, who was transported from Leith to Jamaica on 7 Aug 1685, son of Donald Campbell. [RPCS.XI.329]
CAMPBELL, JOHN, a rebel from Lochwoar, Lorne, who was transported from Leith to Jamaica on 7 Aug 1685, son of Robert Campbell. [RPCS.XI.329]
CAMPBELL, JOHN, a rebel from Carrisk, Lochfyneside, Argyll, who was transported from Leith to Jamaica on 7 Aug 1685. [RPCS.XI.329]
CAMPBELL, JOHN, in Port Royal, Jamaica, probate, 12 Sep 1692, Jamaica
CAMPBELL, JOHN, born in Inveraray, Argyll, during 1674, son of Reverend Patrick Campbell of Torbhlaren and his wife Jean Campbell, from Leith to Darien in 1699, moved to Jamaica in 1700, a planter at Black River, St Elizabeth,

SCOTS IN JAMAICA, 1655-1855

husband of (1) Katherine Clayborn, (2) Elizabeth Gaines, parents of Colin and Ann Campbell or Currie; admitted as a burgess of Glasgow and of Inveraray both in 1716, died in St Elizabeth on 29 Jan 1740, buried at Black River Church. Probate, 1740, Jamaica. [RGD.Jamaica.22/100][MIBWI#340] [F.4.9] [NAS.RS4.396][GBR][IBR][Black River MI, St Elizabeth, Jamaica]

CAMPBELL, JOHN, an indentured servant, from London to Jamaica in 1732. [CLRO/AIA]

CAMPBELL, JOHN, son of Colin Campbell deceased, late of Westmoreland, Jamaica, 1769. [NAS.RD4.223/2.303]

CAMPBELL, JOHN, in Lucca, Jamaica, a letter, 10 July 1769. [NAS.RD4.223/2.303]

CAMPBELL, JOHN, born 1700, master of the St Elizabeth, died 29 July 1766, buried at Orange Bay, Jamaica, 31 July 1766. [MIBWI][Orange Bay MI]

CAMPBELL, JOHN, of Saltspring, Hanover, Jamaica, deed of factory, 1765; a deed, 1770; a sasine, 1771; letter, 1780. [NAS.GD64.1.279.4; RD2.215.143; RS10.10.327][NA.CO137.79]

CAMPBELL, JOHN, Jamaica, married the daughter of Thomas Storer in London, 10 Mar 1774. [GM.44.141]

CAMPBELL, JOHN, of Lancit Hall, Jamaica, married Elizabeth Bell from Glasgow, in Jamaica in 1790. [GM#60.1213]

CAMPBELL, JOHN, Captain of the Royal Artillery, died near Kingston, Jamaica, 30 May 1805. [EEC]

CAMPBELL, JOHN, of Orange Bay, born 1732, former Custos Rotulorum of Hanover, died 16 May 1808. [Orange Bay MI, Jamaica]

CAMPBELL, JOHN, of New Hope, Jamaica, probate, 1802, London. [NA.Prob.11/1379]

CAMPBELL, JOHN, St Mary's, Jamaica, 12 May 1813. [NAS.RD.Argyll.1/112]

CAMPBELL, JOHN, born 1756, of Gibraltar Estate, Trelawney, Jamaica, died 25 Jan 1817. [Bristol Cathedral MI]

CAMPBELL, JOHN, born in Jamaica, first son of Archibald Campbell, matriculated at Glasgow University in 1783. [MAGU]

CAMPBELL, JOHN, youngest son of Dugald Campbell of Carradale, died at Port Royal, Jamaica, 12 June 1804. [SM.66.726]

CAMPBELL, Rev JOHN, born 1749, of St Andrews, Jamaica, died in London on 13 Oct 1813. [GM.83.406]

CAMPBELL, JOHN, born 1788, died at Montego Bay, St James, Jamaica, 21 Dec 1834. [Montego Bay MI]

CAMPBELL, JOHN, third son of Rev. John Campbell of Nicolson Secession Church, Lauriston, Glasgow, died in Kingston, Jamaica, in Oct 1837. [DPCA#1844]

SCOTS IN JAMAICA, 1655-1855

CAMPBELL, JOHN, born 1820, a laborer, with Nancy Campbell born 1817, arrived at Bluefields, Westmoreland, on 23 Jan 1841 aboard the William Pirie, from Stranraer. [NA.CO.140/33]

CAMPBELL, JOHN, first son of the late Rev. Henry Campbell in Jamaica, at Glasgow University in 1850. [MAGU]

CAMPBELL, JOSEPH, second son of Alexander Campbell a merchant in Jamaica, matriculated at Glasgow University in 1783. [MAGU]

CAMPBELL, MARIA, relict of James Whyte in Glasgow, after in Jamaica, testament, 1804, Comm. Glasgow. [NAS.CC9.7.79/68]

CAMPBELL, MARY, born 1745, died 3 Feb 1767 in Jamaica. [St Andrew's MI, Glasgow]

CAMPBELL, Mrs MARY, of Elister, died in Jamaica, 1795. [EEC.21.11.1795]

CAMPBELL, NEILL, in Jamaica, brother of James Campbell of Duntroon, probate, 1 Oct 1801, PCC.

CAMPBELL PATRICK or PETER, a physician in Jamaica, 1779, son of Captain Duncan Campbell of Edinburgh City Guard, [NAS.CS16.1.175]; from Jamaica, settled in Lberton, died at Liberton Kirk, 15 Dec1785, [GM.IX.468/413][EEC]; testament 2 Mar1787, Comm. Edinburgh. [NAS.CC8.8.127][SM.48.623]

CAMPBELL, PATRICK, born 1819, arrived at Bluefields, Westmoreland, on 23 Jan 1841 aboard the William Pirie, from Stranraer. [NA.CO.140/33]

CAMPBELL, PETER, son of Dugald Campbell of Torbhlaren, Kilmory, Argyll, a planter at Fish River, Hanover, Jamaica, husband of Deborah Woodstock, parents Elizabeth, probate 1739, Jamaica; buried at Fish River. [NAS.NRAS#886] [RGD.Jamaica.LOS.22/82]

CAMPBELL, PETER, born 15 Sep. 1775, son of Rev. Peter Campbell and Margaret Scott in Glassary, Argyll, died in Jamaica on 6 Nov 1795. [F.4.7]

CAMPBELL, PETER, at Fish River, Jamaica, father of Peter, Deborah, Louise Henrietta, and Elizabeth, a deed, 1808. [NAS.RD3.331.202]

CAMPBELL, PETER, of Kilmory, born 2 May 1766, settled in Holland and Petersville, Westmoreland, Jamaica, died in Dec 1821. [Petersville MI]

CAMPBELL, PETER, II, of Kilmory, Argyll, and of Jamaica, probate, 1818, London. [NA.Prob.11.1601]

CAMPBELL, REBECCA, daughter of Colin Campbell in Jamaica, relict of Adam Scott of Roundhill, Jamaica, was granted the lands of Lumloch, 3 Feb1818; a deed, 1818. [NAS.RGS.157.23.52; RD5.135.459]

CAMPBELL RIDDELL, a Lieutenant of the 60th Regiment, youngest son of Archibald Campbell of Knockbuy, died in Jamaica, 25 Mar 1807. [SM.69.957]

CAMPBELL, ROBERT, a merchant in Jamaica, 1744. [NAS.RD2.169.74]

CAMPBELL, RODERICK, son of John Campbell (1720-1805) and Margaret McLeod, died in Jamaica. [Dunvegan MI, Skye]

SCOTS IN JAMAICA, 1655-1855

CAMPBELL, SUSANNA, daughter of Colin Campbell in Jamaica, and wife of Dr Robert Jackson in Jamaica, was granted part of the lands of Lumloch on 3 Feb 1818, deeds, 1818. [NAS.RGS.157.23.52; RD5.135.459; RD5.164.29]

CAMPBELL, THOMAS, first son of John Campbell formerly a merchant in Jamaica, matriculated at Glasgow University in 1845. [MAGU]

CAMPBELL, TOMLIN, son of John Campbell of New Hope, Jamaica, a Lieutenant of the 92nd Foot (The Gordon Highlanders), administration, 1808, London. [NA.PROB.11/1452]

CAMPBELL, WILLIAM, son of John Campbell in Jamaica, matriculated at Glasgow University in 1724. [MAGU#227]

CAMPBELL, WILLIAM, a jobber and surveyor, St James parish, Jamaica, 1774. [BL.Add.MS22676/8]

CAMPBELL, WILLIAM, born 16 Nov 1760, in Stuckchapel, Glenfalloch, son of William Campbell and Effie McNicol, emigrated in 1778, a planter in Hanover, Jamaica, died there Oct 1791, probate, 8 June 1793, Jamaica, testament, 12 Nov 1794. [SP.II.195][NAS.RD4.275.233; CC8.8.129]

CAMPBELL, WILLIAM, a merchant in Savannah la Mar, Jamaica, a witness, 1788. [NAS.RD4.244.793]

CAMPBELL, WILLIAM, a mason in Hanover, Jamaica, dead by 1807. [NAS.RD3.318.349]

CAMPBELL, Mrs, born 1713, relict of George Campbell of Orange Grove, Jamaica, died at Enfield in 1801. [GM#1217][GM.71.1217]

CAMPBELL, ..., born in Jamaica on 19 June 1846, son of Lt Col Sir John Campbell. [GM.NS26.313]

CARGILL, JOHN, born 1745, a merchant, died Sep 1780. [Kingston Church MI, Jamaica]

CARGILL, RICHARD, born 1744, an Assemblyman and Militia Colonel, in St Thomas in the East, Jamaica, died Mar 1781, husband of Milborough Hodgins. [Kingston Church MI] [JCTP.1748.360]

CARLISLE, WARRAND, born 12 Nov 1796 in Paisley, 4th son of James Carlyle a craftsman, at Glasgow University 1810, a Presbyterian minister in Brownsville, Jamaica, 1843-1881, died in Hanover, Jamaica, on 25 Aug 1881. [Hanover MI] [MAGU#251]

CARMICHAEL, ELIZABETH, born 1755, via London to Jamaica on the <u>Royal Charlotte</u> in Feb 1774. [NA.T47.9/11]

CARMICHAEL, JOHN, late of Jamaica, died at 18 Downie Place, Edinburgh, on 18 Dec 1841. [AJ#4899]

CARMICHAEL, PETER, from Perthshire, died on Whitehall Estate, St Mary's, Jamaica, in 1803. [AJ#2876]

CARMICHAEL, STEWART, in Hanover, Jamaica, third son of Dr James Carmichael of Balinblae, was granted Balinblae, 20 Dec 1800. [NAS.RGS.132.40.45]

CARMICHAEL, WILLIAM, a Glasgow merchant who settled in Jamaica by 1750. [NAS.B10.15.7166]

CARMICHAEL, WILLIAM, in Jamaica, a deed, 1804. [NAS.RD4.307.832]

CARNABY, THOMAS, a merchant, born 1 Apr1780, son of William Carnaby and Janet Courage in Forres, died at Montego Bay, Jamaica, on 10 July 1807. [AJ#3117][DPCA#272][IJ:9.10.1807]

CARNABY, WILLIAM, born 1806 in Perth, a Special Justice of Claredon, Jamaica, died 18 Mar 1841. [AJ#4870][Old Harbor MI, Jamaica]

CARRUTHERS, CHRISTOPHER, born 1802, son of James Carruthers and Wharrie Richardson in Mouswald Mains, Ruthwell, Dumfries-shire, died 1829 in Jamaica. [Ruthwell MI]

CARRUTHERS, GEORGE, eldest son of the late James Carruthers in Dunwoodie Green, died on Dundee Estate, Trelawney, Jamaica, on 15 July 1796. [GM.66.880]

CARRUTHERS, JAMES, banished to Jamaica for 7 years in 1731. [CM:8.11.1731]

CARRUTHERS, PATRICK, born 1820, a cooper, arrived at Bluefields, Westmoreland, on 23 Jan 1841 aboard the William Pirie, from Stranraer. [NA.CO.140/33]

CATHCART, ANDREW, of Kingston, Jamaica, died in Rhode Island, 1792. [GCr#206]

CATHCART, JOHN, of Carbiston, died in Jamaica, 24 Nov 1791. [GCr#75]

CATHCART, TAYLOR, son of James Cathcart of Pitcairly, educated at Glasgow University around 1793, settled in Jamaica; a planter at Campsarima Estate, Westmoreland, Cornwall, Jamaica, deeds, 1809, 1811. [MAGU#171][NAS.RD3.328.651; RD3.344.574]

CATHCART, WILLIAM, first son of Hugh Cathcart of Gilmorehill a merchant in Jamaica, matriculated at Glasgow University in 1746. [MAGU]

CATHCART, WILLIAM, of Tower, late merchant in Jamaica, was granted Kirklands of Kilmaurs, 2 June 1814. [NAS.RD3.302.346; RGS.149.22; RS54.GR1046/263]

CATHRO, SAMUEL, a shipmaster in Port Royal, Jamaica, probate 4 Sep 1690, Jamaica.

CHALMERS, ANN, from Jamaica, married David Darling, a surgeon in Auchtermuchty, in the Canongate, 21 Dec1798. [Canongate Marriage Register]

CHALMERS, DAVID, in Jamaica, probate, 1792, PCC.

SCOTS IN JAMAICA, 1655-1855

CHALMERS, GILBERT, settled in Charleston, South Carolina, for 12 years, a Loyalist who moved to Kingston, Jamaica, by 1783. [NA.AO12.92.1A; AO12.112.5; AO13.97.224]

CHALMERS, HECTOR, son of James Chalmers a solicitor in Edinburgh, died in Jamaica in Oct 1831, inventory, 1832, Comm. Edinburgh. [NAS] [AJ#4405][EEC#18811]

CHALMERS, JAMES, a merchant in Jamaica, 1765, brother of Ronald Chalmers a farmer in Dilduff, and John Chalmers a merchant in Glasgow. [NAS.CS16.1.125/13]

CHALMERS, WALTER, son of James Chalmers a solicitor in Edinburgh, died on Hampden Estate, Falmouth, Jamaica, on 6 Aug 1827. [AJ#4177]

CHAMBERLAIN, GEORGE, a divinity student, 1823, to Jamaica, 1826, died 1832. [AUPC]

CHAMBERS, HECTOR, son of James Chambers a solicitor in Edinburgh, died in Port Antonio, Jamaica, Oct 1831. [ST.VII.490][NAS.D388]

CHAMBERS, JOHN, in Jamaica, died 9 Dec 1831, inventory, 1833, Comm. Edinburgh. [NAS.SC70.1.33; C929]

CHAPLIN, GEORGE, a merchant in Kingston, Jamaica, died May 1723, testament, 28 May 1724. [NAS.CC8.8.89]

CHAPMAN, THOMAS, in Jamaica, probate, 1748, PCC.

CHARNOCK, JOHN, in Manchester, Jamaica, deeds, 1848, inventory, 1850. [NAS.RD5.811.558/562; 812.156; SC70.1.70]

CHARTERS, GEORGE, from Edinburgh, in Falmouth, Jamaica, died Dec 1841, inventory, 1844. [NAS.SC70.1.65; F28]

CHEYNE, Dr ROBERT, in Kingston, Jamaica, May 1744. [Caribbeana.6.23]

CHISHOLM, CECILIA, in Jamaica, 1790. [NLS.MS5058/40]

CHISHOLM, DANIEL, died in Jamaica, 1791. [GM.61.682]

CHISHOLM, JOHN, born in Ross-shire, a soldier during the French and Indian Wars, then a merchant in Camden, South Carolina, a Loyalist who settled in Jamaica, 1782. [NA.AO12.49.417, etc]

CHISHOLM, ROBERT, in Richmond, Hanover, Jamaica, a letter, 1812. [NAS.RD5.156.32]

CHISHOLM, THOMAS, born 1759, a clerk who emigrated via London to Jamaica aboard the Lady Juliana in Oct 1774. [NA.T47.9/11]

CHISHOLM, WILLIAM, in Jamaica, probate 1746, PCC.

CHISHOLM, WILLIAM, in Jamaica, 6 Aug 1783. [NAS.RGS.121.286]

CHISHOLM, Dr, born 1745, via London to Jamaica aboard the James Dawkins in Feb 1774. [NA.T47.9/11]

CHRISTIE, EDWARD, a coppersmith in St Thomas in the East, Jamaica, a deed, 1789. [NAS.RD3.245.993]

CHRISTIE, FAIRLIE, an Assemblyman, died at Fairfield House, Jamaica, Dec 1806. [GM.77.376]
CHRISTIE, JOHN, born 11 Dec 1772, son of Peter Christie and Isabel Nicol in Inchbrioch, Montrose, died in Jamaica on 6 May 1827. [Inchbrioch MI]
CHRISTIE, JOHN, born 1792 in Forres, Morayshire, died at Montego Bay in Jan 1834. [Montego Bay MI]
CHRISTIE, JOHN, a merchant in Trelawney, Jamaica, 1794. [NAS.RD4.255.660]
CHRISTIE, MARGARET, from New Cargen, Jamaica, died in St Andrews, Scotland, 9 Dec 1862. [S#2337]
CHRISTIE, THOMAS, in St Ann's, Jamaica, oath, 15 Feb 1822, Comm. Moray. [NAS.CC16. 9.12/312]
CHRISTIE, WILLIAM, from Creetown, Kirkcudbright, aboard the Countess of Galloway on 15 Mar 1793 bound for Jamaica, arrived in Kingston in May 1793. [RJG:1.6.1793]
CHRISTIE, WILLIAM, a carpenter at Giffnock Hall, St Elizabeth's, Jamaica, a witness, 1787. [NAS.RD2.243.329]
CHRISTIE, ..., from Greenock aboard the brig Jane bound for Jamaica, arrived there in July 1794. [JRG:2.8.1794]
CHRISTIE, Miss, niece of Fairlie Christie, married Michael Parys, in Kingston, Jamaica, in July 1800. [GM.70.1001]
CHRYSTAL, ROBERT, born 1815, youngest son of William Chrystal in Glasgow, matriculated at Glasgow University in 1829, a merchant in Jamaica. [MAGU]
CHRYSTIE, ROBERT, born 1798, a militia colonel, died in Falmouth, Trelawney, on 19 July 1847. [Falmouth, Jamaica, MI]
CHRYSTIE, WILLIAM, in Kingston, Jamaica, youngest son of Alexander Chrystie of Balchrystie, died in Clifton on 5 June 1844, father of Margaret and others. [NAS.CS313.327][AJ#5036][EEC#18714/21056][W#5.481]
CHRYSTIE, ..., daughter of William Chrystie, was born 11 Oct 1831, in Kingston, Jamaica. [PA#117]
CLACHAR, JOHN S., Jamaica, graduated MD from Edinburgh University, 1814. [EMG#49]
CLAFFORD, Mr., from Glasgow aboard the Betsy and Brothers bound for Jamaica, arrived in Kingston in May 1793. [JRG:25.5.1794]
CLARK, AGNES, born 1834, eldest daughter of Robert Clark a builder in Glasgow, died at Montego Bay on 27 Oct 1857. [Montego Bay MI]
CLARK, ALEXANDER, in Jamaica, 1786. [NLS.MS10925]
CLARK, GEORGE, in Hanover, Jamaica, testament, 1781. [NAS.CC8.8.125]
CLARK, GEORGE, born 1833, second son of William Clark in Inverness, settled on Great Valley Estate, died at Camp Savanna, Jamaica, on 21 June 1858. [Grange Hill MI, Jamaica][Inverness Chapel Yard MI]

CLARK, JOHN, son of Patrick Clark of Holme, late of Kingston, Jamaica, died 1814. [AJ#3454]

CLARK, JOHN, son of Frederick Clark and Elizabeth Kidd in Coupar Angus, died in St Mary's, Jamaica, on 15 May 1833. [Coupar Angus, Perthshire, MI]

CLARK, THOMAS, born 27 Sep 1753 in Kirkgunzeon, Kirkcudbrightshire, eldest son of Rev. William Clark and Janet McKinnel, a physician and HM Botanist in Kingston, Jamaica, deeds, 1778, 1779. [F.2.280][NAS.RD2.226.1; 246/1.458]

CLARK, WILLIAM, born in Jamaica, only son of William Clark formerly a vicar, matriculated at Glasgow University in 1811. [MAGU]

CLARKE, JOHN, son of Edward Clarke formerly of Kingston, Jamaica, matriculated at Glasgow University in 1743. [MAGU]

CLARKE, THOMAS, born 1811, a physician and surgeon, died in St Mary's, Jamaica, on 6 July 1889. [Annetto Bay MI]

CLARKE, ..., a catechist, from Leith to Jamaica in 1800, died there in 1800. [AJ#2750]

CLEGHORN, JAMES, 'after 56 years residence', died in Kingston, Jamaica, 1806. [AJ#3097]

CLEGHORN, LAURENCE, a surgeon in St Mary's, Jamaica, dead by 1757, brother of David Cleghorn a saddler in Kirkcaldy. [NAS.B41.7.7.216; GD237.18.10/8]

CLELAND, GEORGE, in Kingston, Jamaica, 1790. [NAS.RD4.249.727]

CLELAND, JAMES, in St James, Jamaica, dead by 1790. [NAS.RD4.249.727]

CLELAND, SAMUEL, a planter, Paisley Estate, St James parish, Jamaica, 1774. [BL.Add.MS22676/8]

CLELAND, WILLIAM, in Kingston, Jamaica, 1790. [NAS.RD4.249.727]

CLERK, DOUGAL, a rebel and farmer from Otter Gallachie, Argyll, who was transported from Leith to Jamaica on 7 Aug 1685. [RPCS.XI.330]

CLERK, DUGALD, in Jamaica, 1751. [NAS.GD18.5329]

CLERK, GILBERT, steerage passenger from Greenock to Jamaica aboard the Mary of Glasgow in Nov 1773. [NAS.CE60]

CLERK, JAMES, a surgeon and physician in Jamaica, FRCS Edinburgh 1797, FRCP Edinburgh 1817, MD Marischal College, Aberdeen, 1817. [AUL]

CLERK, JOHN, son of Dugald Clerk, from the Clyde to Jamaica in 1749, letters. [NAS.GD18.5239]

CLERK, MARY, a Covenanter in Kirkcudbright, who was transported from Leith to Jamaica on 7 Aug 1685, landed at Port Royal in Nov 1685. [RPCS.XI.330][LJ#30]

CLERK, ROBERT, in Jamaica, 1741. [NAS.GD18.5329]

CLOUSTON, EDWARD, born 27 Sep. 1787 in Orkney, son of Rev. William Clouston and Isabella Traill, a planter in Jamaica, died 1866. [F.7.253][NAS.RS47.173]

SCOTS IN JAMAICA, 1655-1855

CLUNES, JOHN, son of James Clunes [1730-1802] and Jean Mackintosh [1749-1811], in Dyke, Moray, settled in St Mary's, Jamaica. [Dyke MI]
COCHRANE, JOHN, a physician, educated at St Andrews University, settled in Kingston, Jamaica, before 1732. [NAS.NRAS.726.5; GD237.106.5; GD171.4209]
COCHRANE, WILLIAM, a merchant from Glasgow, in Jamaica, 1780. [NAS.CS16.1.179]
COCK, DAVID, a mariner in Jamaica, testament, 3 Aug 1799. [NAS.CC8.8.131]
COCKBURN, Dr JAMES, son of Sir Archibald Cockburn of Langton, was apprenticed to John Jossie an Edinburgh apothecary in 1690, married Sarah ..., father of Archibald (born 1708), William, Thomas, Frances, and Sarah, settled in Jamaica before 1711, died 1717. [CFR#256]
COCKBURN, MARK, formerly surgeon of HMS Harpy, later surgeon of the Naval Hospital at Port Royal, Jamaica, third son of Thomas Cockburn and Janet Bogue in Swinton Quarter, a deed, 1814. [NAS.RD5.60.347]
COCKBURN, THOMAS, in Jamaica, MD Glasgow 1747, probate 1769, PCC.
COCKBURN, THOMAS, in Kingston, Jamaica, a bond, 1793. [NAS.RD3.263.912]
COCKBURN, WILLIAM, in Jamaica, probate 1734, PCC.
COCKBURN, Sir WILLIAM JAMES, in Jamaica, 1789. [NAS.GD216.230]
COHOUNE, JOHN, in St Andrew's, Jamaica, 1670. [SPAWI.1670/270]
COLE, GEORGE, deceased by 1773, formerly of Jamaica, later in Falkland, Fife, natural father of Margaret Cole. [NAS.CS16.1.197/244]
COLLIE, DAVID, born 1800, from Aberdeen, died in St Ann's, Jamaica, 6 Mar 1868. [AJ;15.4.1868]
COLLIE, THOMAS, a clergyman in St Andrew's, Jamaica, died 14 July 1836, inventory, 1839. [NAS.SC70.1.57; C2096]
COLQUHOUN, WALTER, a merchant in Virginia later in Jamaica, 1783, son of Margaret Williamson or Colquhoun. [NAS.CS17.1.2/22.188]
COLTART, WILLIAM, in Kingston, Jamaica, 1821. [NAS.CS17.1.40/166]
COMRIE, WALTER STIRLING, born 1800, settled in Jamaica 1818, died 1 July 1858. [New Hope Estate MI]
CONNELL, DAVID, son of Arthur Connell merchant and Provost of Glasgow, a planter in Westmoreland, Jamaica, deeds, 1786, 1788, 1796, later in Glasgow, 1797. [NAS.RD2.241.725; RD4.244.793; RD3.275.543; NRAS.0623.T-MJ.427/261]
CONNELL, JAMES, a merchant in Port Royal, Jamaica, a burgess and guildsbrother of Ayr, 1710. [AyrBR]
CONNELL, JAMES, son of Arthur Connell a merchant and Provost of Glasgow, a merchant on Green Island, Jamaica, deeds, 1786, 1788. [NAS.RD2.241.725; RD4.244.793]

SCOTS IN JAMAICA, 1655-1855

CONSTABLE, JAMES, born 1763, son of David Constable, '28 years in Jamaica as a medical practitioner', died 24 Oct 1821. [Dundee, Howff, MI]
COOK, FRANCIS M., an attorney and Assemblyman for St Dorothy's, died in Jamaica on 14 Dec 1850. [W.1179]
COOKE, ISABELLA, eldest daughter of A. D. Cooke MD, Custos of St Mary's, married Rev. J. Radcliffe, minister of the Church of Scotland in Kingston, at Green Park, St Ann's, Jamaica, on 29 Jan 1862. [EEC#23693]
COOPER, DAVID, born 26 Mar 1741 in Edzell, Angus, died at Montego Bay, Jamaica, on 11 July 179-. [Montego Bay MI]
COOPER, DAVID, son of George Cooper a merchant in Slateford, Edzell, Angus, died in Jamaica on 4 Jan 1820. [AJ#3663]
COOPER, ESTHER RITCHIE, wife of Alexander Dunlop a bank manager, died at Montego Bay, Jamaica, on 16 May 1844, inventory, 1853. [AJ#5034][EEC#21050] [NAS.SC70.1.53; E3556]
COPLAND, CHARLES, born 9 June 1791, son of Patrick Copland and Elizabeth Ogilvie in Aberdeen, educated at King's College, 1805-1809, died at Old Harbor, Jamaica, on 6 Apr 1820. [EEC#17007][S.4.178][KCA.2.396]
COPLAND, GEORGE, son of William Copland in Jamaica, at King's College, Aberdeen, 1803. [KCA.2.392]
COPLAND, JAMES, son of William Copland in Jamaica, at King's College, Aberdeen, 1816-1817. [KCA.2.427]
CORBETT, JANET, relict of John Balfour late merchant in Glasgow then in Jamaica, was granted Kenmuir, 2 June 1813. [NAS.RGS.148/55]
CORRY, ROBERT, a planter in St John's, Jamaica, a witness, 1771. [NAS.RD2.218.744]
CORVIE, ALEXANDER, born 1800, a laborer, with Janet, born 1806, Margaret, born 1828, George, born 1830, John, born 1831, Alexander, born 1834, James, born 1836, William, born 1839, and Janet, an infant, emigrated from Aberdeen aboard the Rob Roy bound for Jamaica, arrived at Kingston on 11 May 1841. [NA.CO140/33]
COTTER, JAMES, in Jamaica, probate 1793, PCC.
COUPLAND, WILLIAM, a merchant in Jamaica, a witness, 1824. [NAS.RD5.269.131]
COWAN, FRANCIS, born 1825, arrived at Bluefields, Westmoreland, on 23 Jan 1841 aboard the William Pirie, from Stranraer. [NA.CO.140/33]
COX, ELIZABETH, born 1819, daughter of Henry Cox, RN, Elie, Fife, wife of David Mason, died in Savanna la Mar, Westmoreland, Jamaica, on 2 May 1850. [Petersville MI, Jamaica]
CRAIG, AGNES, in Edinburgh, died 22 Oct 1841, inventory, 1842. [NAS.SC70.1.] relict of James McLehose in Jamaica.

SCOTS IN JAMAICA, 1655-1855

CRAIG, ANGUS, in Jamaica, died 22 Oct 1841 in Edinburgh. [NAS.D1568]
CRAIGIE, LAURENCE, eldest son of Laurence Craigie a merchant in Jamaica, matriculated at Glasgow University in 1826. [MAGU]
CRAMOND, JOHN, in Jamaica, probate 1793, PCC
CRAWFORD, ALEXANDER, born 1821, a laborer, arrived at Bluefields, Westmoreland, on 23 Jan 1841 aboard the William Pirie, from Stranraer. [NA.CO.140/33]
CRAWFORD, ANDREW, a witness in Westmoreland, Jamaica, 1741. [see NA.PROB 11/717]
CRAWFORD, DONALD, in Kingston, Jamaica, will, 1813. [NAS.RD5.111.653]
CRAWFORD, GEORGE, from Glasgow, a merchant in Jamaica, testament, 4 Jan 1802. [NAS.CC8.8.133]
CRAWFORD, HENRY JAMES, youngest son of David Crawford of Carronbank, died in Jamaica, June 1803. [AJ#2904][GM.73.882]
CRAWFORD, HUGH, born 1680, a merchant in Kingston, Jamaica, died 17 Dec 1719. [Kingston MI]
CRAWFORD, Dr JAMES, of Lochevat, in Kingston, Jamaica, during 1710. [NAS.AC.Decreets.17.825-835]
CRAWFORD, JAMES, passenger from Greenock to Jamaica aboard the Ross in Nov 1773. [NAS.CE60]
CRAWFORD, JOHN, a rebel from Otter, Argyll, imprisoned in Edinburgh Tolbooth, transported from Leith to Jamaica on 7 Aug 1685. [RPCS.XI.136][ETR#373]
CRAWFORD, JOHN, son of Cornelius Crawford, in Clarendon, Jamaica, testament, 6 Apr 1771. [NAS.CC8.8.123]
CRAWFORD, JOHN, a planter, Bellfield Estate, St James, Jamaica, 1774. [BL.Add.MS22676/8]
CRAWFORD, JOHN, died in Kingston, Jamaica, 1797. [GM.67.804]
CRAWFORD, JOHN INNES, in Jamaica, grandson of Charles Crawford of Kilbride, 1802. [NAS.RS10.1343]
CRAWFORD, Mrs JUDITH, born 1679, died in Spanish Town, Jamaica, 21 Nov 1830. [GM.100.381]
CRAWFORD, LAWRENCE, Jamaica, married Patty Redman in London, May 1750. [GM.20.284]
CRAWFORD, MARY, in Kingston, Jamaica, May 1744. [Caribbeana.6.23]
CRAWFORD, MATTHEW, eldest son of John Crawford a surgeon in Glasgow, of Gilnook Hall, Jamaica, matriculated at Glasgow University in 1762, died at Teviot Row, Edinburgh, 25 Apr 1815. [MAGU]
CRAWFORD, MATHEW, in Giffnock Hall, St Elizabeth's, Jamaica, a witness, 1787. [NAS.RD2.243.329]

SCOTS IN JAMAICA, 1655-1855

CRAWFORD, NINIAN, died in Jamaica, 1790. [GM.60.1214]
CRAWFORD, RICHARD, cabin passenger from Greenock to Jamaica aboard the Mary of Glasgow in Nov 1773. [NAS.CE60]
CRAWFORD, RICHARD, in Giffnock Hall, St Elizabeth's, Jamaica, eldest son of Francis Crawford a wright in Glasgow and Jean Semple, a deed, 1787. [NAS.RD2.243.329]
CRAWFORD, WILLIAM, a Covenanter imprisoned in Edinburgh Tolbooth, transported from Leith to Jamaica on 12 Dec 1685. [RPCS.XI.148][ETR#373]
CRAWFORD, WILLIAM, born 1813, with Sarah Crawford born 1820, arrived at Bluefields, Westmoreland, on 23 Jan 1841 aboard the William Pirie, from Stranraer. [NA.CO.140/33]
CRAWFUIRD, JAMES GRAHAM, of Gartur, youngest son of Archibald Crawfuird, WS, died on Three Mile River Estate, Jamaica, 9 May 1840.[W.54]
CREE, CLELAND, a surgeon at Montego Bay, Jamaica, died 10 Oct 1838, inventory, 1845, Comm. Edinburgh. [NAS.SC70.1.66; F148]
CREE, WILLIAM, son of John Cree and Mary Aitken in Lanark, died in Potose, Jamaica, on 6 Aug 1833. [Lanark MI]
CRICHTON, ELIZABETH DUNDAS, dau of Patrick Crichton in Jamaica, married William Lambie from Jamaica, in Edinburgh, 1820. [GM.90.563]
CRICHTON, ELIZABETH D., born 1798, daughter of Patrick Crichton in Edinburgh, wife of William Lambie in Jamaica, died there on 29 Dec 1821. [EEC#17258][St Andrews Presbyterian MI, Jamaica]
CRICHTON, Dr H. P., died at Bluff Bay, St George's, Jamaica, 1850. [FJ.942]
CRICHTON, JAMES BERTIE MAITLAND MAKGILL, born 1856, second son of Charles J. M. Crichton of Rankeillour Mains, died in Jamaica 29 July 1877, inventory, 1877. [St Andrew's MI, Jamaica][EC#29978][NAS.SC70.1.186]
CRICHTON, ROBERT, son of James Crichton the Customs Collector in Irvine, Ayrshire, died in Jamaica in July 1821. [S.5.249]
CRICHTON, WILLIAM, late of Jamaica, then in Dundee, son of Patrick Crichton of Ruthven, 1786. [NAS.GD48.box 17, fo.812/813]; possibly in Jamaica then in Balhousie, testament, 28 Oct 1788, Comm. St Andrews. [NAS]
CROMAR, ANDREW, eldest son of James Cromar rector of Aberdeen Grammar School, died in Kingston, Jamaica, on 17 Aug 1831. [AJ#4372]
CROMBIE, WILLIAM, in Jamaica, probate 1745, PCC.
CRON, ANNA, ELIZABETH, and JESSY, daughters of Robert Cron from Torthorwald, Dumfries-shire, died in Jamaica, 1831. [Torthorwald MI]
CRON, WILLIAM, born 1758 in Kirkpatrick-Fleming, Dumfries-shire, died in Kingston, Jamaica, on 14 Jan 1778. [Kilpatrick-Fleming MI]

SCOTS IN JAMAICA, 1655-1855

CROW, Reverend FRANCIS, born 1627, son of Patrick Crow of Heughhead and his wife Elizabeth Clapperton, minister of Chirnside, Berwickshire, from 1653 to 1658, emigrated to Jamaica in 1686, died in Essex, England, in 1692. [F.2.33]
CRUIKSHANK, GEORGE, Jamaica, died in London, 22 May 1818. [GM.88.640]
CRUICKSHANK, JOHN, Ballard's Valley, Jamaica, died London 2 Nov 1787, probate 1787, PCC. [GM.57.1127]
CRUICKSHANK, J., Ballard's Valley, Jamaica, died at Berry Hill, St Mary's, Jamaica, 31 Mar 1812. [GM.82.594]
CRUICKSHANK, WILLIAM, late of Jamaica, died in Arbroath, 15 Sep 1817. [S.1.36][GM.87.472]
CULLEN, ISABELLA, died 3 Apr 1834 in Jamaica, inventory, 1854. [NAS.SC70.1.62; F1815]
CUMINE, Reverend ALEXANDER, settled in Beaufort, Port Royal, South Carolina, in 1764 as a schoolmaster, a Loyalist who moved to Kingston, Jamaica, in 1777; an Anglican minister at St Catharine's, 1785; died in Spanish Town, Jamaica, 18 July 1791. [NA.AO12.49.422; AO12.68.81; AO109.120; AO13.138.574][FPA][GM.61.969]
CUMING, GEORGE, first son of Peter Cuming a merchant in St James, Jamaica, matriculated at Glasgow University in 1760. [MAGU]
CUMMINE, WILLIAM, son of William Cummine in Jamaica, at King's College, Aberdeen, 1819-1820. [KCA#2.438]
CUMMING, Sir ALEXANDER, military officer in Nanny Town, Jamaica, 1735. [SPAWI.1735/226]
CUMMING, GEORGE, in Jamaica, probate 1794, PCC.
CUMMING, JANET, born 1815, with Mary, born 1817, emigrated from Aberdeen aboard the Rob Roy bound for Jamaica, arrived at Kingston on 11 May 1841. [NA.CO140/33]
CUMMING, SARAH, a widow from Montego Bay, Jamaica, married Lord Ballenden, in Leith on 26 June 1787. [GM.57.638]
CUMMING, WILLIAM, in Kingston, Jamaica, died 17 Nov 1803, testament, 31 May 1810. [NAS.CC8.8.138]
CUNNINGHAM, Lieutenant ALEXANDER, in Jamaica, probate, 1741, PCC.
CUNNINGHAM, ANNE, 3rd dau of late George Cunningham, Trelawney, Jamaica, married Tudor Castle, Stapleton Grove, Gloucestershire, in London, 14 Oct 1845. [GM.NS24.650]
CUNNINGHAM, CHARLES, a minister sent to Jamaica in 1707. [EMA#22]
CUNNINGHAM, ELIZABETH, daughter of James Cunningham, Jocley's Barn, Jamaica, married Rev. John Thomson, in Hamilton on 18 Sept 1845. [W.609]
CUNNINGHAM, GEORGE, born 1789, of Maxfield & Greenside Estates, died in Jamaica, 9 Oct 1843. [GM.NS21.110]

SCOTS IN JAMAICA, 1655-1855

CUNNINGHAM, HENRY, Governor of Jamaica, died 173-, testament, 30 Aug1739, Comm. Edinburgh. [NAS.CC8.8.102]

CUNNINGHAM, JAMES, imprisoned in Edinburgh Tolbooth, transported from Leith to Jamaica on 7 Aug 1685, landed at Port Royal, Jamaica, and died in Jamaica. [ETR#390][LJ#35]

CUNNINGHAM, JAMES, grandson of Margaret Cleghorn [1723-1803], in Jamaica, 1803. [Kirkliston MI]

CUNNINGHAM, JAMES, Jamaica, married R. Smart's widow, dau of John Willis, in London, 17 Nov 1818. [GM.89.80]

CUNNINGHAM, JOHN, imprisoned in Edinburgh Tolbooth, transported from Leith to Jamaica on 11 Aug 1685. [ETR#369][RPCS.XI.329]

CUNNINGHAM, JOHN, a merchant and cooper, St James, Jamaica, 1774, a deed, 1790. [BL.Add.MS22676/8][NAS.RD4.249.727]

CUNNINGHAM, JOHN, born in Currie, Midlothian, died at Montego Bay, Jamaica, on 8 Dec 1790. [Montego Bay MI]

CUNNINGHAM, JOHN, born in Kirklison, 1738, to Jamaica by 1762, Colonel of St James Militia, died at Montego Bay on 27 Sep 1812. [Montego Bay MI] [GM.82.670]

CUNNINGHAM, SAMUEL, born 1780, died at Roslin Castle, Trelawney, Jamaica, 26 Dec 1844. [GM.NS23.334]

CUNNINGHAM, WILLIAM, a merchant in Glasgow and in Westmoreland, Jamaica, 1744. [NAS.RD2.169.70]

CUNNINGHAM, WILLIAM, Jamaica, died 30 June 1761. [GM.21.334]

CUNNINGHAM, WILLIAM, a merchant in Kingston, Jamaica, died in Somerstown, 29 Aug 1805. [GM.75.884]

CURRIE, AGNES, wife of Rev. Adam Thomson in Jamaica, died 19 Dec 1850, inventory, 1852. [NAS.SC70.1.77; F1553]

CURRIE, ALEXANDER, in Jamaica, died Aug 1828, testament, 25 Aug 1829. [NAS.CC8.8.152]

CURRIE, DANIEL, born 1797, son of Donald Currie and Mary Nicol in Kilmory, Arran, died in Jamaica, 1822. [Kilmory MI]

CURRIE, JOHN, in Westmoreland, Jamaica, probate 1742, London. [NA.Prob.11/717]

CURRIE, JOHN, from Haddington, East Lothian, a merchant in Jamaica, died 1747, testament, 10 Jan 1785, Comm. Edinburgh. [NAS.CC8,8,126]

CUSHNIE, ALEXANDER, a planter in St Thomas, Surry, Jamaica, a deed, 1819, a gentleman in Kingston, Jamaica, a deed, 1821. [NAS.RD5.214.245/263]

CUSHNIE, THOMAS STRATTON, in Kingston, Jamaica, son of Patrick Cushnie in Dunnottar, a deed, 1803. [NAS.RD5.231.364]

SCOTS IN JAMAICA, 1655-1855

CUTHBERT, ANN, widow of George Cuthbert in Jamaica, died in London, 30 Dec 1814. [GM.84.679]

CUTHBERT, GEORGE, born 1747, son of George Cuthbert of Castlehill, Inverness, in St Catherine's, Middlesex, Jamaica, a deed, 1785, Provost Marshal of Jamaica in 1786, died 17 June 1789. [Spanish Town MI] [NAS.RS38.152.186/7; RD4.239.451; RD3.245.210]

CUTHBERT, GEORGE, in Spanish Town, Provost Marshal of Jamaica, 1810; President of the Council of Jamaica, died 25 May 1835. [NAS.CS36.1.41] [GM.NS4.222]

CUTHBERT, JANE, widow of Lewis Cuthbert of Castlehill, Inverness, and of Jamaica, died in Clifton, Gloucestershire, 28 Sep 1830. [Bristol Cathedral MI] [GM.100.380]

CUTHBERT, LEWIS, acting Provost Marshal of Jamaica, son of George Cuthbert of Castlehill, Inverness,1789, 1790, 1795, 1796 1793; died at Clifton Estate, Jamaica, 28 Oct 1802. [NAS.RS38.338; RD3.298.136/140; RD3.391.364; RD4.238.237; RD4.246.447; RD5.50.364; RD5.144.214] [GM.72.1162]

CUTHILL, ALEXANDER, first son of Adam Cuthill a merchant in Jamaica, matriculated at Glasgow University in 1786. [MAGU]

DALL, ALEXANDER, born 1815, son of James Dall [died 1850] and Agnes Black [died 1869], a Customs officer who died in Falmouth, Jamaica, on 8 Sep 1840. [Cupar MI, also Leuchars, Fife, MI][FJ:12.11.1840]

DALL, ROBERT, in Cedar Valley, Jamaica, inventory, 1852. [NAS.SC70.1.77]

DALLAS, ALEXANDER CHARLES, a witness in Kingston, Jamaica, 1819. [NAS.RD5.214.263]

DALLAS, CHARLES ROBERT KING, Jamaica, late of the 32nd Regt., married Julia Maria, dau of Robert Charles Dallas of St Adriesse, Normandy, and Jamaica, in Paris, 3 July 1821. [GM.91.85]

DALLAS, ROBERT, a planter in St Andrew's, Jamaica, 1754; married Mrs John Hewitt, 20 Apr 1769; probate 1769, PCC. [NA.CO137/28/191-196][GM.39.215]

DALLAS, ROBERT, surgeon in Kingston, Jamaica, and Walter Dallas, merchant in Baltimore, Maryland, a decreet, 29 July 1756. [NAS.CS16.1.99/69]

DALLAS, STEWART, a wright in Jamaica, dead by 1774. [NAS.CS16.1.157/282]

DALLAS, WILLIAM, formerly a millwright in Jamaica, then in London, 1774. [NAS.CS16.1.157/282]

DALLING, WILLIAM, a merchant in Jamaica, 1744. [NAS.RS27.130/123]

DALMAHOY, JAMES, in Falmouth, Jamaica, dead by 1822, widow Jane Christie, parents of John Christie Dalmahoy, who was educated at Edinburgh Academy from 1824-1825. [NAS.CS17.1.41/611][Edinburgh Academy Register]

HUGH DALRYMPLE, and his wife Nancy Boswell from Auchenleck, Ayrshire, at St Ann's Bay, Jamaica, a deed, 1790. [NAS.RD2.250.597]

SCOTS IN JAMAICA, 1655-1855

DALRYMPLE, JOHN HAMILTON, born 1777, Customs officer at Montego Bay, Jamaica, son of Hugh Dalrymple of Nunraw, died 7 Aug 1804. [St Andrews MI] [AJ#2963][Montego Bay MI][GM.74.1804]

DALRYMPLE, WILLIAM, son of Sir Hew Dalrymple of North Berwick, in Jamaica. [NAS.GD110.894]

DALRYMPLE, WILLIAM, son of James Dalrymple a merchant in Fraserburgh, at King's College, Aberdeen, 1821-1822, a surgeon in Jamaica, died in Trelawney, Jamaica, 31 Mar1860, inventory, 1863. [KCA.2.444][AJ.9.5.1860][NAS.SC70.1.119; G3263]

DALRYMPLE, Captain, commander of Port Royal Fort, Jamaica, 1730. [SPAWI.1730/627]

DALZELL, GIBSON, husband of Frances Duff, a planter in Jamaica, 1731, Depute Provost Marshal of Jamaica, 1739, probate 1756, PCC. [AUL.ms3175/2201/1; 2227/1][JCTP.1737.595]

DARLING, DAVID, a surgeon at Old Harbour, Middlesex, Jamaica, died 31 Oct 1840, inventory 1851. [NAS.SC70.1.292]

DARLING, ROBERT, born 1797, son of Thomas Darling and Isobel Ponton, died in Jamaica, 3 Aug 1821. [Chirnside, Berwickshire, MI]

DARLING, ..., son of Charles Henry Darling, was born in Jamaica on 6 May 1859. [EEC#23373][CM#21747]

DAUNEY, FRANCIS, at Marischal College, Aberdeen, 1737, a minister in St David's, Jamaica, 1784. [FPA#316]

DAVIDSON, ANDREW, a cooper, St James, Jamaica, 1774. [BL.Add.MS22676/8]

DAVIDSON, CHARLES, second son of John Davidson and Margaret McComie in Tarland, died in Jamaica before 1789. [Tarland MI]

DAVIDSON, HARRY, in Falmouth, Jamaica, inventory, 1874. [NAS.SC70.1.168]

DAVIDSON, JAMES, a surgeon in Jamaica, inventory, 1869. [NAS.SC70.1.141/876]

DAVIDSON, JOHN, son of John Davidson in Kingston, Jamaica, at King's College, Aberdeen, 1798. [KCA.2.383/4]

DAWSON, JAMES, steerage passenger from Greenock to Jamaica aboard the Mary of Glasgow in Nov 1773. [NAS.CE60]

DAWSON, WILLIAM, Jamaica, MD Edinburgh, 1813. [EMG#46]

DEANS, JAMES, a carpenter in St George, Jamaica, a witness, 1813. [NAS.RD5.38.18]

DEANS, WILLIAM, son of John Deans in Jamaica, at King's College, Aberdeen, 1824-1826. [KCA.2.454]

DEMPSTER, ALEXANDER, seventh son of James Dempster a surgeon in Cupar, died on Dunkley's Estate, Vere, Jamaica, 24 Oct 1835. [FH.14.1.1836]

SCOTS IN JAMAICA, 1655-1855

DEMPSTER, Dr ANTHONY, fourth son of James Dempster a surgeon in Cupar, Fife, died in Manchester, Jamaica, in Sep. 1847. [FH: 11.11.1847]

DEMPSTER, Dr DAVID THOMSON, 5th son of James Dempster a surgeon in Cupar, died in Spanish Town, Jamaica, 3 Dec 1834. [FH:19.2,1835]

DENNISTOUN, JAMES, eldest son of James Dennistoun a merchant in Dumfries, educated at Glasgow University, a missionary at Montego Bay 1843-1847, died in Jamaica 1890. [F.7.669]

DESSON, WILLIAM, born 1818, a millwright, with Ann, born 1819, emigrated from Aberdeen aboard the Rob Roy bound for Jamaica, arrived at Kingston on 11 May 1841. [NA.CO140/33]

DEVANEY, JOHN GORDON, from Jamaica, graduated MD at Marischal College, Aberdeen, 13 Sep 1825. [MCA]

DEVINE, FRANCIS, born 1806, a laborer, with Ann, born 1808, John, born 1832, Ann, born 1833, Mary, born 1835, Francis, born 1837, and Margaret, born 1840, emigrated from Aberdeen aboard the Rob Roy bound for Jamaica, arrived at Kingston on 11 May 1841. [NA.CO140/33]

DEWAR, ANNE ELIZA, eldest daughter of Plummer Dewar, died at Montego Bay, 13 Jan 1844. [W.5.4381]

DEWAR, DAVID BURTON, born at Castle Semple 1796, died at Montego Bay on 31 July 1816. [Montego Bay MI]

DEWAR, GEORGINA, daughter of Robert Dewar of Muirbank, married Rev. James Dennistoun of Montego Bay, there on 10 Oct 1843. [SG:XI.1247]

DEWAR, PLUMMER, born 1814, second son of Robert Dewar a merchant in Jamaica, matriculated at Glasgow University in 1830, died in Hamilton, Ontario, on 4 Nov 1878. [MAGU]

DEWAR, ROBERT, 1st son of Robert Dewar a merchant in Jamaica, matriculated at Glasgow University in 1827. [MAGU]

DEWAR, ROBERT, 1st son of Robert Dewar a merchant in Jamaica, matriculated at Glasgow University in 1852, a student of botany. [MAGU]

DEWAR, ROBERT, died at Montego Bay, Jamaica, 15 July 1861. [S#1921]

DEWAR, WILLIAM, born in Paisley on 15 Mar 1801, died at Montego Bay, Jamaica, on 10 July 1858. [Montego Bay MI]

DEWAR, WILLIAM, second son of Robert Dewar a merchant in Jamaica, matriculated at Glasgow University in 1855. [MAGU]

DEWAR, ..., daughter of Plummer Dewar, was born at Montego Bay, Jamaica, on 20 Jan 1839. [SG#8.756]

DICK, DAVID, a merchant in Kingston, Jamaica, co-owner of the Mercury of Glasgow, 1795, [NAS.CE60.11.4/21]; was granted lands of Ellendonan, 1813; a witness, 1816. [NAS.RGS.148.46; RD5.97.266]

DICK, EMILY MARY ANNE, daughter of Archibald Dick late of Jamaica, married George Freer, in Elgin on 28 Jan 1859. [EEC.23319]

DICK, HUGH, of Mt. George, son of Alexander Dick an accountant in Edinburgh, died in Kingston, Jamaica, 1852. [S.14.4.1852]

DICK, JAMES, a merchant in Jamaica, died 4 Mar 1824 in London, testament/inventory, 1824. [NAS.CC8.8.150; SC70.1.32]

DICK, JOHN, an attorney in Kingston, Jamaica, 1801. [NAS.RD2.282.787]

DICK, RICHARD, in Jamaica, graduated MD at Marischal College, Aberdeen, on 15 Nov 1821. [MCA]

DICK, WILLIAM, born 1779, son of John Dick [1747-1833] and Janet Dick [1742-1828] in Bathgate, died in Jamaica, 1803. [Bathgate, Kirkton, MI]

DICKSON, JAMES, schoolmaster of Mannings Free School, Savanna-la-Mar, Jamaica, 1777. [CCGA]

DICKSON, JOHN, planter in Salem, Jamaica, brother of William Dickson a brewer in Lasswade, 1762, 1778. [NAS.RS27.159.164; CS16.1.173/287; CS18/438]

DICKSON, JOHN, of Hillhead, then in Jamaica, 1780. [NAS.CS16.1.179]

DICKSON, JOHN, in Savanna-la-Mar, Jamaica,1780. [NA.CO137.1-35]

DICKSON, JOHN, an attorney in Kingston, Jamaica, 1799, son of John Dickson of Hillhead, Edinburgh. [NAS.CS18.708.8]

DICKSON, RICHARD, son of John Dickson and his wife Ann Crooks, in Hanover, Jamaica, an indenture, 1812. [IRO.Deeds.BA12.1807]; died at Davis's Cove on 26 Jan 1821. [EEC#17145]

DICKSON, ROBERT, born 1763, son of Robert Dickson and Janet Bathgate in Courthill, Nenthorn, Berwickshire, died in Jamaica, 1789. [Nenthorn MI]

DICKSON, WILLIAM, born 1719, son of John Dickson, of Whitstead, to Jamaica 1748, a carpenter in Kingston, Jamaica, deeds, 1765, 1777. [NAS.RD2.197/2.377; RD2.222/2.203]

DIGNUM, Dr HARRY GRAHAM, born 1838, died in Kingston, Jamaica, 24 Jan 1861. [S#1766]

DINGWALL, JOHN, of Salt Savannah Estate, Jamaica, 1856. [NAS.SC48.25.56/239]

DIXON, HENRY, baptised 10 Mar 1785 in Gorbals, son of William Dixon and his wife Janet Smith, died in Cave Valley, Hanover, Jamaica, on 5 Jan 1801. [AJ#2779][GM.71.371]

DIXON, ..., cabin passenger from Greenock to Jamaica aboard the Mary of Glasgow in Nov 1773. [NAS.CE60]

DIXON, WILLIAM, born 1806, with Rose born 1814, Nancy born 1831, John born 1833, and William born 1838, arrived at Bluefields, Westmoreland, on 23 Jan 1841 aboard the William Pirie, from Stranraer. [NA.CO.140/33]

SCOTS IN JAMAICA, 1655-1855

DOBIE, THOMAS, son of a writer in Lockerbie, died in Jamaica, 1803.[AJ.2930]
DOBIE, WILLIAM D., died in Falmouth, Jamaica, 8 Dec 1819. [GM.90.186]
DOD, RALPH, a soldier, to Jamaica on the Grantham in 1659. [SPC.1659/126]
DODD, FRANCIS DUNLOP, born 3 Sep 1818 in Ayrshire, senior magistrate in Hanover, Jamaica, died 7 Nov 1891. [Green Island MI, Jamaica]
DOIG, PAUL, in Jamaica, inventory, 1847. [NAS.SC70.1.67[
DOLLAS, JOHN, son of John Dollas, a tailor in Jamaica, buried in St Nicholas churchyard, Aberdeen, 3 Oct 1754. [ACA]
DONALD, DAVID, born 1739, planter in Hanover, Jamaica, died in London, 30 July 1807. [GM.77.985]
DONALD, DAVID, in Jamaica, son of James Donald a merchant in Kirriemuir, 1777. [NAS.RS35.25.116]
DONALD, JOHN, from Kirriemuir, at Montego Bay, Jamaica, died 19 May 1819, testament, 13 Nov 1819. [NAS.CC8.8.145]
DONALD, MATHEW, was transported from Glasgow to Jamaica on 13 Feb 1669. [Glasgow Burgh Records]
DONALD, ROBERT, in Jamaica, probate 1776, PCC.
DONALDSON, ALEXANDER, Jamaica, died at sea, 24 Mar 1807.[GM.77.487]
DONALDSON, COLIN, a clergyman who emigrated to Jamaica, 1801. [EMA#25]
DONALDSON, GEORGE, son of Alexander Donaldson and Agnes Wightman [1731-1809] in Coldstream, Berwickshire, settled in Jamaica, [Lennell MI]
DONALDSON, JAMES, in Jamaica, probate 1711, PCC
DONALDSON, JAMES, from Maybole, Ayrshire, in Jamaica, died 27 Oct 1828, inventory, 1833. [NAS.SC70.1.49]
DONALDSON, ROBERT, a merchant in Kingston, Jamaica, 1790, a witness. [NAS.RD2.249.1059]
DONALDSON, or BLACK, SUSANNAH, in Jamaica, 1816. [NAS.RS.Burntisland.1.108]
DONALDSON, WILLIAM, a merchant, died in Kingston, Jamaica, 5 Dec 1789. [GM.60.179]
DONALDSON, WILLIAM, late of St John's, New Brunswick, died in Jamaica on 18 Dec 1819. [S.4.167]
DONOVAN, JAMES, a sugar plantation manager, Hope Bay, Jamaica, a witness, 1815. [NAS.RD5.86.256]
DOUGLAS, ANNA CHARLOTTE MURRAY, wife of Henry Lowndes, died in St Thomas in the Vale, Jamaica, 2 Sep 1853. [EEC#22494]
DOUGLAS, CAMPBELL, a gentleman in St Thomas in the East, Jamaica, a deed, 1775; married Agnes, daughter of Robert Marshall a merchant in Glasgow, in Hamilton, 1 July 1793. [NAS.RD4.718.871] [GM.63.670]

DOUGLAS, CHARLES JAMES SHOLTO, the Customs Collector of Jamaica, born after 1710, son of Sir John Douglas of Kelhead and Christian Cunningham. [SP.7.150]

DOUGLAS, DAVID, Assembly printer, Master in Chancery, Judge, died in Spanish Town, Jamaica, 8 Aug 1789. [GM.59.955]

DOUGLAS, EBENEZER, in Jamaica, probate 1797, PCC.

DOUGLAS, JAMES, probate, 1663, Jamaica. [RGO/SpanishTown, liber 1]

DOUGLAS, JAMES, a merchant in Kingston, Jamaica, son of Dr James Douglas in Carlisle, a deed, 1781. [NAS.RD2.23.242]

DOUGLAS, JAMES, in St John's, Jamaica, a deed, 1785. [NAS.RD3.244.520]

DOUGLAS, JAMES CHARLES S., in Jamaica, probate 1783, PCC.

DOUGLAS, JAMES, Jamaica, died aboard the Hope of Bristol bound for Jamaica, 19 July 1791. [GM.61.873]

DOUGLAS, JAMES, formerly in Jamaica, then in Wigtown, 23 Nov 1826. [NAS.MEP]

DOUGLAS, JOHN, son of James Douglas the provost of Gatehouse of Fleet, Wigtownshire, died in Kingston, Jamaica, 1813. [AJ#3410]

DOUGLAS, JOHN, late of Kingston, Jamaica, died in Surrey, 24 Aug 1856. [CM#29879]

DOUGLAS, ROBERT, in Jamaica and in Burntisland, Fife, testament, 28 Aug 1816, Comm. St Andrews. [NAS.CC20.30.204]

DOUGLAS, ROBERT, late in Jamaica, now in Burntisland, husband of Janet Ross, 17 Mar 1848. [NAS.B9.8.1.166]

DOUGLAS, SAMUEL, a merchant in Jamaica, a burgess and guildsbrother of Ayr, 4 Apr 1751. [AyrBR]

DOUGLAS, SAMUEL, possibly from Galloway, formerly in Savannah, Georgia, a Loyalist who settled in Jamaica by 1782, [NA.AO12.71.1]; probate 1823, PCC.

DOUGLAS, Mrs., wife of James Sholto Douglas, died in Spanish Town, Jamaica, in Mar 1777. [CCGA]

DOUGLAS, Mrs., wife of David Douglas, died at an advanced age in Spanish Town, Jamaica, during Apr 1777. [CCGA]

DOUGLAS, Mr., from Glasgow aboard the Mary bound for Jamaica, arrived in Kingston in May 1794. [JRG:18.5.1793]

DOUGLAS, Mr., from Greenock aboard the brig Jane bound for Jamaica, arrived there in July 1793. [JRG:2.8.1794]

DOVE, JAMES, a merchant in Jamaica, married Jean Kirkcaldie in Edinburgh, 1 Mar 1761. [Edinburgh Marriage Register]

DOW, JOHN, born 3 Jan 1760, son of Rev. Robert Dow and Janet Adie in Ardrossan, a merchant in Jamaica. [F.3.79]

DOW, ..., a planter in St Andrew's, Jamaica, 1754. [NA.CO137/28]

SCOTS IN JAMAICA, 1655-1855

DOWNIE, ADELAIDE, daughter of Rev. Thomas Downie, late in Nova Scotia, died in Kingston, Jamaica, 9 Jan 1867. [S#7350]
DOWNIE, JOHN, a Covenanter who was transported from Leith to Jamaica in Aug 1685. [RPCS.XI.130]
DOWNIE, J., in Clarendon, Jamaica, died 14 Dec 1812. [GM.83.386]
DOWNIE, MARTHA, born 1812, arrived at Bluefields, Westmoreland, on 23 Jan 1841 aboard the William Pirie, from Stranraer. [NA.CO.140/33]
DRUMMOND, ANDREW, in Mocha, Jamaica, died 4 Jan1851, inventory, 1859. [NAS.SC70.1.100; E3546]
DRUMMOND, ARCHIBALD, born 1775, died 2 Feb 1815. [Kingston, Jamaica,MI]
DRUMMOND, JAMES, probate, 1745, Jamaica. [RGO/SpanishTown, liber25]
DRUMMOND, JAMES, a clerk in Greencastle, St Mary's, Jamaica, eldest son of Thomas Drummond of Deanstone and Jacobina Stewart, a deed, 1786. [NAS.RD3.246.892]
DRUMMOND, JAMES, in St James, Cornwall, Jamaica, died in Old Monklands, testament, 1817, Comm.Hamilton. [NAS.CC10.7.3.183]
DRUMMOND, JOHN, born 1717, a physician who died in Westmoreland, Jamaica, on 10 June 1754. [Savanna la Mar MI, Jamaica]
DRUMMOND, JOHN, steerage passenger from Greenock to Jamaica aboard the Mary of Glasgow in Nov 1773. [NAS.CE60]
DRUMMOND, JOHN, probate, 1806, PCC.[Pitt, Q.122]
DRUMMOND, Dr JOHN, died in Westmoreland, Jamaica, 14 Aug 1804. [GM.74.690]
DRUMMOND, or HOWARD, KATHERINE, daughter of James Drummond in Kelty, died in Kingston, Jamaica, during 1806. [SM.69.77] [NAS.GD16.43.57]
DRUMMOND, ROBERT, late of Jamaica, died in Edinburgh on 8 July 1798. [AJ#2647][NAS.RD4.264.460]
DRUMMOND, STEPHEN, probate, 1720, Jamaica.[RGO/SpanishTown/16/F9]
DRUMMOND, WILLIAM, an attorney in Kingston, Jamaica, 1801. [NAS.RD2.282.787]
DRYSDALE, JOHN, a physician and surgeon, Kingston, Jamaica, will, 1786. [NAS.RD2.264.402]
DUFF, ANTOINETTE ALEXINA, wife of David Hutchison, late of Coffee Grove, Jamaica, died in Lockport, Niagara County, 11 Feb1860. [DC#23483][S#1476]
DUFF, JAMES, in Jamaica, 1 Jan 1782. [NAS.RD4.272.599]
DUFF, JOHN, born 1812, a carpenter, emigrated from Aberdeen aboard the Rob Roy bound for Jamaica, arrived at Kingston on 11 May 1841. [NA.CO140/33]
DUN, JAMES, from Edinburgh, a merchant in Maryland, later in Jamaica, 1760. [NAS.CS16.1.107/276]

SCOTS IN JAMAICA, 1655-1855

DUNBAR, ALEXANDER, in St Elizabeth, Jamaica, probate 30 Jan 1679, Jamaica.
DUNBAR, ALEXANDER, a merchant from Nairn, died in Kingston, Jamaica, 1794. [GM.64.768]
DUNBAR, DAVID, born 1757, son of Patrick Dunbar and Marion Dunshee in the Mains of Dalquharren, Dailly, Ayrshire, a planter on Rozelle Estate, Jamaica, died 1786. [Dailly MI][NAS.NRAS.3572/40/20]
DUNBAR, HECTOR, probate 1683, Jamaica.[RGO/SpanishTown.liber 4]
DUNBAR, JAMES, late of Jamaica, graduated MD at King's College, Aberdeen, on 8 Nov 1742. [KCA#128]
DUNBAR, JAMES, in Jamaica, probate 1743, PCC.[Boycott.Q/260]
DUNBAR, JOHN LAWRENCE, a planter, Lathy Estate, St James, Jamaica, 1774. [BL.Add.MS22676/8]
DUNBAR, JANET, died at Orangehill, Jamaica, on 8 Mar 1829. [S#973]
DUNBAR, ROBERT, died at Orangehill, Jamaica, 8 Mar 1829. [EEC#18322]
DUNBAR, STEPHEN, son of Walter Dunbar in Forres, Morayshire, died on Eden Plantation, Jamaica,in Sep 1780. [SM.42.617][GM.III.381]
DUNCAN, ALEXANDER, in Jamaica, 1751. [NAS.RH15.69.2]; a burgess of Edinburgh, 1758. [EBR]
DUNCAN, ALEXANDER, born 1809, a laborer, with Isabella, born 1810, William, born 1835, Margaret, born 1837, and Isabella, born 1840, emigrated from Aberdeen aboard the Rob Roy bound for Jamaica, arrived at Kingston on 11 May 1841. [NA.CO140/33]
DUNCAN, H., in Savanna-la-Mar, 1780. [NA.CO137.1-35]
DUNCAN, HECTOR, in St Thomas, Jamaica, probate 30 Aug 1684, Jamaica
DUNCAN, JAMES, born 1813, son of John Duncan and Margaret Ferrier in Strathcathro, Angus, died in Jamaica during 1854. [Brechin MI]
DUNCAN, JOHN, born 1814, a carpenter, emigrated from Aberdeen aboard the Rob Roy bound for Jamaica, arrived at Kingston on 11 May 1841. [NA.CO140/33]
DUNCAN, WILLIAM, born 1695, a cooper in Kingston, Jamaica, died on 16 Dec 1729. [Kingston MI]
DUNCANSON, DAVID, probate, 1708, Jamaica. [RGO/SpanishTown.liber12]
DUNCANSON, JAMES, son of Walter Duncanson town clerk of Dunbarton, died in Jamaica, 5 Apr1797. [CM.11824][GM.67.528]
DUNDAS, ALEXANDER, probate, 1748, Jamaica. [RGO/Spanish Town, liber 27]
DUNDAS, ALEXANDER, died in Jamaica, by Feb 1792. [GCr.70]
DUNDAS, JAMES, manager of Taylor's Caymanas the property of James Ewing, died in Jamaica on 11 Dec 1850. [W#1179]
DUNDAS, Major, and his servant, from Greenock to Jamaica aboard the Mary of Glasgow in Nov 1773. [NAS.CE60]

SCOTS IN JAMAICA, 1655-1855

DUNLOP, ALEXANDER, a planter in Jamaica, 1782, son of Professor Alexander Dunlop and Mary Leitch. [NAS.RS10.45]

DUNLOP, ALEXANDER, manager of the Colonial Bank at Montego Bay, Jamaica, 1843. [NAS.RS10.475]

DUNLOP, JOHN, MD, born 6 Feb 1823, son of John Dunlop of Cairbraid, died in St Andrew's, Jamaica, on 30 July 1867. [Up Park Camp MI, Jamaica]

DUNLOP, JOHN ALEXANDER GRAHAM, born 7 May 1844, infant son of Alexander Dunlop, a bank-manager at Montego Bay, died 28 Sep 1844, testament, 1853. [EEC#21111][W#5.47/516][NAS.SC70.1.80; F1714]

DUNLOP, ROBERT BRUCE ELLIS, born 1844, 6th son of Henry Dunlop of Craigtoun and Alexina Rankin, died in Kingston, Jamaica, Jan 1877. [EC#28837] [Dean MI, Edinburgh]

DUNN, QUENTIN, a Covenanter who was transported from Leith to Jamaica on 11 Aug 1685. [RPCS.XI.329][ETR#369]

DURANT, THOMAS and BENJAMIN, from Jamaica, apprentice millwrights in Alloa, Clackmannanshire, 1790. [NAS.RD2.274.61]

DURNO, JOHN, an advocate from Aberdeen, in Jamaica by 1809, died 1816. [NAS.GD171.914][S.1.6]

DUTHIE, ALEXANDER, a planter in Jamaica, later in Aberdeen, buried 24 May 1765 in St Nicholas churchyard, testament, 19 June 1769, Comm. Aberdeen. [NAS][ACA]

DUTHIE, ARCHIBALD, in Savanna-la-Mar, Jamaica, 1780. [NA.CO137.1-35]

DUTHIE, GEORGE, probate, 1735, Jamaica. [RGO/SpanishTown.liber 20]

DUTHIE, JAMES, sometime of Jamaica, died in Stirling, 1817. [S.1.17]

DUTHIE, JOHN, probate 1729, Jamaica. [RGO/SpanishTown.liber 18/F69]

EASSON, GEORGE, an overseer in Jamaica, 1823. [NAS.SC48.49.25.19/242]

EASSON, or OCHTERLONY, MARGARET, in Tophill, Little London, Westmoreland, Jamaica, 1880. [NAS.SC49.48.25.80/156]

EASTON, JOHN, MD, a surgeon at Kingston Royal Hospital, eldest son of Rev. Dr Easton in Kirriemuir, died in Kingston, Jamaica, on 13 Aug 1841. [AJ#4886]

ECCLES, GEORGE, a merchant in Jamaica, died 1799, testament, 18 Dec 1812. [NAS.CC8.8.138]

EDGAR, ALEXANDER, of Netherhouses, formerly in Jamaica, 1747. [NAS.RD4.176/1.482/4]

EDGAR, ALEXANDER, born in Hamilton, Lanarkshire, first son of Alexander Hamilton of Martha Brae, Jamaica, matriculated at Glasgow University in 1787. [MAGU]; a planter in Trelawney, Cornwall, Jamaica, a deed, 1791. [NAS.RD4.250.1260]

EDGAR, ALEXANDER, in Jamaica, an inventory, 1821. [NAS.SC70.1.21]

EDGAR, ALEXANDER, late in Jamaica, then in Edinburgh, 1839. [NAS.RS38.841]

EDGAR, ARCHIBALD, in Jamaica, probate, 1795, PCC.
EDGAR, HANDISYDE, a physician in Trelawney, Cornwall, Jamaica, at Montego Bay, deeds, 1791, 1798; in St James, Cornwall, Jamaica, testament, 8 Apr1814. [NAS.RD4.250.1260; RD3.282.716; RD4.253.272; CC8.8.140]; his widow died in London on 13 July 1819. [GM.89.93]
EDGAR, JAMES, a planter in St Mary's, Jamaica, 1779. [NAS.CS16.1.174]
EDGAR, JAMES, a physician in Trelawney, Cornwall, Jamaica, a deed, 1793. [NAS.RD4.253.272]
EDGAR, JAMES, of Auchingrammont, Hamilton, and of St George's, Surrey, Jamaica, testament, 20 Feb 1811, Comm. Hamilton. [NAS.CC10.7.2.7]
EDGAR, MARY, third daughter of Alexander Edgar of Wedderley, wife of Dr James Henry Archer, died in Springmount, Jamaica, on 9 Oct 1831. [AJ#4383]
EDGAR, THOMAS, son of the late Archibald Edgar in Jamaica, at King's College, Aberdeen, 1795. [KCA.2.379]
EDMONSTONE, WILLIAM, in Jamaica, 1774. [NAS.CS16.1.334]
EDMONSTONE, ..., of Ednam, in Port Royal, Jamaica, 1712. [NAS.Admiralty Decreet.17.825-835]
EDWARDS, BRYAN, a stipendiary judge of Westmoreland, Jamaica, married Lydia Myra, daughter of Joseph Bowen of Saltspring, Jamaica, at Montego Bay, on 7 Nov 1835. The said Bryan Edwards died on 13 Nov 1835 in New Savanna, Westmoreland, Jamaica. [AJ#4592]
EDWARDS, HUGH, in Jamaica, graduated MD at Marischal College, Aberdeen, on 26 May 1823. [MCA]
EDWARDS, JOHN, the Receiver General of Jamaica, died 18 Jan 1848, inventory, 1849. [NAS.SC70.1.1869; E1917]
EDWARDS, MARY MACKENZIE, daughter of Alexander Mackenzie Edwards and Mary Chambers, died in Jamaica, 1875. [Dean MI, Edinburgh]
ELDER, PATRICK, a carpenter at Seven Rivers, St James, Jamaica, 1792. [NAS.RS52.2767]
ELLIOT, JAMES, born in Portobello, Midlothian, during 1789, a Lt. Col. of the Trelawney Militia in Jamaica, husband of Margaret Hunter [1797-1885], died on 2 June 1862. [Portobello Episcopal MI]
ELLIOT, JOHN, in Port Royal, Jamaica, probate 16 May 1671, Jamaica
ELLIOT, JOHN, a Covenanter in Teviotdale who was transported from Leith to Jamaica in Aug 1685, landed at Port Royal, Jamaica, in Nov 1685. [RPCS.XI.329][LJ#44]
ELLIOT, THOMAS, son of Thomas Elliot in Jamaica, at King's College, Aberdeen, 1816. [KCA.2.428]
ELLIS, ADAM GIBB, an advocate in Jamaica, inventory, 1895. [NAS.SC70.1.337]

SCOTS IN JAMAICA, 1655-1855

ELLIS, FRANCIS, born 1820, with Mary Ann Ellis born 1818, arrived at Bluefields, Westmoreland, on 23 Jan 1841 aboard the William Pirie, from Stranraer. [NA.CO.140/33]

ELLIS, JOHN, son of William Ellis in Jamaica, at King's College, Aberdeen, in 1801. [KCA.2.389]

ELLIS, ROBERT, passenger from Greenock to Jamaica aboard the Ross in Nov 1773. [NAS.CE60]

ELMSLIE, JOHN, in Jamaica, 1790. [NLS.ms5028/40]

ELPHINSTONE, WILLIAM, in Jamaica, 1749. [NAS.RH4.70.bundle 53]

ELRICK, ANDREW, a merchant in Jamaica, a burgess and guildsbrother of Ayr, 4 Apr1751. [AyrBR]

ERSKINE, ALEXANDER, second son of John Erskine in Jamaica, at Glasgow University in 1791, died 1855. [MAGU]

ERSKINE, DAVID, 2nd son of John Erskine in Jamaica, at Glasgow University, 1793. [MAGU]

ERSKINE, DAVID, at Montego Bay, Jamaica, testament, 6 Jan 1798. [NAS.CC8.8.131]

ERSKINE, JOHN, a planter, Lima Estate, St James, Jamaica, son of Alexander Erskine a merchant in Montrose, Angus, died at Montego Bay in 1768; 1774. [NNQ.IX.20] [BL.Add.MS22676/8]

ERSKINE, JOHN, in St James, Cornwall, Jamaica, probate 25 Oct 1786, Jamaica. [NAS.GD123.142.340; CS17.1.1/144, 148]

ERSKINE, JOHN, a merchant from Greenock, died in Kingston, Jamaica, 17 Sept 1795. [GM.65.969]

ERSKINE, JOHN JAMES, in Jamaica, MD Edinburgh University, 1791. [EMG#23]

ESSON, THOMAS, planter, St Mary's, Jamaica, a witness, 1802. [NAS.RD3.300.1112]

EXILE, [?], ELIZA, born 1825, emigrated from Aberdeen aboard the Rob Roy bound for Jamaica, arrived at Kingston on 11 May 1841. [NA.CO140/33]

EWART, HELEN, in Kingston, Jamaica, inventory, 1891. [NAS.SC70.1.298]

EWART, MATHILDE, in Kingston, Jamaica, inventory, 1891. [NAS.SC70.1.298]

EWART, Dr ROBERT, in Jamaica, 1750. [NAS.NRAS.Tweedie-Stoddart pp, bundle 47]

EWING, THOMAS, born 1803, son of Peter Ewing in Arbroath, Angus, died in Kingston, Jamaica, 1832. [Arbroath Abbey MI]

FAIRFULL, ALEXANDER, from St Andrews, died in Kingston, Jamaica, on 21 July 1852. [FJ#1026]

FAIRLIE, JAMES, from Kingston, Jamaica, died in Bellfield, 19 May 1819. [GM.88.586]

SCOTS IN JAMAICA, 1655-1855

FAIRWEATHER, ROBERT, Custos of St Mary's, Jamaica, died there on 28 Apr 1843. [AJ#4982]

FALCONER, DANIEL, born 1816, a millwright, emigrated from Aberdeen aboard the Rob Roy bound for Jamaica, arrived at Kingston on 11 May 1841. [NA.CO140/33]

FALCONER, GEORGE, a planter in Jamaica, a witness, 1781. [NAS.RD2.231.242]

FALCONER, JAMES, born 1759, died in Jamaica on 5 Mar 1828. [St Andrew's MI, Jamaica]

FALCONER, JAMES C., from Inverness, graduated MA from King's College, Aberdeen, in Mar 1847, later a teacher in Jamaica. [KCA#299]

FALCONER, ROBERT, in Spanish Town, 1801, son of Rev. John Falconer, died in Jamaica, 1802. [AJ#2839][NAS.PS3.CC16.9.10/88]

FALCONER, WILLIAM, in Spanish Town, Jamaica, a lease, 1808, Comm. Moray. [NAS.CC16.9.10.88]

FALCONER, WILLIAM GORDON, born 1806, third son of David Falconer a merchant in Forres, died at the Orange River, Jamaica, in Oct 1832. [AJ#4438][NAS.GD23.6.663]

FALCONER, WILLIAM, of Rosehill, Jamaica, 1845. [NAS.RS38.GR2272/262]

FAREW, JOHN, steerage passenger from Greenock to Jamaica aboard the Mary of Glasgow in Nov 1773. [NAS.CE60]

FARQUHAR, ANDREW, born 1800, eldest son of Andrew Farquhar in Mains of Caskieben, Aberdeenshire, died in Spanish Town, Jamaica, on 2 Oct 1834. [AJ#4536]

FARQUHAR, DAVID, a merchant in Kingston, Jamaica, died 1758, testament, 7 Apr1763. [NAS.CC8.8.119]

FARQUHAR, GEORGE, cabin passenger from Greenock to Jamaica aboard the Mary of Glasgow in Nov 1773. [NAS.CE60]

FARQUHAR, JOHN, a planter in Jamaica, 1715. [NAS.RD4.117.589]

FARQUHAR, JOHN, from Edinburgh, a merchant in Spanish Town, Jamaica, testament, 22 June 1767. [NAS.CC8.8.120]

FARQUHAR, THOMAS, in St David's, Jamaica, probate 3 Jan 1694, Jamaica

FARQUHARSON, ALEXANDER, of Jobshill, died in Jamaica on 21 Sep 1821. [AJ#3865]

FARQUHARSON, CHARLES, in Jamaica, MD Edinburgh University, 1806. [EMG#39]

FARQUHARSON, CHARLES, a planter in St Ann's, Middlesex, Jamaica, a deed, 1807; father of Charles Miller Farquhar, born 1815, at Edinburgh Academy, 1827-1831. [NAS.RD5.271.168] [EAR]

SCOTS IN JAMAICA, 1655-1855

FARQUHARSON, ELIZABETH FRANCES, only dau of Matthew Farquharson, St Elizabeth, Jamaica, married Robert Henry Robertson, 2nd son of Duncan Robertson, St Elizabeth, in London, 19 Mar 1864. [GM.NS2/16.521]

FARQUHARSON, F., Lieutenant Colonel of the 7th Royal Fusiliers, married Thomasine, youngest daughter of T. Nasmyth, in Jamaica on 27 June 1833. [DPCA.5.7.1833]

FARQUHARSON, JAMES, of Invercauld, via Greenock to Jamaica on the Rosamund, Feb 1793. [NAS.NRAS#61.6.1]

FARQUHARSON, JOHN, RN, born 1771, died in Jamaica, 30 Jan 1792.[GCr.93]

FARQUHARSON, JOHN, son of James Farquharson of Coldrach, died in Jamaica on 14 Oct 1808. [EA#4711][SM.71.237]

FARQUHARSON, MATTHEW, in St Elizabeth's, died at the Rectory, Montego Bay, on 22 Mar 1840. [AJ#4819]

FARQUHARSON, THOMAS, attorney at law in Kingston, Jamaica, only son of Paul Farquharson in Perth, a deed, 1774. [NAS.RD2.216.923]

FARQUHARSON, Mrs, wife of Charles Farquharson of Persie, died in Spring Vale, Jamaica, on 28 Dec 1822. [EEC#17424][DPCA#1076]

FARQUHARSON, WILLIAM, from Edinburgh, died in Kingston, Jamaica, in 1805. [AJ#3024]

FERGUS, JOHN, died in Falmouth, Jamaica, on 25 Nov 1825. [AJ#4080]

FERGUSON, AGNES, who was transported from Leith to Jamaica in Aug 1685, landed at Port Royal, Jamaica, in Nov 1685. [RPCS.XI.136][LJ#18]

FERGUSON, ALEXANDER, in Jamaica, died 12 Dec 1836, inventory, 1837, Comm. Edinburgh. [NAS.SC70.1.55; D1020]

FERGUSON, ALEXANDER EDMUND, born 1801, son of Alexander Ferguson of Baledmund, Perthshire, died on St Iago Estate, Clarendon, Jamaica, on 6 June 1831. [AJ#4366]

FERGUSON, ALLISON, died at the house of her aunt Mrs Rankine in Westmoreland, Jamaica, on 30 Jan 1834, [SG#232]

FERGUSON, ANDREW, MD, born 1813, son of Andrew Ferguson in Aberdeen, died in Kingston, Jamaica, 30 Aug 1853. [AJ.5.10.1853]

FERGUSON, ANGUS, was transported from Leith to Jamaica in Aug 1685. [RPCS.XI.149]

FERGUSON, ANGUS, son of Rev. John Ferguson in Uphall, died in Jamaica on 28 June 1819. [S.3.143]

FERGUSON, CHARLES, born in Aug 1708, son of Rev, Adam Ferguson and Mary Goprdon in Crathie, died in Port Royal, Jamaica, Oct 1743. [F.4.189]

FERGUSON, DONALD, a Covenanter in Ruchoard was transported from Leith to Jamaica in Aug 1685. [RPCS.XI.136]

SCOTS IN JAMAICA, 1655-1855

FERGUSON, DUNCAN, a Covenanter who was transported from Leith to Jamaica in Aug 1684. [RPCS.IX.95]

FERGUSON, DUNCAN, a farmer in Polmaise, St Ninian's, Stirlingshire, imprisoned in Edinburgh Tolbooth, was transported from Leith to Jamaica in Aug 1685. [RPCS.XI.136][ETR#373]

FERGUSON, ELIZABETH, born 1757, a spinster who emigrated via London to Jamaica aboard the Royal Charlotte in Feb 1774. [NA.T47.9/11]

FERGUSON, EUPHEMIA, born 1758, a spinster who emigrated via London to Jamaica aboard the Royal Charlotte in Feb 1774. [NA.T47.9/11]

FERGUSON, JAMES, late of Hanover, Jamaica, married Eliza, only daughter of Duncan MacDiarmid in Kynachan, at Dunfallandie, 1809. [EA#XCI.4733]

FERGUSON, JAMES, of Middlehaugh, late of Jamaica, testament, 1 June 1819. [NAS.CC7.8.160]

FERGUSON, JANET, widow of William Jameson a merchant and wharfinger in Kingston, Jamaica, 1850. [NAS.CS313.15]

FERGUSON, JOHN, a physician in Kingston, Jamaica, died in Clapham, 22 July 1856, inventory, 1856. [NAS.SC70.1.92][GM.NS2/1.391]

FERGUSON, PATRICK, born 27 Oct 1717, son of Rev. Adam Ferguson and Mary Gordon, died in Port Royal, Jamaica, on 18 Mar 1747. [F.4.189]

FERGUSON, ROBERT, in St Thomas, Jamaica, 1670. [SPAWI.1670/270]

FERGUSON, ROBERT, a merchant in Jamaica, 1824. [NAS.NRAS.0623.JMT/2]

FERGUSON, ROBERT, a merchant in Wigton, Jamaica, late of Manchester, Jamaica, second son of Thomas Ferguson, Peebles, formerly of Leith, died at Howard House, Detroit, Michigan, 12 Sep 1855, inventory, 1857. [EEC#322800] [NAS.SC70.1.93; H221]

FERGUSON, Dr THOMAS, born 1706, died in Jamaica 1791. [GM.61.1065]

FERGUSON, WILLIAM, first son of James Ferguson a merchant in Jamaica, matriculated at Glasgow University in 1785. [MAGU]

FERRIER, DAVID, an attorney in Kingston, Jamaica, died Mar 1819 in Edinburgh, inventory, 1855. [NAS.SC70.1.88; E4439]

FERRIER, JOHN, in Jamaica, married Elizabeth Watson in Edinburgh, 29 Mar 1788. [EMR]

FERRIER, WILLIAM, a Jacobite rebel, transported via Liverpool to Jamaica, arrived 21 Mar1748. [NA.T53/44]

FIDDES, ALEXANDER, born 1817, FRCS, Edinburgh, died in Kingston, Jamaica, on 25 Dec 1869. [S#8273]

FIFE, LAURENCE, son of Laurence Fife in Jamaica, at King's College, Aberdeen, 1814-1817. [KCA#2/421]

FIFE, WILLIAM, brother of Barclay Fife a merchant in Leith, died in Jamaica, 6 Jan1810. [PC#63]

SCOTS IN JAMAICA, 1655-1855

FINDLATOR, ALEXANDER JAMES, son of James Findlator in Jamaica, was admitted as a burgess of Banff in 1777; a clerk in Jamaica, a witness, 1790. [BBR][NAS.RD4.249.727]; died in London, 8 Jan 1815. [GM.85.180]

FINDLATOR, JAMES, a planter, Leogan Estate, St James, Jamaica, 1774. [BL.Add.MS22676/8]

FINDLATOR, Miss PEGGY, died at Montego Bay, 2 July 1798. [AJ#2649]

FINDLAY, THOMAS, son of James Findlay an Excise Surveyor, died in Jamaica on 15 Apr 1816. [GrA: 25.6.1816]

FINDLAY, WILLIAM, born 1797, a ploughman, emigrated from Aberdeen aboard the Rob Roy bound for Jamaica, arrived at Kingston on 11 May 1841. [NA.CO140/33]

FINLAYSON, ALEXANDER LOCKHART, in Jamaica, son of William Finlayson WS in Edinburgh, a deed, 1808. [NAS.RD3.326.769]

FINGZEIS, J. K., born 1804, son of James Fingzeis and Christian Kay, died in Kingston, Jamaica, on 14 Feb 1874. [Potymoak MI]

FINGZEIS, Mrs MARY, born in Elgin on 27 May 1819, wife of Major F. K. Fingzeis, died in Kingston, Jamaica, on 26 Mar 1870. [St Andrew's Presbyterian Church MI, Jamaica]

FINLAY, ALEXANDER, Lt.Col. of the 3rd West Indian Regt. in Jamaica, died in Nairn, 1851. [NAS.RS29.6.17]

FINLAY, JAMES, in Jamaica, 1782, 1794, brother of William Finlay of Moss. [NAS.CS17.1.1/46; GD46.1.147]

FINLAYSON, ALEXANDER LOCKHART, son of William Finlayson depute clerk of the Bills in Edinburgh, died in Savanna-la-Mar, 23 July 1823. [EEC#17515][NAS.RD33.326.769]

FINLAYSON, CHARLOTTE, wife of Alexander Finlayson, died Aug 1809. [Trelawney MI, Jamaica]

FINLAYSON, DAVID, in Savannah-la-Mar, 1780, [NA.CO137.1-35]; Member of the House of Assembly for Westmoreland, Jamaica, died in Edinburgh, 3 Feb 1799. [SM.61.210][AJ#2666]

FINLAYSON, DAVID, attorney at law in Jamaica, eldest son of William Finlayson a writer in Edinburgh, 1808. [NAS.RD3.325.1183; RD3.326.769; RD3.271.96]

FINLAYSON, DAVID F., born 8 Jan 1770, Member of the House of Assembly for Westmoreland 1797-1831, Speaker 1821-1830, died in Spanish Town, Jamaica, 7 Mar 1834[St Catherine's MI, Jamaica][AJ#4505]

FINLAYSON, JOHN, youngest son of William Finlayson, Depute Clerk of the Bills, died in Savanna-la-Mar, Jamaica, 1800. [AJ#2732]

FINLAYSON, JOHN HOYES, born 1820, son of Rev. John Finlayson in Cromarty, died in Kingston, Jamaica, on 2 Dec 1849. [AJ#5324][W#1077]

SCOTS IN JAMAICA, 1655-1855

FINNISON, JOHN, a Covenanter who was transported from Leith to Jamaica in Aug 1685. [RPCS.XI.329]

FISHER, JAMES, in Jamaica since 1766, eldest son of John Fisher late of the Waulkmill of Crombie; 1782; died 1789, testament, 4 Oct 1804. [NAS.CS97.110.18; CS17.1.1/46; CC8.8.135]

FISHER, JAMES DICKSON, only son of James Fisher a settler in Jamaica, matriculated at Glasgow University in 1793. [MAGU#172]

FISHER, JOHN, youngest son of Charles Fisher, SSC, in Edinburgh, died in Irwin, Jamaica, 14 Mar 1879. [EC#29503]

FISHER, SAMUEL, born 1822, arrived at Bluefields, Westmoreland, on 23 Jan 1841 aboard the William Pirie, from Stranraer. [NA.CO.140/33]

FITCHET, ALEXANDER, born 1792, son of John Fitchet a merchant in Montrose, Angus, died in Jamaica on 20 Feb 1822.

FLEMING, CHRISTOPHER, born 1813, with Catherine born 1822, arrived at Bluefields, Westmoreland, on 23 Jan 1841 aboard the William Pirie, from Stranraer. [NA.CO.140/33]

FLEMING, WILLIAM, born 15 Feb 1842, eldest son of James Fleming and Isabella McLaren in Glasgow, a coppersmith who died in St Andrew's, Jamaica, on 3 Sep. 1862. [Hampden MI, Jamaica]

FLETCHER, DUNCAN, a rebel who was transported from Leith to Jamaica in Aug 1685. [RPCS.XI.136]

FLETCHER, JOHN, a rebel in Rumcadle, Kintyre, Argyll, who was transported from Leith to Jamaica in Aug 1685. [RPCS.XI.329]

FOGO, WILLIAM, a planter in Clarendon, Jamaica, a bond, 1784. [NAS.RD2.236/1.571]

FORBES, ALEXANDER, born in Edinburgh 27 July 1689, second son of Sir David Forbes of Newhall, died in Jamaica on 15 Nov 1729. [Spanish Town Cathedral MI, Jamaica]

FORBES, ALEXANDER, a Jacobite from Wemyss, Fife, who was transported to Jamaica in 1747. [NA.CO137.58]

FORBES, ALEXANDER, in Jamaica, probate, 1771, PCC.

FORBES, ALEXANDER, in Kingston, Jamaica, died 30 Apr 1803, testament, 9 Mar 1804. [NAS.CC8.8.136][GM.73.1254]

FORBES, ALEXANDER, born 1761, late in Jamaica, died in Aberdeen on 15 Feb 1814. [AJ#3451]; testament, 6 Feb 1815, Aberdeen. [NAS]

FORBES, ALEXANDER, born 1800, died in Kingston, Jamaica, on 17 Mar 1833. [St Andrew's MI. Jamaica]

FORBES, ANNE, born 1762, died 14 Nov 1842. Kingston MI, Jamaica]

FORBES, CHARLES, steerage passenger from Greenock to Jamaica aboard the Mary of Glasgow in Nov 1773. [NAS.CE60]

FORBES, Rev. DUNCAN, in Little London, Westmoreland, Jamaica, 1875. [NAS.RS.Dysart.5/269]

FORBES, GEORGE, died in Thatchfield, St Elizabeth's, Jamaica, 13 Nov 1823. [EEC#17567]

FORBES, HENRY, jr., married Mary Anne, youngest dau of James Smith, g'dau of Alexander Aikman, in Kingston, Jamaica, 2 Nov 1831. [GM.101.644]

FORBES, JAMES, a time-served indentured servant who emigrated from Barbados to Jamaica on the Two Brothers, master Rice Jeffreys, on 13 Feb 1678. [NA.CO1.44.47][H#367]

FORBES, JOHN, son of Alexander Forbes a gentleman in Jamaica, at King's College, Aberdeen, 1812-1816. [KCA#2/415]

FORBES, JONATHAN, of Waterton, Col. of the St Catherine's Regiment, died in Jamaica 15 Dec 1820. [S.5.213]

FORBES, JONATHAN, born 1802, son of James Forbes in Old Meldrum, Aberdeenshire, a surgeon who died in Bognie, Westmoreland, Jamaica, 31 Jan 1831. [EEC#18632]

FORBES, MUNGO, from Jamaica, died 6 Apr 1807 in Bristol. [GM.77.489]

FORBES, NATHANIEL, a wharfinger, St James, Jamaica, 1774. [BL.Add.MS22676/8]

FORBES, WALTER, a merchant in Savannah la Mar, Jamaica, a witness, 1788. [NAS.RD4.244.793]

FORBES, WILLIAM, in Jamaica, probate 1773, PCC.

FORBES, WILLIAM, from Callendar, Perthshire, a physician in Port Royal, Jamaica, letters, 1808/1809. [NAS.RH1/2.796]

FORDYCE, EMILIA, daughter of Alexander Fordyce, married John Stennet, a physician in St James, Jamaica, in Edinburgh, Mar 1791, and died in Jamaica, Mar 1803; a deed, 1792. [DF][NAS.RD3.270.433]

FORFAR, ALEXANDER, born 1753, a clerk, via London to Jamaica on the Reward in Dec 1773. [NA.T47.9/11]

FORREST, JAMES, son of James and Marion Forrest, a Covenanter from Cambusnethan, Lanarkshire, transported from Leith to Jamaica in Aug 1685, landed at Port Royal, Jamaica, in Nov 1685. [RPCS.XI.329][LJ#17]

FORRESTER, JOHN, a planter in Jamaica, relict Elizabeth Somerville, 1750. [NAS.RH18.3.278]

FORRESTER, SOMERVILLE, in Westmoreland, Cornwall, Jamaica, died 1 Oct 1804, testament, 20 Apr1811. [NAS.CC8.8.138]

FORRESTER, WALTER, only son of Somerville Forrester a merchant in Jamaica, matriculated at Glasgow University in 1817. [MAGU]

FORSYTH, AMBROSE, born 1840, son of William Forsyth [1797-1846], died in Jamaica 28 Feb 1870. [St Michael's MI, Dumfries]

FORSYTH, JAMES, a printer in Jamaica, a burgess and guildsbrother of Ayr, 4 Apr 1751. [AyrBR]
FORSYTH, JOHN ALEXANDER, born 25 Feb 1770, son of Rev. William Forsyth and Margaret Turner in Aboyne, died in Jamaica, 20 Feb 1800. [F.6.78]
FORSYTH, JOHN, in St Anne's, Jamaica, inventory, 1854. [NAS.SC70.1.82]
FORSYTH, JOSEPH, Jamaica, MD Edinburgh University, 1814. [EMG#47]
FORSYTH, WILLIAM, born 1757, a husbandman, via London to Jamaica on the Royal Charlotte in Feb 1774. [NA.T47.9/11]
FORTESCUE, JAMES, second son of .... Fortescue in Cameron, Fife, died at Orange Park, St David's, Jamaica, 7 Oct 1837. [DPCA#1845]
FORTUNE, JOHN, son of John Fortune and Margaret Gray, died in Kingston, Jamaica, on 1 Oct 1853. [St Andrews MI]
FOSTER, JOHN, first son of John Smith in Jamaica, matriculated at Glasgow University in 1765. [MAGU]
FOTHERINGHAM, Dr GEORGE, a physician in Jamaica, 1772. [NAS.CS16.1.151]
FOUBISTER, PETER ALEXANDER, born 10 Apr 1801, a chaisemaker in Kingston, Jamaica, died 8 Aug 1835. [Kingston MI]
FOWLAR, JAMES, in Jamaica, 21 Apr 1802; later in Rosemarkie, 1829. [NAS.RD4.271.842; CS17.1.46/384]
FOWLAR, JAMES, son of Reeves Fowlar MD in New Providence, died at Florida Settlement, Falmouth, Jamaica, 18 Mar1840. [EEC#20053]
FOWLAR, JOHN, in Trelawney, Jamaica, father of Sarah, wife of George Budge, a Lieutenant of the Ross-shire Militia, 1816. [NAS.PS3.16.281]
FOWLIS, JOHN, a carpenter at Morant Bay, Jamaica, testament, 2 Feb 1804. [NAS.CC8.8.135]
FRAME, WILLIAM, in Clarendon, Jamaica, 1670. [SPAWI.1670/270]
FRANKLYN, PETER, in Jamaica, 9 Dec 1820. [NAS.RD400.738]
FRASER, DAVID, a merchant in Jamaica, 1771. [NAS.RS27.192.342]
FRASER, DAVID, at Martha Brae, Trelawney, Jamaica, 1790. [NAS.GD21.395]
FRASER, DONALD, settled in Georgia 1768, Customs Controller for Sunbury, a Loyalist who settled in Jamaica 1783. [NA.AO12.109.140]
FRASER, DUNCAN, Jamaica, married Mrs Slater, 1 Aug 1794. [GM.64.764]
FRASER, FORBES, born 1817, a blacksmith, with Ann, born 1817, emigrated from Aberdeen aboard the Rob Roy bound for Jamaica, arrived at Kingston on 11 May 1841. [NA.CO140/33]
FRASER, HUGH, in Nairn, formerly in Spanish Town, Jamaica, 25 Dec 1825. [NAS.RS.Nairn.2/36]
FRASER, JAMES, in Jamaica, 6 Nov 1798. [NAS.SC20.33.13]
FRASER, JAMES, in Trelawney, Jamaica, dead by 1823.[NAS.GD16.43.67]
FRASER, JAMES, in Coolshade, St Ann's, Jamaica, 1803-1815. [NAS.GD57.651]

SCOTS IN JAMAICA, 1655-1855

FRASER, Dr JOHN, eldest son of James Fraser in Glasgow, died in Kingston, Jamaica, 1794. [GM.64.768]

FRASER, JOHN, attorney in Kingston, Jamaica, pre 1803. [NAS.RD3.326.1403]

FRASER, JOHN, born 13 May 1789, son of Rev. John Fraser in Libberton, Lanarkshire, died in Jamaica on 16 Nov 1821. [EEC#17262][F.1.255]

FRASER, MARGARET, born 1827, from Aberdeen, died at Montego Bay, 1852. [AJ:16.6.1852]

FRASER, THOMAS, born 1824, 3rd son of Thomas Fraser and Jane Suter, died in Mandeville, Jamaica, 1 June 1860. [Chapel Yard MI, Inverness][S#1571]

FRASER, Dr WILLIAM, a physician in Jamaica, died in Edinburgh, testament, 13 July 1769, Comm. Edinburgh. [NAS.CC8.8.121]

FRASER, WILLIAM, formerly a Captain of the Prince of Wales Fencibles, died in Jamaica, June 1802. [CM#121790][GM.73.882]

FRASER, WILLIAM, a merchant from Forfar, died in Kingston, Jamaica, 12 June 1839, inventory, 1844, Comm. Edinburgh. [NAS.SC70.1.66; E286][SG#788]

FRASER, Rev. WILLIAM, born 1764, rector of Trelawney, and a chaplain to the Forces, died at Rectory House, Falmouth, Jamaica, on 1 Apr 1844.[AJ#5028]

FRASER, WILLIAM, son of James Fraser a surgeon and Eliza Hoyle in Dumfries, to Jamaica 1830, died in Spanish Town, Jamaica, 1863. [St Michael's MI]

FREDERICK, Mr., from Glasgow aboard the Mary bound for Jamaica, arrived in Kingston in May 1793. [JRG:18.5.1793]

FREEBAIRN, DAVID, a merchant in Kingston, Jamaica, 1787. [NAS.AC.Decreets.52]

FRENCH, BARBARA, relict of Peter Jamieson a merchant in Kingston, Jamaica, testament, 28 Sep 1801. [NAS.CC1.6.W39]

FREW, ALEXANDER, born 1794, died in Jamaica on 10 Oct 1826. [Bathgate, Kirkton, MI]

FREW, FANNY, born 1823, daughter of Rev. J M Frew, rector of St Thomas in St Thomas in the East, Jamaica, died in Kingston, 24 Mar 1842. [GSP.718]

FREW, SOPHIA LOUISA, infant daughter of Rev. J M Frew, rector of St Thomas in the East, died in Grenada, 24 Feb 1842. [GSP#718]

FRIGG, ANDREW, a skipper in Jamaica, died 1769, son of John Frigg a merchant in Findhorn, Morayshire, 1780. [NAS.CS16.1.179; CC8.8.123]

FRISSELL, WILLIAM, probate 25 June 1677, Jamaica.

FRIZELL, JOHN, in St John's, Jamaica, 1670. [SPAWI.1670/270]

FULLARTON, ALEXANDER, born 1730, a former Assemblyman, died on Hopewell Estate, Jamaica, 1806. [AJ#3069]

FULLARTON, ALEXANDER, born 1788, Ordnance storekeeper in Jamaica, died 4 Jan 1850. [Kingston MI]

FULLARTON, GEORGE, in Jamaica, probate 1750, PCC.

SCOTS IN JAMAICA, 1655-1855

FULLERTON, HUGH, a jobber, St James, Jamaica, 1774. [BL.Add.MS22676/8]
FULLARTON, Mrs, wife of Alexander Fullarton, born 1806, died 7 Nov 1855. [Kingston MI]
FULTON, ARTHUR RANKIN, a seaman in Jamaica, inventory, 1881. [NAS.SC70.1.209]
FULTON, SAMUEL, born 1810, a laborer, with Rebecca born 1814, Isabella born 1827, Samuel born 1834, and Alexander born 1836, arrived at Bluefields, Westmoreland, on 23 Jan 1841 aboard the William Pirie, from Stranraer. [NA.CO.140/33]
FYFFE, CHARLES, youngest son of David Fyffe of Drumgeith, died in Jamaica, 15 Oct 1801. [CM#121847][GM.74.86]
FYFE, CHARLES GORDON, in Jamaica, died 24 July 1859 at Up Park Camp, inventory, 1863. [NAS.SC70.1.118; H1562]
FYFFE, DAVID, from Dundee, a planter on Black River Estate, Jamaica, from 1761 to 1773, was admitted as a burgess of Banff, 1775, and as a burgess and guildsbrother of Glasgow in 1789, later in Drumgeight, Dundee. [BBR][GBR] [NLJamaica.ms1655][NAS.RS35.PR28/374; RS35.39]
FYFE, LAURENCE, born in Banffshire 1765, died at Harmony Hall, St Mary's, Jamaica, 15 Aug 1838. [AJ#4796]
FYFFE, ROBERT, son of Barclay Fyffe a merchant in Leith, died in Kingston, Jamaica, 1 Aug 1794. [GM.64.958]
FYFE, WALTER, a coppersmith at Anetto Bay, Jamaica, died in May 1821, testament, 18 Oct 1824. [NAS.CC8.8.150]
FYFFE, WILLIAM, in Westmoreland, Jamaica, 1797, 1799. [NAS.NRAS.0623.T-MJ.427/26][GA.T-ARD#13/1]; died in Kingston, 6 Jan 1810.[GM.80.284]
GAIRDEN, GEORGE, in Jamaica, probate 1795, PCC.
GAIRDNER, THOMAS, in Jamaica, probate 1794, PCC.
GAIRDYN, GEORGE, an attorney in St Mary's, Jamaica, was admitted as a burgess of Banff, 1784. [BBR]
GALBRAITH, ARCHIBALD, died at Wynter's Prospect Pen, Jamaica, 1798. [AJ#2649]
GALBRAITH, DAVID, born 1770, son of John Galbraith and Janet Galloway in Anniston, Lanarkshire, a surgeon in Jamaica, died 13 Oct 1793. [Symington MI]
GALBRAITH, Rev EDWARD, Hanover, Jamaica, died in Lucca, Jamaica, 19 June 1859. [GM.NS2/9.196]
GALBRAITH, WILLIAM, in Jamaica, testament, 23 June 1768. [NAS.CC8.8.121]
GALBREATH, ARCHIBALD, a merchant in Savannah la Mar, Jamaica, 1801. [GA.T-ARD#13/1]
GALLIE, ALEXANDER, died 1831 in Jamaica, inventory, 1858. [NAS.SC70.1.90; H47]

SCOTS IN JAMAICA, 1655-1855

GALLOWAY, JAMES, born 1748, "56 years in Jamaica", of Unity Hall, St James's, Jamaica, died in Trelawney 28 Aug 1833. [Falmouth MI, Jamaica]
GALLOWAY, ROBERT, in St Andrew's, Jamaica, 1670. [SPAWI.1670/270]
GALLOWAY, WILLIAM, in Jamaica, probate 1783, PCC.
GALLY, ALEXANDER, a cooper in Kingston, Jamaica, a witness, 1783. [NAS.RD2.234.1440]
GALLY, THOMAS, a writer in Edinburgh, later an attorney in Kingston, Jamaica, 1770. [NAS.CS16.1.141/343]
GALVOY, RALPH, from Glasgow aboard the Nancy bound for Jamaica, arrived in Kingston in June 1793.[JRG:22.6.1793]
GAMMELL, ALBERT, born 1841, died in Spanish Town, Jamaica, 14 June 1868. [S#7795]
GARDINER, CHRISTINE, guilty of infanticide, imprisoned in Edinburgh Tolbooth, then transported from Leith to Jamaica in Aug 1685. [ETR#369][RPCS.XI.330]
GARDINER, JAMES, son of James Gardiner [1720-1790] and Elspet Wilson [1720-1795], settled in Jamaica before 1813. [Banff MI]; testament 30 Oct 1830. [NAS.CC1.6.W993]
GARDINER, JAMES, in St James, Jamaica, 1827. [NAS.SC48.49.25.23/97]
GARDINER, MARGARET, relict of James Gardiner late of Jamaica, died in Banff, 8 Dec 1831. [AJ#4379]
GARDNER, ALEXANDER, possibly from Perth, a surgeon and physician in Westmoreland, Jamaica, dead by 1788. [NAS.B59.38.6.184]
GARDNER, ALEXANDER, born 1789, son of Alexander Gardner, a farmer, and Elizabeth Morrison, died in Jamaica, 25 Oct 1811. [Abernyte MI]
GARDNER, ANDREW, in Duanscale, Trelawney, Jamaica, a deed, 1797. [NAS.RD3.278.840]
GARDNER, JAMES, a merchant in Jamaica, testament, 22 Oct 1802. [NAS.CC8.8.133]
GARDNER, JOHN, eldest son of Alexander Gardner a jeweller in Edinburgh, a Writer to the Signet, 21 Dec 1786, later an attorney in Jamaica, died 1794. [HWS#76]
GARDNER, JOHN, merchant at Montego Bay, Jamaica, a witness, 1818. [NAS.RD5.144.504]
GARDNER, WILLIAM, born in Drymen, Stirlingshire, settled in Jamaica 1764, died in Kingston 28 Dec 1820. [EEC#17132][S.5.218]
GAULD, ALEXANDER, in Jamaica, dead by 1851, husband of Isabella Neil. [NAS.CS228.B.19.40]
GAVIN, JAMES, 1st son of William Gavin a merchant in Jamaica, matriculated at Glasgow University in 1811. [MAGU#256]

SCOTS IN JAMAICA, 1655-1855

GAVINE, JAMES, a Covenanter from Douglas, Lanarkshire, imprisoned in Edinburgh Tolbooth, husband of Helen Dickson, transported from Leith to Jamaica in Aug 1685, returned to Scotland after 1695, and died in Douglas. [ETR#369][RPCS.XI.330][Douglas MI]

GEDDES, ALEXANDER, born 1800, son of John Geddes [1753-1817] and Helen Tod [1771-1837], of Annandale and Murphy's Hill, St Ann's, Jamaica, died at Murphy's Hill on 1 Apr 1864. [Bellie MI, Morayshire][Ocho Rios MI, Jamaica]

GEDDES, DAVID, born 1821, a tailor, arrived at Bluefields, Westmoreland, on 23 Jan 1841 aboard the <u>William Pirie</u>, from Stranraer. [NA.CO.140/33]

GEDDES, ELEANOR, wife of George Geddes, Woodford Bridge, died in Jamaica, 12 July 1852. [GM.NS38.433]

GEDDES, GEORGE, born 1808, son of John Geddes and Helen Tod, died in Jamaica, 24 May 1864. [Bellie MI]

GEDDES, JOHN, born 1788, son of John Geddes and Margaret Anderson, an assistant surgeon of the 54th Regiment, died in Jamaica, Nov 1808. [Bellie MI]

GEDDES, JOHN, born 1822, emigrated from Aberdeen aboard the <u>Rob Roy</u> bound for Jamaica, arrived at Kingston on 11 May 1841. [NA.CO140/33]

GEDDES, JOHN, born 1829, son of Alexander Geddes and Jean Ramsay, died in Westmoreland, Jamaica, on 27 Aug 1857. [Cupar MI]

GENTLE, WILLIAM, a planter of Clarendon, Jamaica, before 1807. [NAS.B59.38.6.247]

GENTLEMAN, DAVID, master of the <u>Elizabeth of Montrose,</u> died in Jamaica, 1717. [NAS.CS16.1.23.100; 26.908]

GERARD, JOHN, died at Montego Bay, 17 Feb 1849. [AJ#5282]

GIBB, JOHN, a Covenanter, transported from Leith to Jamaica in Aug 1685. [RPCS.XI.329]

GIBB, JOHN, born 1786, son of George Gibb in Leith, died in Jamaica 24 Mar 1803. [AJ#2692][EEC#14272]

GIBB, ROBERT, born 1769, died in Kingston, Jamaica, 1805. [AJ#2986]

GIBB, ROBERT, born 1768, died in Kingston, Jamaica, 1 Jan 1804.[CM#13032]

GIBB, ROBERT CHARLES, in Ludlow, Clarendon, Jamaica, deeds, 1797, 1811. [NAS.RD3.276.932; RD4.265.570; RD4.295.254]

GIBBON, GEORGE, from Glasgow, died at St Anne's Bay, Jamaica, Oct 1800. [GM#70.1214]

GIBSON, DAVID, at Montego Bay, Jamaica, 1783. [NAS.CS17.1.2/233]

GIBSON, DAVID, in Jamaica, then in Edinburgh, 1821. [NAS.CS17.1.40/178]

GIBSON, JAMES, born 1822, arrived at Bluefields, Westmoreland, on 23 Jan 1841 aboard the <u>William Pirie</u>, from Stranraer. [NA.CO.140/33]

GIBSON, LAURENCE, died in Holmwood, Racetown, Jamaica, 21 Jan 1857. [EEC#21043]

SCOTS IN JAMAICA, 1655-1855

GIBSON, PETER, from Greenock, surgeon at Hope Bay, Jamaica, a deed, 1815. [NAS.RD5.86.256]

GIBSON, PETER, planter in Trelawney, Cornwall, Jamaica, a deed, 1818. [NAS.RD5.150.4]

GIBSON, WILLIAM, son of Alexander Gibson master of Perth Academy, servant to John Ritchie, Virgin Valley, St James, Jamaica, 1797-1800. [NAS.B59.37.4.29]

GILCHRIST, ALEXANDER, a planter in Hanover, Jamaica, administration, 1766, London. [NA.Prob.11/961]

GILCHRIST, GEORGE, a planter and millwright in Hanover, Jamaica, dead by 1777. [NAS.GD217.685]

GILCHRIST, WILLIAM, in St Andrew's, Jamaica, probate 10 Dec 1677, Jamaica.

GILCHRIST, WILLIAM, a millwright in Jamaica, 1772. [JCTP.1772.298]

GILLESPIE, CHARLES, born 1813, son of John Gillespie in Caerlaverock, Dumfries-shire, died in Jamaica, 11 Sep 1836. [Caerlaverock MI]

GILLESPIE, JAMES, an attorney in Jamaica, 1767. [NAS.GD345.1171.1.128]

GILLESPIE, JOHN, a gentleman in Kingston, Jamaica, a witness, 1765. [NAS.RD2.197/2.377]

GILLESPIE, THOMAS, a merchant in Kingston, Jamaica, died 19 Apr 1799, [AJ#2688][GM.69.621]; probate 1799, PCC.

GILLESPIE, URQUHART, MD, married Eliza, daughter of Lt. Green of the Royal Marines, in Jamaica, 1806. [AJ#3086]

GILLESPIE, WILLIAM, from Edinburgh, died 1812 in Jamaica, inventory, 1859. [NAS.SC70.1.-; H750]

GILLIS, MCLAURIN, a merchant at Montego Bay, Jamaica, trading with Greenock, 1796. [NAS.E504.15.73]

GILLIES, ROBERT MCLAURIN, third son of Reverend John Gillies, born 1 Apr 1750 in Glasgow, matriculated at Glasgow University in 1766, later a merchant in Jamaica, died 3 Jan 1778. [MAGU][F.3.399]

GILMORE, JOHN, born 1811, with Elizabeth born 1812, Robert born 1837, and Mary born 1839, arrived at Bluefields, Westmoreland, on 23 Jan 1841 aboard the <u>William Pirie</u>, from Stranraer. [NA.CO.140/33]

GILROY, RALPH, late of Jamaica, died in Gainslaw, Berwick, 12 Nov 1825. [AJ#4063][EEC#17815]

GIRVAN, THOMAS, an engineer in Surrey, Jamaica, inventory, 1889. [NAS.SC70.1.278]

GLAS, ROBERT, born 1786, son of Provost Glas of Stirling, died in Belmont, Jamaica, 1804. [AJ#2945]

GLAS, WILLIAM BRYCE, born 1806, 6th son of John Glas in Stirling, died on St Toolies Estate, Jamaica, 16 Jan 1825. [AJ#4032][BM.XVII.760]

SCOTS IN JAMAICA, 1655-1855

GLASS, GEORGE, in Trelawney, Cornwall, Jamaica, a deed, 1790; died in Edinburgh, testament, 29 Dec 1796.[NAS.RD3.253.864; CC8.8.130]

GLASS, JOHN, born 1819, arrived at Bluefields, Westmoreland, on 23 Jan 1841 aboard the William Pirie, from Stranraer. [NA.CO.140/33]

GLASS, JOHN, in Newton of Balcanquhal, late of Jamaica, died in Portobello, Midlothian, 30 Jan 1845. [EEC#21305]

GLASS, REBECCA, in Kingston, Jamaica, a deed, 1785. [NAS.RD4.239.1064]

GLASS, Captain, in Jamaica, 1753. [NAS.B59.38.2.263]

GLEIG, ALEXANDER, a planter, Bellisle Estate, Westmoreland, Jamaica, a witness, 1784. [NAS.RD2.238/1.940]

GLEN, GEORGE, born 1805, eldest son of George Glen of HM Customs at Greenock, died in Jamaica on 8 Jan 1834. [GrAd:5.5.1834]

GLEN, WILLIAM, in Westmoreland, Jamaica, died 17 Sep 1845, inventory, 1851. [NAS.SC70.1.73]

GLOVER, CHRISTIAN YOUNG, wife of Rev. Duncan Forbes a United Presbyterian minister, died at St George's Manse, Jamaica, 23 May 1860. [S#1567]

GOLDIE, Rev. ALEXANDER, born 1804 in Midlothian, educated at Edinburgh University, minister of St Andrew's Presbyterian Church in Jamaica from 22 Nov 1846, died in Kingston 22 July 1847. [St Andrew's, MI][F.7.669]

GOLDSMITH, CATHERINE ELIZA, wife of Gilbert McNab MD, died in Kingston, Jamaica, 9 June 1851. [W#1238]

GOOD, HUGH, late a writer in Edinburgh, died in Kingston, Jamaica, 2 June 1820. [AJ#3787]

GOODBRAND, ALEXANDER, a Jacobite transported via Liverpool to Jamaica, landed 21 Mar 1748. [NA.T53/44]

GOODFELLOW, ROBERT, in Jamaica, died 23 Oct 1827, inventory, 30 Aug 1828, testament, 1828, Comm. Edinburgh. [NAS.CC8.8.152; SC70.1.39; B1367]

GOODIN, DEHANY, fourth son of David Goodin formerly a merchant in Jamaica, matriculated at Glasgow University in 1754. [MAGU]

GORDLET, ..., from Greenock to Jamaica on the Bell, arrived in Kingston in Jan 1793. [JRG:19.1.1793]

GORDON, ADAM GARDEN, youngest son of James Gordon of Rosieburn, died in Viewfield, St John, Spanish Town, 11 Nov 1850. [EEC#22068][W.1183]

GORDON, ALEXANDER, steerage passenger from Greenock to Jamaica aboard the Mary of Glasgow in Nov 1773. [NAS.CE60]

GORDON, ALEXANDER, a planter in Jamaica, died 178-, testaments, 6 May 1780, 17 Nov1783. [NAS.RD2.234.1086; CC8.8.126]

GORDON, ALEXANDER, in Jamaica, probate, 1784, PCC.

SCOTS IN JAMAICA, 1655-1855

GORDON, ALEXANDER, in Belmont, Jamaica, a sasine, 29 Sep 1786. [NAS.RS8.512]
GORDON, CHARLES, of Cairness, died in Jamaica, 1755. [AUL.ms1160/5/7]
GORDON, CHARLES, son of Dr Charles Gordon in Jamaica, apprenticed in Edinburgh, 1772. [REA]
GORDON, CHARLES, a merchant in Jamaica, dead by 1773. [NAS.GD67/105]
GORDON, CHARLES, attorney and overseer of Albion Estate, St Mary's, Jamaica, died there 27 Feb 1842. [ASG#11/1080]
GORDON, ELIZABETH, in Jamaica, probate, 1790, PCC.
GORDON, ELIZABETH, born 1816, daughter of Dr W. Gordon at Montego Bay, wife of R. W. Gordon, died in Kingston, Jamaica, 24 Jan 1845. [AJ#5075]
GORDON, Mrs FRANCES, born 1753, died in Jamaica, 30 Oct 1837. [GM.NS7.447]
GORDON, FRANCIS, Kenmore, Jamaica, only bro of Sir John Gordon of Earlston, died in Spanish Town, Jamaica, 27 July 1823. [GM.93.647]
GORDON, GEORGE, a surgeon in Jamaica, husband of Elizabeth Denholm, 1753. [NAS.RS27.142.349]
GORDON, GEORGE, in Jamaica, probate, 1759, PCC.
GORDON, GEORGE, a carpenter, St James, Jamaica, 1774. [BL.Add.MS22676/8]
GORDON, GEORGE, in Hanover, Jamaica, testament, 13 Dec 1781. [NAS.CC8.8.125]
GORDON, HENRY, a jobber, St James, Jamaica, 1774. [BL.Add.MS22676/8]
GORDON, ISABELLA MARIA, in Spanish Town, Jamaica, 1850.[NAS.GD366/5]
GORDON, JAMES ALEXANDER, died in Jamaica, 1757. [GM.27.338]
GORDON, JAMES, a carpenter, St James, Jamaica, 1774. [BL.Add.MS22676/8]
GORDON, JAMES, formerly Captain of the Aberdeenshire Militia, died in Port Maria, St Mary's, Jamaica, 20 Nov 1820. [S.5.217]
GORDON, JAMES COLQUHOUN, Hanover, Jamaica, dead by 1820. [NAS.RD5.282.690]
GORDON, JAMES IRVING, of Carlton, born 1839, youngest son of Sir John Gordon of Earlston, died 3 Nov 1862. [Earlston MI, Montego Bay]
GORDON, JANE CAROLINE, eldest daughter of George Gordon, married John Wallace Harris, Kingston, Jamaica, on George Island Estate, Jamaica, 24 July 1834. [AJ#4522]
GORDON, JOHN, a planter, Glasgow Estate, St James, Jamaica, 1774. [BL.Add.MS22676/8]
GORDON, JOHN, an Assemblyman, St Anne's, Jamaica, died 1774. [GM.44.494]
GORDON, JOHN, in Jamaica, probate, 1774, PCC.
GORDON, JOHN, in Jamaica, probate, 1775, PCC.

SCOTS IN JAMAICA, 1655-1855

GORDON, JOHN, born 24 Mar 1782, son of Rev.Thomas Gordon and Elizabet Michie in Aboyne, at King's College, Aberdeen, 1795-1799, MA, settled in Jamaica. [KCA#2/379][F.6.78]

GORDON, Sir JOHN, of Earlston, married Julia, daughter of J. Gallimore, at Water Valley, Jamaica, Dec 1811. [GM.81.585]

GORDON, JOHN, son of William Gordon MD in Jamaica, at King's College, Aberdeen, 1824. [KCA#2/458]

GORDON, JOSEPH, sometime in Jamaica then in Edinburgh, testament, 1800, Comm. Edinburgh. [NAS]

GORDON, MICHAEL, born 1818, arrived at Bluefields, Westmoreland, on 23 Jan 1841 aboard the <u>William Pirie</u>, from Stranraer. [NA.CO.140/33]

GORDON, RANDOLPH NORMAN, in Jamaica, inventory, 1894. [NAS.SC70.1.330]

GORDON, RICHARD, in Jamaica, probate, 1795, PCC.

GORDON, ROBERT, third son of William Gordon military commander of Jamaica, matriculated at Glasgow University, 1741. [MAGU]

GORDON, ROBERT, in Jamaica, probate, 1768, PCC.

GORDON, ROBERT, a planter, Windsor Estate, St James, Jamaica, 1774. [BL.Add.MS22676/8]

GORDON, ROBERT HOME, son of Dr John Gordon of Greencastle, Jamaica, 1780; was granted Embo, 1785. [NAS.RS38.51; RGS.123.108]

GORDON, ROBERT, in Jamaica, probate, 1786, PCC.

GORDON, ROBERT, in Kingston, Jamaica, a witness, 1793. [NAS.RD3.276.101]

GORDON, ROBERT DANIEL, son of Robert Gordon of Auchress, died in Clarendon, Jamaica, 1802. [AJ#2853]

GORDON, ROBERT, Jamaica, died in Windsor, 12 Feb 1833. [GM.103.187]

GORDON, ROBERT, born 1799, second son of William Gordon of Halmyre, died in Kingston, Jamaica, 14 Nov 1831. [EEC#18789]; in Clifton Mount, St Andrew's, Jamaica, deeds, 1822, 1824. [NAS.RD5.235.477; RD5.269.131]

GORDON, SAMUEL, in Jamaica, probate, 1778, PCC.

GORDON, THOMAS, an attorney in Jamaica, 1752. [NAS.GD345.1162.4.7]

GORDON, THOMAS, in Jamaica, probate, 1753, PCC.

GORDON, THOMAS, in Jamaica, probate, 1781, PCC.

GORDON, THOMAS, born 1 July 1768, son of Rev. George Gordon and Cecilia Reid in Keith, settled in Overhall, Port Maria Bay, Jamaica, died 15 June 1807. [F.6.321][DPCA#265]

GORDON, WALTER, an overseer at Airy Castle, Jamaica, died 1782, testament, 16 May 1783. [NAS.CC8.8.126]

GORDON, WILLIAM, in Jamaica, probate, 1740, PCC.

GORDON, WILLIAM, in Jamaica, a burgess of Edinburgh, 1743. [EBR]

GORDON, WILLIAM, in Jamaica, probate, 1763, PCC.
GORDON, WILLIAM, son of John Gordon of Hallhead, settled in Jamaica as a merchant by 1723, husband of Susanna ..., parents of William, [1723-1798], Susanna born 1729, Thomas born 1730, and Robert died 1768. [SNQ.IX.172/210]
GORDON, WILLIAM, Montego Bay, Jamaica, died 1766. [GM.36.390]
GORDON, WILLIAM, from Peterhead, in Jamaica, testament, 16 May 1783. [NAS.CC8.8.126]
GORDON, Dr WILLIAM, in Villa de Medici, St Andrew's, Jamaica, son of William Gordon of Halmyre, a deed, 1824. [NAS.RD5.269.131]
GORDON, WILLIAM, in Jamaica, MD Aberdeen, 23 Nov 1822, died in St Andrew's, Jamaica, 18 Sep 1836. [AJ#4639][AUL]
GORDON, WILLIAM, son of William Gordon MD in Jamaica, at King's College, Aberdeen, 1822-1826, a surgeon HEICS, later in Jamaica. [KCA#2/447]
GORDON, WILLIAM, born 1814, son of Rev. John Gordon, a surgeon who died at Newcastle Barracks, Jamaica, 7 Dec 1836. [Speymouth-Dipple MI]
GORDON, WILLIAM, in Jamaica, died 5 Oct 1838, inventory, 1839.[NAS.SC70.1]
GORDON, Mrs, born 1788, wife of Dr William Gordon, died at Montego Bay, 31 Dec 1817. [AJ#3660]
GOURDON, GEORGE, in St John's, Jamaica, probate 16 July 1685, Jamaica
GOURLAY, JOHN, from Lebanon, Cupar, then in Jamaica, 1835. [NAS.SC20.34.18.175/180]
GOW, ROBERT, a planter, St James, Jamaica, 1814. [NAS.RD5.271.425]
GOWANS, Dr JAMES, in Belmont, Jamaica, 1807. [NAS.GD417.211]
GOWRIE, ALEXANDER, born 1751, a carpenter, via London to Jamaica on the Great Marlow in Apr 1774; at Amatto Bay, Jamaica, a witness, 1792. [NA.T47.9/11][NAS.RD3.270.433]
GRACE, PETER, son of Dr Grace in Cupar, died in Jamaica, 26 Apr 1824. [FH]
GRAEME, JOHN ALEXANDER, 1st son of Alexander Graeme of Serge in Jamaica, matriculated at Glasgow University in 1789. [MAGU#157]
GRAEME, LAURENCE, in Williamsfield, St Thomas in the Vale, Jamaica, son of James Graeme of Garvock, a deed, 1798; in Pemberton Valley, Jamaica, before 1803. [NAS.RD3.281.48; B59.38.6.242]
GRAHAM, ANN, St James, Jamaica, 1774. [BL.Add.MS22676/8]
GRAHAM, ANNE CATHERINE, wife of David Littlejohn, Kingston, Jamaica, 1796. [NAS.CS17.1.15/817]
GRAHAM, BRICE, born 1783, merchant in Kingston, Jamaica, died at Latimer's Pen, 19 May 1849. [GM.NS32.334]

SCOTS IN JAMAICA, 1655-1855

GRAHAM, DUNCAN, MD, in Jamaica, married Elizabeth, daughter of James Kerr a writer in Edinburgh, there on 10 Mar1771; 1774. [EMR][NAS.RS27.216.215]

GRAHAM, FERGUS, in Jamaica, eldest son of William Graham of Mossknow who died before 1764, and Isobel Herries who died in 1737, letters 1768-1792. [NAS.GD1.403.42; GD206.229/244].

GRAHAM, FRANCIS, former Assemblyman for St Thomas in the Vale, died in Villa Pen, Spanish Town, Jamaica, 1 Feb 1820.[EEC#16975][S.4.167]

GRAHAM, GEORGE, son of John Graham, in Jamaica by 1765, a burgess of Stirling, 1768. [NAS.GD29.2054/2167]

GRAHAM, IVOR, a rebel from Innerneil, Argyll, who was transported from Leith to Jamaica in Aug 1685. [RPCS.XI.329]

GRAHAM, JACOB, a jobber, St James, Jamaica, 1774. [BL.Add.MS22676/8]

GRAHAM, JAMES, in Jamaica, 1737. [JCTP.1737.595]

GRAHAM, JAMES, from Airth, settled in Jamaica by 1783. [NLS.ms10925/5]

GRAHAM, JAMES, died in Westmoreland, Jamaica, July 1795. [George's Plain MI, Jamaica]

GRAHAM, JAMES, fourth son of Robert Burdon Graham of Feddel, at Glasgow University 1788, died Jamaica, 16 Jan 1806. [Carribeana#4.17]

GRAHAM, JAMES F., Assemblyman, St Thomas in the Vale, Jamaica, died at Villa Pen, Spanish Town, Jamaica, 1 Feb 1820. [GM.90.281]

GRAHAM, JAMES, born in Jedburgh, formerly a forester on Cromarty Estate, died at Seamore, Garden Plantation, Jamaica, Aug 1841. [AJ#4892]

GRAHAM, JOHN, master of the Oxford, died in Jamaica, pro.12 Mar 1739, PCC.

GRAHAM, JOHN, a planter at Taylor's Caymannas, Jamaica, 15 Nov 1776. [NAS.RS10.11.233]

GRAHAM, JOHN, of Gartur, late of Westmoreland, Jamaica, and Matilda, daughter of James Erskine of Cardross, a marriage contract, 1799. [NAS.GD15.826]

GRAHAM, JOHN, to Jamaica 1749, a merchant who died in Kingston, Jamaica, 13 Mar 1799. [AJ#2685][Kingston MI][GM.69.527]

GRAHAM, JOHN, second son of John Graham of Drunkie, died in Trelawney, Jamaica, 1802. [AJ#2679]

GRAHAM, JOHN, born 1820, arrived at Bluefields, Westmoreland, on 23 Jan 1841 aboard the William Pirie, from Stranraer. [NA.CO.140/33]

GRAHAM, ROBERT CUNNINGHAME, 2nd son of Nicholas Graham of Dartmore, at Glasgow University in 1748, later a planter and Receiver General of Jamaica, died in Gartmore on 11 Dec 1797. [MAGU][NAS.GD22.1.566]

GRAHAM, ROBERT, 10th son of John Graham formerly a merchant in Jamaica, matriculated at Glasgow University in 1816. [MAGU]

GRAHAM, ROBERT, born 1816, 2nd son of John Graham and Mary McFie in Greenock, died in Jamaica on 4 Mar 1836. [GrAd: 21.4.1836][Inverkip MI]
GRAHAM, THOMAS, of Buchlyvie, Receiver General of Jamaica, died 12 Dec 1763. [NAS.GD22.sec.3/208]
GRAHAM, WALTER, died in Jamaica by 1785. [NAS.GD22.1.210]
GRAHAM, WILLIAM, a witness in Hanover, Jamaica, 1744. [see RGD.Jamaica.LOS24/330]
GRAHAM, WILLIAM, formerly a surgeon and physician in Westmoreland, Jamaica, a burgess of Dumfries, 1753, in Westmoreland, Jamaica, 1757; now of Mossknow, 1764. [NAS.GD1.403.42/71; GD219.290]
GRAHAM, WILLIAM LECKIE, 2nd son of John Graham formerly a merchant in Jamaica, matriculated at Glasgow University in 1817. [MAGU]
GRAHAM, Mr., from Glasgow aboard the Betsy and Brothers bound for Jamaica, arrived in Kingston in May 1793. [JRG:25.5.1794]
GRAHAM, ..., son of Lionel Graham, Assistant Commissary of the Ordnance Dept., was born in Kingston, Jamaica, 12 Sep 1877. [EC#29022]
GRAHAME, DUNCAN, sometime in Jamaica then in Edinburgh, a sasine, 13 Sep 1779. [NAS.RS10.11.476]
GRAHAME, PETER, an overseer in Windsor, Jamaica, died Sep 1755, testament, 12 Mar 1776. [NAS.CC8.8.123]
GRANT, ALEXANDER, of Auchoyranie, residing in Jamaica. 1765. [NAS.RGS.108.212]
GRANT, ALEXANDER, in Jamaica, probate, 1780, PCC.
GRANT, ALEXANDER, in Jamaica, son of William Grant a merchant in Kirkcaldy, Fife, testament, 27 June 1789, Comm. Edinburgh. [NAS]
GRANT, ALEXANDER, born 1800, second son of David McDowell Grant of Arntully, died on Eden Estate, Jamaica, 31 Dec 1817. [AJ#3658]
GRANT, ALEXANDER, born 1793, eldest son of Patrick Grant in Glenbeg, Strathspey, Judge of the Quarter-sessions in Lucca and Westmoreland, Member of the Jamaica House of Assembly, died on Greenland Estate, Jamaica, 27 Aug 1846. [AJ#5155]
GRANT, ANDREW, from Berwickshire, a merchant in Jamaica then in London, 1774. [NAS.RS19.16.317]
GRANT, CHARLES, born 1741, died in Kingston, Jamaica, 4 Oct 1825. [AJ#4070]
GRANT, CHARLES, eighth son of Nathaniel Grant SSC, died in Jamaica, in Jan 1832. [AJ#4399][EEC#18795]
GRANT, COLQUHOUN, from Jamaica, married Margaret, daughter of the late Dr Abernethie in Jamaica, in London 28 Jan 1798. [SM.60.148]
GRANT, DANIEL, a planter, Maggotty Estate, St Andrew's, Jamaica, 1754. [NA.CO137/28]

SCOTS IN JAMAICA, 1655-1855

GRANT, DANIEL, born 1809 in Fife, '14 years in Jamaica', died on Hopewell Estate, Trelawney, Jamaica, 27 Sep. 1841. [AJ#4902]

GRANT, Dr DAVID, in Jamaica, graduated MD at King's College, Aberdeen, 16 Apr 1764. [KCA#131]

GRANT, DAVID, son of Dr David Knox Grant in Jamaica, at King's College, Aberdeen, 1792. [KCA.2/373]

GRANT, DAVID, formerly a merchant in Grantown, died in Jamaica, 1846. [Inverallen MI]

GRANT, FRANCIS, born 1722, MA, a schoolmaster who died 6 Sep 1779. [Kingston, Jamaica, MI]

GRANT, FRANCIS, of Kilgraston, late in Jamaica, a burgess of Edinburgh, 29 July 1795. [EBR]

GRANT, GEORGE, son of John Grant a merchant in Leith, a merchant in Jamaica and a burgess of Stirling, 1768. [NAS.GD29.2167]

GRANT, GEORGE, late of Jamaica, was granted Thornhill in 1795, died 22 Jan 1796. [NAS.RGS.128.145; RS29.410]

GRANT, GEORGE COLE, a surgeon, 7th son of Rev. Dr Grant in Dundee, died in Jamaica, June 1801, testament, 9 Mar 1802. [AJ#2803][NAS.CC8.8.133]

GRANT, GEORGE W. N. C., born 1815, son of Major John Grant of Auchterblair, died at Lucky Hill Estate, St Mary's, Jamaica, 1834. [AJ: 4.2.1835]

GRANT, GEORGINA, born 1828, late of George Square, Edinburgh, died in Lucea, Hanover, Jamaica, 7 Feb 1856. [CM#20730]

GRANT, GEORGINA, 4th daughter of Alexander Grant, died in Spot Valley, Pen, Jamaica, 23 July 1877. [EC#29979]

GRANT, JAMES, son of Isaac Grant WS, died at Montego Bay, 1802. [AJ.2854]

GRANT, JAMES, a merchant in Kingston, Jamaica, died 5 Oct 1826.[AJ.4118]

GRANT, JAMES, from Abernethy, Strathspey, late of St Thomas in the Vale, Jamaica, died in St Croix 28 Oct 1830. [AJ#4351]

GRANT, JAMES, in Windsor Park, St Catherine's, Jamaica, son of James Grant tacksman of Midfodderlatter, Banffshire, a deed, 1813.[NAS.RD5.44.858]

GRANT, JAMES, born 28 Aug 1804 in the parish of Cross and Burness, son of Rev. William Grant and Isabella Haggart, died in Jamaica. [F.7.259]

GRANT, JAMES MACDOWAL, son of David Grant of Arntilly, at King's College, Aberdeen, 1817, a planter in Jamaica. [KCA#2.431]

GRANT, JAMES COLQUHOUN, in Hanover, Jamaica, 1822. [NAS.NRAS#0771/612]

GRANT, JOHN, in Spanish Town, Jamaica, 1774. [NAS.GD248.61.2]

GRANT, JOHN, of Kilgraston, Chief Justice of Jamaica, 1784; in Spanish Town, 1787; died Edinburgh 1793. [NA.CO137.38/39; GD248.61.2; RGS.124.166]

GRANT, JOHN, a coppersmith, St James, Jamaica, 1774. [BL.Add.MS22676/8]

SCOTS IN JAMAICA, 1655-1855

GRANT, JOHN, a planter in Jamaica, 1790. [NAS.RD2.274.61]
GRANT, JOHN, in Jamaica, a burgess of Banff 1775, testament, 19 Nov 1807. [NAS.CC1.6.W329][BBR]
GRANT, JOHN LACHLAN, second son of Lt. Col. Alexander Grant in Elgin, died in Cascade, Hanover, Jamaica, 22 Oct 1837. [AJ#4695]
GRANT, JOHN, son of Patrick Grant of Glenlochy [1709-1783] and Beatrice Grant [1711-1780]. Chief Justice of Jamaica. [Kirkmichael MI, Banffshire]
GRANT, JOHN, born 1821, son of Peter Grant and Christian Grant in Culnafiadh, Abernethy, Inverness-shire, died in Jamaica, 1850. [Abernethy MI]
GRANT, LACHLAN, died in Jamaica, 1791. [GM.61.1065]
GRANT, Col. LEWIS, in Jamaica, 1742. [NA248.99.5.24][NAS.GD248.86.1]
GRANT, LEWIS, on Maggotty Estate, Jamaica, 1774. [NAS.GD248.51.2]
GRANT, PATRICK, Crown Surveyor of Jamaica, son of Alexander Grant of Corimony, died in Jamaica, 1818. [AJ#3657]
GRANT, PATRICK, Sergeant at Arms to the House of Assembly, son of Sir Ludovic Grant of Dalvey, died at Salt Ponds, Jamaica, 25 Oct 1820. [S.4.200]
GRANT, RICHARD, in Jamaica, probate, 1714, PCC.
GRANT, RICHARD, in St Thomas in the East, 1776. [NLS.Acc.8793]
GRANT, ROBERT LAING, born 29 Apr 1794, in Cross and Burness parish, second son of Rev. William Grant in Sanda, Orkney, died in St Ann's, Jamaica, 17 July 1824. [EEC#17647][F.7.259]
GRANT, THOMAS, a ship's carpenter from Jamaica who died in Deptford, Kent, during 1700. Probate, 5/1148, PCC.
GRANT, Dr WALTER, in Jamaica, 1763. [NAS.GD345.1180]
GRANT, WILLIAM, son of Alexander Grant in Fort Augus [1757-1805] and Mary Macintosh [1750-1812], settled in Jamaica by 1812. [Petty MI] [Invermoriston MI]
GRANT, WILLIAM, born 29 Apr 1794, third son of Rev. William Grant in Sanday, Orkney, died in Jamaica, 1818. [EEC#16820][F.7.259][S.3.115]
GRANT, Dr WILLIAM FORSYTH, in Jamaica, died 2 Aug 1833, inventory, 1835, Comm. Edinburgh. [NAS.SC70.1.52; C1316]
GRANT, Dr., from Leith to Jamaica on the Roselle, arrived in Kingston in Apr 1793. [JRG:27.4.1793]
GRASSIE, MARGARET, born 1820, emigrated from Aberdeen aboard the Rob Roy bound for Jamaica, arrived at Kingston on 11 May 1841. [NA.CO140/33]
GRAY, ADAM, born 1781, son of Adam Gray and Elspet Paul in Coull, late from Jamaica, died in Aberdeen, 12 June 1845. [Coull MI]; a planter in St George, Jamaica, 1813. [NAS.RD5.38.18]
GRAY, Dr ALEXANDER, born 1792, '30 years in Jamaica', died in Corunna, St Andrew's, Jamaica, 18 May 1846. [AJ#5142]

GRAY, GEORGE, in Kingston, Jamaica, 1728-1730. [NAS.GD18.5365]
GRAY, GEORGE, of Milne's Court, Edinburgh, died in Lucca, Jamaica, 1802. [AJ#2839]
GRAY, JAMES B., second son of Mr Gray a solicitor in Edinburgh, died in Coldstream, Jamaica, 20 Oct 1819. [AJ#3758][S.4.156]
GRAY, JAMES, formerly of Jamaica, married Margaret, only daughter of Captain Archibald Weir, in Greenock on 5 June 1826. [GrAd:6.6.1826]
GRAY, JOHN, in Port Royal, Jamaica, 1742. [NAS.NRAS.0508/dr.6]
GRAY, JOHN, an overseer, St James, Jamaica, 1774. [BL.Add.MS22676/8]
GRAY, PATRICK, on overseer, St James, Jamaica, 1774. [BL.Add.MS22676/8]
GRAY, PATRICK, born 1746, settled on Friendship Estate, Hanover, Jamaica, died at Glendoick House, Perth, 24 July 1806. [Kinfauns MI]
GRAY, PATRICK, possibly from Glamis, Angus, at Montego Bay and Hanover, Jamaica, husband of Sarah Gray, administration, 1807, London. [NA.Prob.11/1459]
GRAY, PETER, born 1808, son of Peter Gray and Marion Mason, died in Port Royal, Jamaica, 12 Apr 1835. [Duns MI]
GRAY, ROBERT, in Jamaica, decreets, 1773/1774. [NAS.CS16.1.81/405; CS16.1.154/223]; a planter, Industry and Virgin Valley Estates, St James, Jamaica, 1774. [BL.Add.MS22676/8]
GRAY, ROBERT, born 1782, a surgeon, died in Jamaica 25 June 1812. [Dundee, Constitution Road MI]
GRAY, WILLIAM, an attorney in Kingston, Jamaica, son of Patrick Gray tacksman of Easter Lairg, 1760. [NAS.RD37.12.268]
GRAY, WILLIAM, of Iter Boreale, Jamaica, former Postmaster General of Jamaica, 1776. [NAS.RS3.360/436]
GRAY, WILLIAM, of Herboreal, late Provost Marshal of Jamaica, a bond, 1776; died Jamaica Apr 1788. [NAS.RD4.233.1221; CS17.1.1][GM.58.658]
GRAY, WILLIAM, born 1808, eldest son of John Gray of Williamsfield, Dumfries, died on Potosi Estate, St Thomas in the East, Jamaica, 23 Oct 1829. [S.1057]
GRAY, WILLIAM, son of John Gray [1744-1794] and Jean White [1750-1817], died on Brimmershall Estate, St Mary's, Jamaica, 16 Nov 18..., aged 40. [West Linton MI]
GREEN, ALEXANDER, born 1807, son of William Green and Helen Stewart, died in Jamaica, 22 Apr 1834. [Aberlour MI]
GREEN, JAMES, born 1802, son of William Green and Helen Stewart, died in Jamaica, 14 July 1847. [Aberlour MI]
GREEN, JOSEPH, in St Mary's, Middlesex, Jamaica, brother of John Green in Petersburg, Virginia, a deed, 1798. [NAS.RD3.281.13]

SCOTS IN JAMAICA, 1655-1855

GREEN, JOSEPH, in Kingston, Jamaica, died 14 Apr 1851. [NAS.SC70.1.70; F1119]

GREGORY, ARTHUR, a planter in St Andrew's, Jamaica, 1754. [NA.CO.137/28]

GREGORY, GEORGE, from Edinburgh, a merchant in Kingston, died in Jamaica, 25 May 1822. [EEC#17330]

GREIG, ALEXANDER, a physician and planter in Jamaica, testament, 23 Feb 1776. [NAS.CC8.8.124]

GREIG, WALTER, late Jamaica, died 17 Feb 1784. [GM.54.236]

GREIG, WILLIAM, a planter in St Andrew's, Jamaica, 1754. [NA.CO137/28]

GRIER, JAMES, a Covenanter from Dalry who was transported from Leith to Jamaica in Sep. 1685, landed at Port Royal, Jamaica, in Nov 1685. [RPCS.XI.153][LJ#17]

GRIERSON, JOSEPH, in Greenpark, Jamaica, died 8 Oct 1849. inventory, 1851. [NAS.SC70.1.71; F1156]

GRIEVE, ARCHIBALD, son of Thomas Grieve a merchant in Edinburgh, died in Kingston, Jamaica, 26 Nov 1851. [W#1287]

GRIEVE, JAMES, a former merchant in Edinburgh, eldest son of John Grieve, died in St Thomas in the East, Jamaica, 20 Dec 1830. [EEC#18621]

GRIFFIN, ..., from Greenock aboard the Friends bound for Jamaica, arrived there in Oct 1794. [JRG:25.10.1794]

GRIGOR, ROBERT, son of Robert Grigor a writer in Elgin, at Marischal College, Aberdeen, 1827, later a sugar refiner in Jamaica. [MCA.II.465]

GRUBB, JAMES, born 1804, eldest son of James Grubb the stamp distributor in Forfar, died on Hyde Estate, Trelawney, Jamaica, 14 Feb 1838. [AJ.4711]

GUILD, WILLIAM, Jamaica, son of Provost John Guild, a burgess of Dundee, 1817. [DBR]

GUNN, JOSEPH, in St John's, Jamaica, 1670. [SPAWI.1670/270]

GUTHRIE, JAMES, in Jamaica, 1712. [NAS.GD44.14.4.9]; died in Westmoreland, Jamaica, 10 July 1728. [Cross Path MI, Jamaica]

GUTHRIE, JAMES, on Friendship Estate, Jamaica, 1801. [DCA.H2]

GUTHRIE, JOHN, born 1687, arrived in 1700 via Darien (?), died in Westmoreland, Jamaica, 13 June 1739. [Cross Path MI, Jamaica]

GUTHRIE, MOLLY, in Kingston, Jamaica, 1780. [NAS.CS16.1.177]

GUTHRIE, PATRICK, son of John Guthrie and Helen Yeaman, born Dundee 8 Oct 1776, a merchant, died at Montego Bay, 21 Dec 1821; a deed, 1818. [Montego Bay MI][NAS.RD5.144.504]

GUTHRIE, WILLIAM, at Two Mile Wood, St Elizabeth's, Jamaica, son of Rev. Harry Guthrie and Rachel Milne in Edinburgh, a deed, 1774; died in Edinburgh, 1814.[NAS.RD3.733.387][GM.84.195]

SCOTS IN JAMAICA, 1655-1855

HACKET, ALICIA, born 1823, eldest daughter of Dr Hacket the Deputy Inspector General, died in Kingston, Jamaica, 17 Jan 1846. [EEC#21312][PC#2008]

HADDOW, GAVIN, late a merchant in Jamaica, married Margaret Young, in Edinburgh, 18 Dec 1763. [EMR]

HAIG, JOHN, a witness in Jamaica, 1775. [NAS.RD4.718.871]

HALDANE, GEORGE, Governor of Jamaica, 16 Aug 1758; died 26 July 1759. [NAS.RS10.9.147][GM.29.497]

HALDANE, HENRY, an attorney in Spanish Town, Jamaica, 1808; late of Kingston, Jamaica, died in Haddington, 9 Dec 1826. [NAS.RD3.326.769] [AJ#4120]

HALIBURTON, GAVIN, in Kingston, Jamaica, May 1744; a planter, St Andrew's, Jamaica, 1754. [Caribeanna.6/23][NA.CO137/28]

HALKET, JAMES, a physician in Jamaica, admitted as a burgess of St Andrews, Fife, 2 Oct 1770. [St ABR]

HALL, HUGH, St James, Jamaica, 1774. [BL.Add.MS22676/8]

HALL, HUGH KIRKPATRICK, a planter, Kirkpatrick Estate, Irwin Estate and Tryall Estate, St James, Jamaica, 1774. [BL.Add.MS22676/8]

HALL, JAMES, a rebel from Kintyre, Argyll, who was transported from Leith to Jamaica in Aug 1685. [RPCS.XI.136]

HALL, JAMES H., in Jamaica, 1806, only son of John Hall of Benacres. [NAS.CS17.1.19/294]

HALL, JAMES, late in Jamaica, married Mary, daughter of James Anderson of Rispond, Sutherland, there, 13 Sep 1854. [EEC#22634]

HALL, MARK, in St Mary's, Jamaica, 1740. [NAS.GD206.229/244]

HAMILTON, ALEXANDER, at Morant Bay, 1776. [NLS.Acc.8793]

HAMILTON, ALEXANDER WEST, Lt. Col. and ADC to the Governor of Jamaica, 1800. [NAS.GD142/34]

HAMILTON, Lord ARCHIBALD, Governor of Jamaica, 1711-1715. [Rawl.A/312]

HAMILTON, ARCHIBALD, in St Ann's, Jamaica, died 1799, testament, 9 Mar 1801. [NAS.AC7.76; CC8.8.132]

HAMILTON, CHARLES, St James, Jamaica, 1774. [BL.Add.MS22676/8]

HAMILTON, CHARLES, Customs Collector at Montego Bay, 1766-1784. [NAS.GD232.10.3; 237.67; NRAS#2177/1111][BL.Add.ms38218/293]

HAMILTON, GEORGE R., a planter, Success Estate, St James, Jamaica, 1774. [BL.Add.MS22676/8]

HAMILTON, GEORGE DUNDAS, born 1811, son of John Hamilton of Sundrum, died at Hyde Hall, Trelawney, Jamaica, 17 Feb 1833. [Hyde Hall MI]

HAMILTON, GEORGE WILLIAM, son of John Hamilton and Helen Bogle in Northbank, Glasgow, a planter in Tulloch, St Thomas in the Vale, Jamaica, 5 Sep 1829. [NAS.RD398.536]

HAMILTON, JAMES, late in Jamaica, then in Falkirk, testament, 8 Nov 1796, Comm. Stirling. [NAS]
HAMILTON, JAMES, a planter in St George's, Jamaica, dead by 1800. [NAS.NRAS.0620.GDB, bundle 2]
HAMILTON, JAMES, born 1801, son of James Hamilton and Agnes Watson in Biggar, died in Jamaica, 3 Jan 1824. [St Mary's, Biggar, MI]
HAMILTON, JOHN, in Jamaica, burgess of Edinburgh, 1735, [EBR][NAS.GD3.2.109][JCTP.1737.595]; probate 1747, PCC.
HAMILTON, JOHN, son of the late John Hamilton, a merchant in Jamaica, was granted lands in the barony of Alloway, Ayrshire, 1754. [NAS.GD3.1.8.3.1]
HAMILTON, JOHN, in Jamaica, testament, 7 Aug 1786, Comm. Edinburgh. [NAS.CC8.8.127]
HAMILTON, JOHN, born 1781, 1st son of John Hamilton a merchant in Glasgow, Lord Provost of Glasgow, at Glasgow University in 1793, died in Kingston, Jamaica, on 4 Nov 1801. [MAGU#172][GM.72.181][Caribeanna.4.17]
HAMILTON, MATTHEW, a rebel and husbandman from Kintyre, Argyll, imprisoned in Edinburgh Tolbooth, was transported from Leith to Jamaica in Aug 1685.[ETR#369] [RPCS.XI.329]
HAMILTON, PATRICK, born Glasgow 6 Sep 1757, son of Rev. John Hamilton and Mary Bogle, died in Jamaica, 15 Jan 1788. [F.3.458]
HAMILTON, PRIMROSE, daughter of John Hamilton in Jamaica deceased, 1780. [NAS.CS16.1.179]
HAMILTON, ROBERT, a merchant in Jamaica, later of Bourtreehill, 1742. [NAS.GD3.1.8.12.9; RGS.97.187]
HAMILTON, ROBERT, fourth son of John Hamilton an officer of Glasgow, at Glasgow University in 1801, a merchant in Jamaica, died in London 1840. [MAGU][NAS.C2482; RD5.193.513]
HAMILTON, THOMAS, from Kelso [?], in Kingston, Jamaica, 1807. [NAS.RD5.389.42]
HAMILTON, WILLIAM, 3rd son of John Hamilton of Redhall, died in Jamaica in July 1799. [AJ#2691]
HAMILTON, WILLIAM, born June 1748, 4th son of James Hamilton a merchant in Edinburgh and Helen Baillie, a merchant in Jamaica, husband of Elizabeth Nisbet, died 15 Dec 1802 in Edinburgh. [SP.II.55]
HANDYSIDE, ANDREW, in Jamaica, 22 Feb 1826. [NAS.RD5.320.246]
HANDYSIDE, ROBERT, born 1776, died in Jamaica, 4 Sep 1796. [Edinburgh, Greendykes MI]
HANNAH, ANDREW, from Creetown, Kirkcudbright, aboard the Countess of Galloway on 15 Mar 1793 bound for Jamaica, arrived in Kingston in May 1793. [RJG:1.6.1793]

HANNAY, WILLIAM, a carpenter and merchant in Spanish Town, Jamaica, later in Wigton, testament, 1760, Wigton. [NAS]
HARPER, ALEXANDER, late of Jamaica, died in Banff 12 July 1843. [AJ#4987]
HARPER, ROBERT, Lt. of the 15th Foot, died in Jamaica, 16 Apr 1828, inventory, 1832, Comm. Edinburgh. [NAS]
HARRIS, GEORGE, in Kingston, Jamaica, graduated MD at Marischal College, Aberdeen, 1768. [MCA]
HARRIS, JOHN, in Kingston, Jamaica, graduated MD at Marischal College, Aberdeen, 1767. [MCA]
HARRIS, MARY, in Kingston, 1787. [NAS.B56.16.132]
HARRIS, ROBERT WILLIAM, Assemblyman for St Thomas in the Vale, died in St Catherine's, Jamaica, 27 Mar 1830. [PA#45]
HARRISON-OLIPHANT, JOHN, in Jamaica, 1784, 1788. [NAS.CS17.1.3/204; 7/19]
HART, JAMES, born in Girvan, Ayrshire, settled in Jamaica, dead by 1811. [NAS.GD2.252]
HARVEY, ..., a planter, Great River Estate, St James, Jamaica, 1774. [BL.Add.MS22676/8]
HARVEY, ..., daughter of Mr Harvey, born 12 Apr 1838 at Deanery Park, Kingston, Jamaica. [AJ#4717]
HARVIE, W. I., in Jamaica, 1836. [NAS.RD5.548.549]
HASTIE, WILLIAM, a Covenanter from Carluke, Lanarkshire, was transported from Leith to Jamaica in Aug 1685. [RPCS.XI.136]
HAY, ALEXANDER, a merchant in Kingston, Jamaica, co-owner of the Commerce of Glasgow, 1793. [NAS.CE60.11.3/65]
HAY, ALEXANDER, born 1807, son of George Hay a farmer in Turriff, died on Duckenfield Estate, Jamaica, 3 Aug 1857. [AJ.9.9.1957]
HAY, BEATRIX, eldest daughter of Rev. James Hay in Roberton, wife of John Jamieson late planter in Jamaica, died in Portsoy, 24 Feb 1845. [EEC#21157]
HAY, CHARLES, Clifton Pen, Jamaica, died in Aberdeen, 14 Aug 1805. [GM.75.882]
HAY, FRANCIS, born 1773, died in Jamaica 1811. [Dundonald MI]
HAY, JAMES, born 1696, Judge of the Grand Court of Jamaica, died 7 Oct 1735. [Spanish Town Cathedral MI]
HAY, Sir JAMES, died in Kingston, Jamaica, Aug 1794. [GM.64.1054]
HAY, PETER, late of Jamaica, 19 Jan 1783. [NAS.RS8.150]
HAY, JOHN, son of A. Hay a japanner in Aberdeen, died on Low Ground Estate, Jamaica, 21 June 1853. [AJ.7.9.1853]
HAY, MICHAEL, in Kingston, Jamaica, died 12 Dec 1762. [GM.32.241]

SCOTS IN JAMAICA, 1655-1855

HAY, PETER, born 1777 in Drumblade, in the West Indies for 69 years, died in Kingston, Jamaica, 24 May 1869. [AJ.22.9.1869]

HAY, ROBERT GRAY, in Jamaica, probate 1797, PCC.

HAY, WILLIAM, born 1681, settled in Westmoreland, Jamaica, died 16 Apr 1717. [Kingston MI][NAS.GD477.410.3]

HAY, WILLIAM, in Jamaica, married Helen,[born 1752], 8th daughter of Alexander Innes an advocate and Anne Rose, 30 Sep.1784. [SAA]

HAZEL, JOHN, in Kingston, Jamaica, then in Ayr, testament, 24 Oct 1820, Glasgow. [NAS.CC9.7.81/106]

HEADRICK, Dr WILLIAM, 4th son of Rev. James Headrick in Dunnichen, died on Blue Hole Estate, Jamaica, 17 Dec 1848. [AJ#5280][EEC#21784]

HEATH, BENJAMIN, a physician from Jamaica, married Marion Wallace, widow of John Galbreath a merchant in Glasgow, in Edinburgh, 3 Nov 1790.[EMR]

HEMMING, ..., from Greenock to Jamaica on the Bell, arrived in Kingston in Jan 1793. [JRG:19.1.1793]

HENDERSON, BALFOUR, and CHRISTIAN HENDERSON, of Jamaica, 1816. [NAS.CS38.14.75]

HENDERSON, CHARLES, a planter in Jamaica, inventory, 1864, Edinburgh. [NAS.SC70.1.13/641]

HENDERSON, or COSGROVE, CHRISTINE, in Spanish Town, Jamaica, 18 Nov 1839. [NAS.RS27.49.250]

HENDERSON, DONALD, overseer at Alexandria, Jamaica, died Dec 1828, inventory, 1830, Comm. Edinburgh. [NAS]

HENDERSON, ELLEN ELIZABETH, born 1840, eldest daughter of George Henderson from Edinburgh, died in Kingston, Jamaica, 9 Feb1868. [S#7675]

HENDERSON, GEORGE, a merchant in Kingston, Jamaica, son of George Henderson in Newton Stewart, 1787. [NAS.RS61.177]

HENDERSON, HUME, born 1784, son of James Henderson and Jean Tait in Ayton, died in Jamaica, 14 Dec 1807. [Coldingham MI]

HENDERSON, JAMES, surgeon in Jamaica, testament, 2 Jan 1756, Comm. Edinburgh. [NAS]

HENDERSON, JAMES, son of Adam Henderson MD in Jamaica, at King's College, Aberdeen, 1784-1788, graduated MD in 1793. [KCA.2.364]

HENDERSON, JAMES, born 1784, son of Robert Henderson in Hoddam, died in Kingston, Jamaica, 15 Feb 1808. [Hoddam MI, Dumfries-shire]

HENDERSON, JAMES, a contractor from Craigie Clove, died in Jamaica 20 Apr 1835. [Dalmeny MI]

HENDERSON, JANE, at Anotto River Plantation, Jamaica, died 29 May 1829, inventory, 1854. [NAS.SC70.1.85; F1958]

HENDERSON, JOHN, from Edinburgh, a saddler in Jamaica, died 1755. [NAS.CC8.8.116]

HENDERSON, JOHN, first son of John Henderson MD formerly in Jamaica, at Glasgow University in 1768. [MAGU]

HENDERSON, JOHN HALLY, son of Rev. John Henderson in Wanlockhead, of the Ordnance Office in Jamaica, died 3 Oct 1820. [F.3.329]

HENDERSON, JOHN, son of William Henderson in Dunfermline, died in Perth, Trelawney, Jamaica, 14 Apr 1845. [W#579]

HENDERSON, JOHN JAMES, MD, born 1817, from Aberdeen, died in East Street, Kingston, Jamaica, 6 Dec 1861. [AJ#5948]

HENDERSON, J.B., son of the late John Henderson a surgeon in Port Glasgow, died in Jamaica on 16 Apr 1821. [GrA: 31.8.1821]

HENDERSON, PATRICK, a cooper, *"a middle size fellow, marked with the small pox, aged 18 years, talks broad Scotch"*, an indentured servant who absconded from the ship Antelope at Montego Bay 12 June 1754. [JC#295]

HENDERSON, ROBERT, in Jamaica then in Elgin, testament, 28 May 1824. [NAS.CC16.4.10.497]

HENDERSON, WILLIAM, son of William Henderson in Jamaica, at King's College, Aberdeen, 1820-1824, LCRS of Edinburgh, 1826, settled in Jamaica. [KCA.2.440]

HENDERSON, Dr WILLIAM FORSYTH, in Pleasant Hills, married Maria, daughter of Robert Mein, Retreat Pen, Portland, Jamaica, there 16 June 1836. [AJ#4627]

HENDERSON, Mrs, from Jamaica, was buried in St Nicholas churchyard, Aberdeen, 1 May 1788. [ACA]

HENDERSON, ..., son of W. F. Henderson, MD, born in Bath, St Thomas in the East, Jamaica, 20 May 1847. [AJ#5194]

HENDRY, E. H., in Jamaica, 9 June 1813. [NAS.RD5.321.87]

HENDRY, PETER, died in Jamaica by 1768. [NAS.GD26.13.658]

HENDRY, WILLIAM, a merchant in St Andrews, died in Shortwood, Jamaica, 1805. [AJ#2981]

HENRY, ALEXANDER, a merchant in Kingston, Jamaica, co-owner of Glasgow registered ships, 1794. [NAS.CE60.11.3; 6/59/106]

HENRY, JOHN, a merchant in Jamaica and co-owner of the Flora of Greenock, 1801. [NAS.CE60.11.7/68]

HENRY, ROBERT, a merchant in Kingston, Jamaica, and co-owner of Scots registered ships, 1801/1803. [NAS.CE60.11.7/68; 8/27]

HEPBURN, PENELOPE, daughter of William Hepburn in Jamaica, married Arthur Law of Pittiloch, in Edinburgh, 24 Nov 1789. [EMR]

SCOTS IN JAMAICA, 1655-1855

HEPBURN, WILLIAM, born 1712, son of John Hepburn of Urr and Emilia Nisbet, an apprentice surgeon in Edinburgh 1724, a surgeon in Jamaica, a witness in Hanover, Jamaica, 1744, died at Dalskairth 30 May 1775. [TDG#23/235] [see RGD.Jamaica.LOS24/330]

HERRIES, WILLIAM, born 1778, son of John Herries and Margaret Caven in Kirkgunzeon, Kirkcudbright, died in Jamaica, 17 Nov 1805. [Kirkgunzeon MI]

HERRING, NATHANIEL, in Jamaica, a burgess of Glasgow, 1716. [GBR]

HERON, ANDREW, a clerk in Kingston, Jamaica, a witness, 1790. [NAS.RD2.249.1059]

HILL, ROBERT, son of James Hill and Agnes Muirhead, a surgeon who died in Jamaica, 26 July 1737. [F.2.285]

HILL, ROBERT, son of Peter Hill cess collector in Edinburgh, died in Jamaica in May 1827. [AJ#4153]

HINCKSMAN, RICHARD, a merchant from Glasgow, died in Jamaica, June 1797. [GM.67/711]

HISLOP, LAWRENCE, jr., eldest son of John Hislop in Biggar, died on Leogan Estate, Montego Bay, Jamaica, 16 Apr 1839. [SG#8/777]

HISLOP, LAURENCE, late of Jamaica, died at Leith Links 4 Jan 1856.[CM.20679]

HODGE, DAVID, son of J. Hodge a Customs officer in Alloa, a planter in Jamaica. [NNQ.IV.137]

HODGE, ELIZABETH, widow of Ebenezer Reid, in Kingston, Jamaica, died 13 Mar1845, inventory, 1846. [NAS.SC70.1.67; F409]

HOGG, ANDREW, son of William Hogg in Haddington, at Marischal College, Aberdeen, 1835, a missionary in Jamaica. [MCA.II.495]

HOGG, CHARLES, in Jamaica, probate 1732, PCC.

HOGG, MARGARET, daughter of John Hogg an attorney in Jamaica, married Robert Primrose a surgeon, in Edinburgh, 10 Nov 1776. [EMR]

HOGG, ..., son of A. G. Hogg, was born 26 Dec 1846 in New Broughton, Manchester, Jamaica. [AJ#5171]

HOLMES, ALEXANDER, born 9 May 1789 in Edinburgh, editor of the *Cornwall Chronicle*, died at Montego Bay, 18 Sep 1861. [Montego Bay MI]

HOLMES, JAMES, a merchant in Falmouth, Jamaica, deceased, his widow Mary Ann Barker, and his father John Holmes a merchant in Greenock, 1820. [NAS.SC53.56.2/217]

HOLMES, MARGARET, a prisoner in Edinburgh Tolbooth who was transported from Leith to Jamaica in Aug 1685. [ETR#369][RPCS.XI.330]

HOME, CHARLES, only son of Dr George Home, in Jamaica, 1715. [NAS.RD4.117.295]

SCOTS IN JAMAICA, 1655-1855

HOME, Dr GEORGE, in St Andrew's, Leguan, Jamaica, only brother of James Home of Castlelaw and uncle of Robert Home a wright in Edinburgh, 1715. [NAS.RD4.117.295]

HOME, JOHN, in St Andrew's, Jamaica, 1670. [SPAWI.1670/270]

HOME, ROCHEAD, a merchant in Port Royal, Jamaica, 1715. [NAS.RD4.117.295]

HOOD, DAVID, overseer on Dundee plantation, Jamaica, 1792. [NAS.GD241.189.1]

HOPE, THOMAS, a soldier, died 1699 in Jamaica, testament, 1707. [NAS.CC8.8.83]

HOPETON, ALEXANDER, WALDRON, first son of David Hopeton a planter in Jamaica, matriculated at Glasgow University in 1840, a medical student. [MAGU]

HOPKINS, JAMES, from Jamaica, died in Greenock on 25 Dec 1813. [GrAd: 31.12.1813][NAS.RS10.2902]

HOPKIRK, GEORGE, born 1765, son of Alexander Hopkirk and Jean Briggs in Dryburgh, Roxburghshire, died at Dryburgh Castle, Jamaica, 11 Mar1813. [Dryburgh MI]

HOSACK, MARY ANN, born 4 Apr 1810, wife of John Bell, died in Woodstock, Jamaica, 28 Sep 1838. [Girvan MI]

HOSIE, GEORGE, born 1776, son of George Hosie and Janet Gregg, died at Davies Cove, Jamaica, 1800. [Abercorn MI]

HOSSACK, ..., son of William Hossack at Buff Bay River Estate, was born in Montpelier, St George's, Jamaica, 8 July 1844. [W.5.498]

HOSSACK, ..., daughter of William Hossack at Buff Bay River Estate, was born in Montpelier, St George's, Jamaica, 13 July 1852. [W.1359]

HOUSTOUN, AGNES, in Jamaica, inventory, 1853. [NAS.SC70.1.77]

HOUSTOUN, JOHN, in Trelawney, Jamaica, 1814. [NAS.RD5.271.425]

HOUSTOUN, WILLIAM, in Kingston, Jamaica, 9 Dec 1730. [BM.Sloane.4051/141]

HOUSTOUN, WILLIAM, son of Allen Houstoun a teacher in Glasgow, a merchant in Jamaica, died there 15 Oct 1808. [GM.79.85]

HOUSTOUN, WILLIAM, born 1821, arrived at Bluefields, Westmoreland, on 23 Jan 1841 aboard the William Pirie, from Stranraer. [NA.CO.140/33]

HOWIE, JOHN, a Covenanter imprisoned in Edinburgh Tolbooth who was transported from Leith to Jamaica in Aug 1685. [ETR#369]

HOWIE, JOHN, a merchant in Kingston, Jamaica, died 9 Sep 1847, inventory, 1849. [NAS.SC70.1.69; E1451]

HOWIE, SAMUEL, a Covenanter imprisoned in Edinburgh Tolbooth who was transported from Leith to Jamaica in Aug 1685. [ETR#369][RPCS.XI.329]

HOWNAME, WALTER, a Covenanter from Teviotdale, who was transported from Leith to Jamaica in Aug 1685, landed at Port Royal, Jamaica, in 1685. [RPCS.XI.330][LJ#15/17]

HUGHES, WALTER, a planter in St Andrew's, Jamaica, 1754. [NA.CO137/28]

HUIE, THOMAS, a merchant in Kingston, Jamaica, and co-owner of a Glasgow ship, 1805. [NAS.CE60.11 8/63]

HUME, JOHN, a naval surgeon in Port Royal, Jamaica, 1753. [NAS.RS27.142.273]

HUME, ROBERT, youngest son of Alexander Hume of Coldingham Law, died at Bagnals, St Mary's, Jamaica, 12 Jan 1804. [GM.74.596]

HUNTER, JAMES, in Jamaica, testament, 26 Feb 1800, Comm. Edinburgh. [NAS]

HUNTER, JOHN, a planter in Jamaica, married Eliza Mary, daughter of Col. Robert Ballingall, in Canongate, 20 Oct 1794. [CMR]

HUNTER, JOHN, born 1780, son of Robert Hunter [1745-1816], died in Kingston, Jamaica, 17 Dec 1799. [Inverkip MI]

HUNTER, MARGARET, widow of Walter Miller a merchant in Jamaica, died 18 Dec 1847 in Granton, Edinburgh, inventory, 1852. [NAS.SC70.1.77]

HUNTER, ROBERT, grandson of Professor Hunter of Edinburgh University, died in Jamaica, 1 Jan 1805. [AJ#2985][CM#13033]

HUNTER, ROBERT, a cabinetmaker in Falmouth, Jamaica, then in Lochwinnoch, 1815. [NAS.SC58.59.6.23]

HURD, JEAN, born 1808, a teacher, with Margaret, born 1828, William, born 1830, Arthur, born 1832, Elspeth, born 1835, Elizabeth, born 1836, and Charles, born 1840, emigrated from Aberdeen aboard the Rob Roy bound for Jamaica, arrived at Kingston on 11 May 1841. [NA.CO140/33]

HUTCHEON, JOHN, in Jamaica, testament, 23 June 1812. [NAS.CC16.9.10.423]

HUTCHESON, GEORGE, in Kingston, Jamaica, May 1744; a burgess and guildsbrother of Ayr, 30 Apr 1750. [Caribbeanna.6.23][AyrBR]

HUTCHESON, ROBERT, who was transported from Leith to Jamaica in Aug 1685. [RPCS.XI.136]

HUTCHINSON, LEWIS, born 1733, to Jamaica in 1760s as an estate administrator, settled at Edinburgh Castle, St Ann's, a serial killer, hanged in Spanish Town on 16 Mar 1773. [Jamaica Gleaner]

HUTCHISON, ALEXANDER MCCONACHIE, in Glasgow, son of Robert Hutchison in Jamaica, testament, 13 July 1793, Comm. Glasgow. [NAS]

HUTCHISON, WILLIAM, settled in Jamaica by 1694, and in Port Royal in 1700. [SPAWI.1699.443][DP#352]

HYSLOP, ANDREW, in St James, Jamaica, 1814. [NAS.RD5.271.425]

HYSLOP, JEAN, in Jamaica, died 9 Nov 1811, testament, 19 Sep 1817. [NAS.CC8.8.143]

SCOTS IN JAMAICA, 1655-1855

HYSLOP, MAXWELL, a merchant in New York, then in Kingston, Jamaica, 1809, son of William Hyslop of Lochend deceased. [NAS.CS17.1.28/400]

HYSLOP, WELLWOOD, a merchant in New York, then in Kingston, Jamaica, 1809, son of William Hyslop of Lochend deceased. [NAS.CS17.1.28/400]

INGLIS, ALEXANDER, rector of St Andrew's, Jamaica, probate, 15 July 1749, PCC

INGLIS, FRANCES, died 9 Jan 1791. [Kingston MI, Jamaica]

INGLIS, GEORGE, in Savanna-la-Mar, Jamaica, 1780. [NA.CO137.1-35]

INGLIS, JAMES, a carpenter in St James, Jamaica, probate, 24 Sep 1789, PCC.

INGLIS, JAMES, a merchant, married Mary Jane Brock in Kingston, Jamaica, 12 Sep 1799. [SM.61.907]

INGLIS, JAMES, born 1773, son of Cornelius Inglis, a surgeon, and Euphemia Weir in Lanark, late of Kingston, Jamaica, died in Walthamstow, England, Nov 1814. [Lanark MI]

INGLIS, JAMES, late in Kingston, Jamaica, died in Musselburgh, 3 Oct 1823. [DPCA.1107]

INGLIS, PATRICK, born Apr 1701, 3rd son of John Inglis of Langbyres, Registrar of Chancery in Jamaica, died 1737. ['Family of Inglis', p.10.]

INGLIS, THOMAS, a merchant in Charleston, South Carolina, a Loyalist who settled in Kingston, Jamaica, by 1784. [NAS.AO12.52.249; AO12.92.1]

INNES, ALEXANDER, chief carpenter, HM Dockyard, Port Royal, Jamaica, 31 Aug 1784. [NAS.RS29.99]

INNES, HUGH, died in Jamaica, 6 Oct 1803. [EEC#14354]

INNES, JAMES, in Jamaica, probate, 1797, PCC.

INNES, JOHN, a merchant in Port Royal, Jamaica, probate 16 Sep 1692, Jamaica

INNES, JOHN, a planter in St Andrew's, Jamaica, 1754. [NA.CO137/28]

IRELAND, JOHN, a Covenanter imprisoned in Edinburgh Tolbooth who was transported from Leith to Jamaica in Aug 1685. [ETR#369][RPCS.XI.114]

IRVINE, Dr CHARLES, born 1720, son of Arthur Irvine and Cecilia Barclay, sometime in Friendship Estate, St Thomas, Jamaica, later in Aberdeen, died 30 May 1791; testament, 11 June 1794, Comm. Aberdeen. [NAS]; probate, 1794, PCC; [NAS.NRAS.0051, deed-box 75][St Nicholas MI, Aberdeen][NLS.Acc.8793]

IRVINE, JOHN, born 1811, a laborer, emigrated from Aberdeen aboard the Rob Roy bound for Jamaica, arrived at Kingston on 11 May 1841. [NA.CO140/33]

IRVINE, WILLIAM, from Leith, in Jamaica by 7 Dec 1810. [NAS.RS27.2.257]

IRVING, AEMILIUS, born 1746, died in St James, Jamaica, 22 Jan 1794. [St James MI]

IRVING, Dr JAMES, in Jamaica, 1757, brother of John Irving of Bonshaw. [NAS.GD219.290]

SCOTS IN JAMAICA, 1655-1855

IRVING, JAMES, a planter, Hartfield Estate, St James, Jamaica, 1774. [BL.Add.MS22676/8]
IRVING, Hon. JAMES, a planter, Ironshore Estate, St James, Jamaica, 1774. [BL.Add.MS22676/8]
IRVING, JAMES, a surgeon, late in Jamaica, died in Gatehouse, 25 Nov 1821. [S.5.252]
IRVING, JAMES, born 1816, with Eliza born 1815, William born 1834, and Christopher born 1836, arrived at Bluefields, Westmoreland, on 23 Jan 1841 aboard the William Pirie, from Stranraer. [NA.CO.140/33]
IRVING, JOHN, a doctor, St James, Jamaica, 1774. [BL.Add.MS22676/8]
IVAR, JOHN, who was transported from Leith to Jamaica in Aug 1685. [RPCS.XI.136]
JACK, JAMES, in Chatham Estate, Jamaica, dead by 1785. [NAS.GD23.6.441]
JACK, JAMES, from Greenock, died in Jamaica on 4 Aug 1847. [GrA: 28.9.1847]
JACK, MARGARET, born 1811, spouse of Alexander McEwan, died at King's House, Jamaica, on 12 June 1844, buried at St Catherine's Cathedral there. [Lochwinnoch MI]
JACK, WILLIAM, born 1819, arrived at Bluefields, Westmoreland, on 23 Jan 1841 aboard the William Pirie, from Stranraer. [NA.CO.140/33]
JACKSON, GEORGE, born 1822, a cooper, arrived at Bluefields, Westmoreland, on 23 Jan 1841 aboard the William Pirie, from Stranraer. [NA.CO.140/33]
JACKSON, ISAAC, Copse Estate, Hanover, Jamaica, died 3 Aug 1856, inventory, Comm. Edinburgh, 1857. [NAS.SC70.1.94; G3543]
JACKSON, JOHN, a Covenanter from Braestob in Glasgow, who was transported from Leith to Jamaica in Aug 1685, landed at Port Royal in Nov 1685, settled in Spanish Town. [RPCS.XI.329][LJ#81]
JACKSON, ROBERT, a planter, Hampton Estate, St James, Jamaica, 1774. [BL.Add.MS22676/8]
JAFFRAY, THOMAS, in Jamaica, probate, 1767, PCC.
JAMES, ELIZABETH L., relict of Rev. William Fraser rector of Trelawney, Jamaica, and of Findrack, Aberdeenshire, died in Falmouth, Jamaica, 22 June 1850. [AJ#5353]
JAMESON, MARY JANE, wife of Dr Thomas Ross Jameson of the Medical Staff in Jamaica, died in Kingston, 14 Dec 1839. [EEC#20009]
JAMESON, ..., son of Rev. William Jameson in Goshen, Jamaica, died in St Ann's, Jamaica, 12 July 1839. [SG#798]
JAMIESON, ALEXANDER, a Covenanter and a servant in Mauchline, Ayrshire, imprisoned in Edinburgh Tolbooth, transported from Leith to Jamaica in Aug 1685. [ETR#369][RPCS.XI.136]

SCOTS IN JAMAICA, 1655-1855

JAMIESON, ALEXANDER, son of John Jamieson a merchant in Elgin, died in Clarendon, Jamaica, Jan 1803. [AJ#2932]

JAMIESON, ANN, a widow, St James, Jamaica, 1774. [BL.Add.MS22676/8]

JAMIESON, ELIZABETH, daughter of John Jamieson an overseer in Jamaica, married John Chirnside a farmer, 15 July 1790. [Canongate MR]

JAMIESON, JOHN, youngest son of John Jamieson town clerk of Dysart, died in Belmont, Jamaica, 4 Nov 1819. [EEC#16950][S.4.159]

JAMIESON, MARY JANE, wife of Dr Thomas Ross Jamieson, died in Kingston, Jamaica, 15 Dec 1839. [AJ#4804]

JAMIESON, MARY WILSON, youngest daughter of Rev. John Jamieson in Methven, married William Milne of Halifax Estate, Jamaica, at Lucky Hill Pen, St Mary's, Jamaica, 16 Apr 1846. [AJ#5133]

JAMIESON, PETER, a merchant in Kingston, Jamaica, married Barbara, daughter of advocate John French, in Aberdeen, 9 June 1796; testament, 28 Sep 1801, Comm. Aberdeen. [AJ][NAS]

JAMIESON, WILLIAM, a merchant in Jamaica, a burgess and guildsbrother of Ayr, 1751, [Ayr BR]; probate, 1761, PCC.

JARDINE, FERGUS, a minister in Kingston, Jamaica, 1871-1875. [F.7.670]

JARDINE, WALTER, born 1806, late of Jamaica, died in Lilliesleaf, 19 Sep 1837. [Lilliesleaf MI]

JARDINE, WILLIAM, a carpenter in Jamaica, 1798. [NAS.CS313.1114]

JOHNSON, GEORGE, fourth son of James Johnson formerly a merchant in Jamaica, matriculated at Glasgow University in 1785. [MAGU]

JOHNSON, ROBERT, first son of Adam Johnson a merchant in Jamaica, matriculated at Glasgow University in 1786. [MAGU]

JOHNSON, ROBERT, eldest son of Joseph Johnson a writer in Edinburgh, died in Jamaica, 1816. [S#3]

JOHNSTON, ADAM, an overseer in St Elizabeth's, Jamaica, died July 1795, testament, 12 Mar 1796. [NAS.CC8.8.130]

JOHNSTON, ALEXANDER, graduated MA from Marischal College, Aberdeen, in 1758, a physician in St Ann's, Jamaica, from 1763, partner of Dr Alexander Fullerton. [HSP.1582/29B, box 1, ledger 1760-1772; box 2, folder 1]

JOHNSTON, ANDREW, a schoolmaster who emigrated to Jamaica in 1706. [EMA#37]

JOHNSTON, ANDREW, a planter on Whitehall Plantation, St Andrew's, Jamaica, 1754. [NA.CO137.28]

JOHNSTON, CATHERINE, 2nd daughter of Robert Johnston of Annandale, Jamaica, died on passage from New York to St Ann's, Aug 1839.

JOHNSTON, DONALD, a Covenanter who was transported from Leith to Jamaica in Aug 1685. [RPCS.XI.136]

SCOTS IN JAMAICA, 1655-1855

JOHNSTON, DUNCAN, in St Catherine's, Jamaica, 1783. [NAS.CS17.1.3/373]

JOHNSTON, Rev. FRANCIS, in Vere, Jamaica, 1794. [NAS.RS8.349]

JOHNSTON, Rev. GEORGE, "18 years a Wesleyan Methodist in the West Indies", died at Morant Bay, Jamaica, 5 Oct 1821. [Morant Bay MI]

JOHNSTON, JAMES, son of Alexander Johnston MD in Jamaica, at King's College, Aberdeen, 1797-1800, graduated MA. [KCA.2/382]

JOHNSTON, JOHN, son of Alexander Johnston MD in Jamaica, at King's College, Aberdeen, 1791. [KCA.2/374]

JOHNSTON, JOHN, a merchant in Jamaica, 1821. [NAS.CS17.1.40/180]

JOHNSTON, JOHN, late in Kingston, Jamaica, then in Edinburgh, died in Balcurvie on 21 May 1829.[FH]

JOHNSTON, MORRICE, son of James Johnston in Aberdeen, died in Kingston, Jamaica, 17 Apr 1853. [AJ.25.5.1853]

JOHNSTON, ROBERT, son of Alexander Johnston MD in Jamaica, at King's College, Aberdeen, 1790-1803, graduated MA. [KCA.2/386]

JOHNSTON, ROBERT, son of Joseph Johnston a writer in Edinburgh, died in Jamaica, 1816. [S.1.4]

JOHNSTON, ROBERT, of Annandale, Jamaica, died in St Ann's, Jamaica, Aug 1839. [AJ#4789]

JOHNSTON, ROBERT, born 1789, first son of Andrew Johnston an articifer in Dunfermline, matriculated at Glasgow University in 1815, a Secession minister from 1828 to 1832, died in Dunlin Castle, Jamaica, in Jan 1853.[MAGU]

JOHNSTON, SAMUEL, in Jamaica, probate, 1766, PCC.

JOHNSTON, SPENCE, a surgeon who died at Dry Harbour, St Ann's, Jamaica, 1804. [AJ#2945]

JOHNSTON, THOMAS, born 1686, died in Jamaica 30 Oct 1744. [St Andrew's MI, Jamaica]

JOHNSTON, THOMAS, in Jamaica, 1817. [NAS.CS17.1.36/500]

JOHNSTONE, ADAM, an overseer, St Elizabeth's, Jamaica, testament, 1796, Comm. Edinburgh. [NAS]

JOHNSTONE, ALEXANDER, in Jamaica, a letter, 1798. [NAS.GD1.616.302]

JOHNSTONE, JOHN, in Kingston, Jamaica, died 21 May 1828 in Edinburgh. [NAS.C89]

JOHNSTONE, Dr THOMAS, born 1810, died in St Ann's, Jamaica, 20 Aug 1858. [Brown's Town, MI, Jamaica]

JOHNSTONE, THOMAS, from Dumfries-shire, in Jamaica, died Dec 1830. [NAS.D600]

JOPP, ALEXANDER, born 26 Oct 1764, son of James Jopp [1722-1794] and Jean Moir [1730-1782], at King's College, Aberdeen, 1778, died in Kingston, Jamaica, 26 Jan 1798. [St Nicholas MI, Aberdeen][KCA#2/351]

SCOTS IN JAMAICA, 1655-1855

JOPP, ANDREW, in Jamaica, 21 Jan 1786. [NAS.RS8.445, PR30.128]

JOPP, DAVID, born 1814, son of Andrew Jopp an advocate in Aberdeen, died in Manchester, Jamaica. 1842. [AJ.2.11.1842]

JOPP, KEITH, a merchant in Jamaica, co-owner of the Magnet of Glasgow, 1800. [NAS.CE60.11.6/18]

JOPP, WALTER HART, son of Robert Jopp in Leith, died in Falmouth, Jamaica, 21 Nov 1824. [AJ#4031][EEC#17713]

JUNOR, WILLIAM, born 1790. From Edinburgh, manager of the Colonial Bank in Jamaica, died 9 May 1853. [St Andrew's MI, Jamaica]

KAY, WILLIAM, a missionary catechist in Jamaica, died Oct 1841, inventory, 1842. [NAS.SC70.1.61; D1619]

KEILLER, JOHN, master of the Greyhound, died at Montego Bay 1 Nov 1831. [EEC#18615]

KEILLER, MARGARET, born 1800, daughter of James Keiller [1759-1846] a merchant in Dundee, wife of Archibald McGowan MD, died in Portland, Jamaica, 29 Nov 1822. [Dundee Howff MI][Machineal MI, Jamaica]

KEIN, PATRICK, a prisoner on Edinburgh Tolbooth who was transported from Leith to Jamaica in Aug 1685. [ETR#162]

KEITH, Sir ALEXANDER, born 1741, Lt.Col. 88th Regiment, died 3 Oct 1781. [Kingston MI, Jamaica]

KEITH, BASIL, Governor of Jamaica, 1774-1777, son of Robert Keith, died 15 June 1777. [Spanish Town Cathedral MI]

KELL, NEIL, who was transported from Leith to Jamaica in Aug 1685. [RPCS.XI.130]

KELLIE, MARTHA, wife of John Fisher, died in Bryan Castle, Rio Bueno, Jamaica, 27 June 1868. [S#7800]

KELLY, JOHN, eldest son of Mr Kelly a merchant in Greenock, died aboard the Britannia of Greenock at Jamaica on 19 July 1808. [GrA: 19.9.1808]

KEMP, ALEXANDER, born 1821, a clerk, emigrated from Aberdeen aboard the Rob Roy bound for Jamaica, arrived at Kingston on 11 May 1841. [NA.CO140/33]

KENNEDY, ALEXANDER, born 1795 in Kelton, Kirkcudbrightshire, an overseer on Hopewell Estate, Jamaica, died 19 Jan 1832. [Falmouth MI, Jamaica]

KENNEDY, ARCHIBALD, youngest son of John Kennedy of Underwood, died at Machineal, St Thomas in the East, Jamaica, 28 Oct 1843. [EEC#20696]

KENNEDY, Dr D., born in Glasgow, died at Waterloo, St Ann's, Jamaica, 25 Nov 1827. [AJ#4178]

KENNEDY, ELIZA, born 1822, arrived at Bluefields, Westmoreland, on 23 Jan 1841 aboard the William Pirie, from Stranraer. [NA.CO.140/33]

KENNEDY, JOHN, a Covenanter who was transported from Leith to Jamaica in Aug 1685. [RPCS.XI.329]

KENNEDY, JONATHAN BROWN, born 1803, died in Jamaica, 4 Dec 1840. [Wigtown MI]

KENNEDY, SARAH, born 1799, a servant, arrived at Bluefields, Westmoreland, on 23 Jan 1841 aboard the William Pirie, from Stranraer. [NA.CO.140/33]

KER, ALAN, born 7 Dec 1819, first son of Robert Ker a merchant in Renfrewshire, matriculated at Glasgow University in 1833, Ouisne Judge of the Supreme Court of Jamaica from 1861-1885, died in Kingston on 20 Mar 1885. [MAGU]

KERR, ALEXANDER, son of George Kerr a merchant in Greenock, died in Jamaica on 5 June 1816. [GrA: 2.8.1816]

KERR, CHARLES, servant to John Hamilton a merchant in Kingston, Jamaica, a burgess and guildsbrother of Ayr, 24 June 1735. [Ayr BR]

KERR, CHARLES HOPE, born 1817, died in Jamaica 31 Dec 1840. [St Andrew's MI, Jamaica]

KERR, DAVID, born 1745, a surgeon who emigrated via London to Jamaica on the Dawes in Dec 1775. [NA.T47.9/11]; possibly in Trelawney, Jamaica, 1783. [NLS.Melville ms3591/115-130]; born 1745, late of Jamaica, died 1829. [Montrose Episcopal MI]

KERR, DAVID, son of William Kerr a writer and provost of Forfar [1745-1777]. A Major General with 37 years service in the Cornwall Militia, died 1805. [Montego Bay MI, Jamaica]

KERR, DAVID, born 1845, eldest son of David Kerr, of Edinburgh and Jamaica, was lost at sea 23 Dec 1861 in the Pentland Firth when bound for Jamaica on the brig Columbus of Leith. [S#2065]

KERR, FRANCES ELIZABETH, infant daughter of Herbert J. Kerr, died 2 Nov 1878, on Kent Estate, Trelawney, Jamaica. [EC#29385]

KERR, HENRY, born 1816, arrived at Bluefields, Westmoreland, on 23 Jan 1841 aboard the William Pirie, from Stranraer. [NA.CO.140/33]

KERR, JAMES, planter at Moor Park, St James, Jamaica, 1774; probate, 1785, PCC. [NA.Prob.11/1127][BL.Add.MS22676/8]

KERR, JAMES, in Jamaica, a burgess and guildsbrother of Glasgow, 11 Aug 1779. [GBR]

KERR, JAMES, Jamaica, MD Edinburgh University, 1794. [EMG#25]

KERR, JAMES, a planter in Kingston, Jamaica, testament, 20 Dec 1817. [NAS.CC10.7.3.208]

KERR, JOHN, born 30 Nov 1745 in Carmunnock, son of Rev. John Kerr and Susanna McGoun, settled in St Elizabeth, Jamaica. [F.3.380]

SCOTS IN JAMAICA, 1655-1855

KERR, ROBERT, in Jamaica, his widow Elizabeth McConachie in Gatehouse of Fleet, testament, 1814, Comm. Kirkcudbright. [NAS]

KERR, Dr THOMAS, born 1781, son of John Kerr and Janet Irving in Lochmaben, died in Jamaica, 12 Aug 1803. [Lochmaben MI, Dumfries-shire]

KERR, THOMAS, youngest son of Gilbert Kerr of Gateshaw, died in Jamaica, 6 Aug 1821. [S.5.247]

KERR, WILLIAM, passenger from Greenock to Jamaica aboard the Ross in Nov 1773. [NAS.CE60]

KERR, WILLIAM, only son of William Kerr a merchant in Jamaica, matriculated at Glasgow University in 1785. [MAGU]

KERR, WILLIAM, Spring Garden, Jamaica, married Margaret, daughter of James Hunter of Frankfield, in Edinburgh, 18 Oct 1791. [EMR]

KERR, WILLIAM, in Greenwood, Jamaica, an inventory, 1899. [NAS.SC70.1.381]

KETTLES, WILLIAM, born 1794, died in Machineal, Jamaica, 22 Nov 1836. [AJ#4649]

KIDD, DAVID, born 1824, emigrated from Aberdeen aboard the Rob Roy bound for Jamaica, arrived at Kingston on 11 May 1841. [NA.CO140/33]

KIDD, JAMES, in Jamaica, possibly from Scone, Perthshire, dead by 1820. [NAS.B59.38.5.66]

KIDSTONE, ALEXANDER, in Jamaica, 1850; of Queen St., Edinburgh, died 15 Aug 1850, inventory, 1850, Comm. Edinburgh. [NAS.RD5.863.409/431/440; SC70.1.71; E2366]

KILGOUR, MARGARET, wife of James Carr, died at Montego Bay on 22 Nov 1842. [AJ#4957]

KING, DAVID, in Forest Pen, Black River, Jamaica, 1880. [NAS.SC48.25.80/155]

KING, FIFE ELLISON, first son of Thomas King a merchant in Jamaica, matriculated at Glasgow University in 1780. [MAGU]

KING, HENRY CURZON, born 1811, 2nd son of the late John King of Springbank, Port Glasgow, died in Kingston, Jamaica, on 14 Nov 1830. [GrA: 11.2.1831]

KING, HUGH, a millwright in Jamaica, died 1740, testament, 3 Feb 1744. [NAS.CC8.8.108]

KING, JOHN, a merchant in Kingston, Jamaica, eldest son of George King a merchant in Paisley, 1779. [NAS.CS16.1.175]

KING, Dr THOMAS, in Savanna la Mar, Jamaica, 1778. [NLS.ms5332.236/265]

KING, THOMAS, born in Jamaica, second son of Thomas King a doctor, matriculated at Glasgow University in 1782. [MAGU]

KINGHORN, GEORGE, born 1750, died 6 Sep 1823. [Kingston, Jamaica, MI]

KINKEAD, GEORGE, born 1770, a merchant in Kingston, Jamaica, died 12 Mar 1811. [Kingston MI]

SCOTS IN JAMAICA, 1655-1855

KINLOCH, GEORGE OLIPHANT, born 1723 in Angus, owner of Grange Estate, Westmoreland, Jamaica, died 1770. [NAS.GD1.8.35/36][Savanna la Mar MI]
KINLOCH, GEORGE, sugar plantation manager, Hope Bay, Jamaica, a witness, 1815. [NAS.RD5.86.256]
KINLOCH, MARGARET, 3rd daughter of George Kinloch in Jamaica, married Thomas Kinnear a writer in Stonehaven, there 4 May 1805. [CM#13053]
KINNISON, JOHN, born 1824, minister at Accompang and Mount Trinity, Jamaica, 1875-1881, died 24 July 1887. [F.7.670]
KIRKPATRICK, HUGH, born in Irvine, Ayrshire, on 23 Oct 1671, emigrated to Jamaica in 1693, married Ann Goodin, settled in Westmoreland, father of Hugh, James, James, Edward, and Mary, died 8 Dec 1746. [Llandilo MI, Westmoreland, Jamaica]
KIRKWALL, ELIZABETH, who was transported from Leith to Jamaica in Aug 1685. [RPCS.XI.329]
KIRKWOOD, THOMAS, a doctor, St James, Jamaica, 1774. [BL.Add.MS22676/8]
KNIGHT, JOSEPH, a black slave who was brought from Jamaica to Scotland as a servant by Sir John Wedderburn of Ballindean pre 1774, successfully petitioned for his liberty in the Court of Session, 1774-1778. [NAS.CS235.K.2.2]
KNUBLEY, SIMON, in Jamaica, died 26 Sep 1836, inventory, 1837. [NAS.SC70.1.55; C1783]
LAING, ALEXANDER MORRISON, a physician and surgeon in Kingston, Jamaica, inventory, 1894. [NAS.SC70.1.330]
LAING, ARCHIBALD, born 1780, MD, died Port Royal, Jamaica, 21 Apr 1826. [Port Royal MI]
LAING, JAMES, in Jamaica, died 15 Dec 1827, inventory, 1845. [NAS.SC70.1.66; E49]
LAING, ELEANOR, died 29 Sep 1747. [Kingston MI, Jamaica]
LAING, JAMES, born 1765, in Jamaica by 19 Jan 1803, died 15 Dec 1827. [NAS.RD2.287.802] [Spanish Town Cathedral MI]
LAING, MALCOLM, born 1718, died 1 Aug 1781, probate, 1782, PCC. [Kingston MI, Jamaica][NLS.ms5028/40]
LAIRD, JAMES, Jamaica, MD Edinburgh University, 1803. [EMG#35]
LAING, Mr., from Kingston, Jamaica, in June 1793 aboard the Roselle bound for Leith. [JRG:29.6.1793]
LAMB, DAVID, a jobber, St James, Jamaica, 1774. [BL.Add.MS22676/8]
LAMB, JOHN, a planter in St James, Cornwall, Jamaica, testament, 1766. [NAS.CH2.542.11]
LAMBIE, ELISABETH DUNDAS, in Jamaica, died 19 Dec 1821. [NAS.D145]
LAMBIE, NEIL, in St Thomas in the East, Jamaica, 1776. [NLS.Acc.8793]

SCOTS IN JAMAICA, 1655-1855

LAMBIE, WILLIAM, planter in St Thomas in the East, Jamaica, 1769. [NAS.B10.15.7303]

LAMBIE, WILLIAM, born 28 Dec 1758, third son of Rev. Archibald Lambie and Catherine McLachlan in Kilmartin, matriculated at Glasgow University in 1771, died in Jamaica on 29 July 1794. [MAGU][F.4.14]

LAMBIE, WILLIAM, Jamaica, married Elizabeth Dundas Crichton daughter of Patrick Crichton in Jamaica, in Edinburgh 1820, died on Quebec Estate, Jamaica, 29 Aug 1832. [GM.90.563][EEC#18871][FH#556]

LAMOND, ANDREW, son of Andrew Lamond [1705-1778] and Agnes Michie [1703-1787], in Migvie, Aberdeenshire, died in Jamaica. [Migvie MI]

LAMOND, JOHN, son of Andrew Lamond [1705-1778] and Agnes Michie [1703-1787],in Migvie, Aberdeenshire, died in Jamaica, 1789. [Migvie MI]

LAMONT, MATHEW, youngest son of John Lamont of Kockdow, died in Kingston, Jamaica, 2 Apr 1825. [AJ#4040]

LANDELL, JAMES, born 9 Nov 1783, son of Rev. James Bell and Janet Heriot, a Lieutenant of the 60th Foot, died in Port Antonia, Jamaica, 26 July 1803. [Coldingham MI]

LANDELL, JOHN, a witness in Jamaica, 1813. [NAS.RD5.55.275]

LANDELL, THOMAS, born 1786, son of Rev. James Bell and Janet Heriot, died in Jamaica, 25 Nov 1815. [Coldingham MI]

LANDLE, J., from Leith to Jamaica on the Roselle, arrived in Kingston in Apr 1793. [JRG:27.4.1793]

LANG, ALEXANDER MORRISON, a physician, Kingston, Jamaica, 1888, brother of David Lang an advocate in Edinburgh who died 29 Apr1886. [NAS.SH.1888]

LANG, MALCOLM, a planter in St Andrew's, Jamaica, 1754. [NA.CO137/28]

LANG, ROBERT, a planter in St Thomas in the East, Jamaica, 1789. [NAS.RS54.1190]

LAUDER, GEORGE, of Pitscandly, once a merchant in Jamaica, dead by 1760. [NAS.B18.4.8.16]

LAUDER, ALEXANDER, born 1796, eldest son of John Lauder, Queen's Head Inn, Kelso, died in Jamaica, 17 Jan 1823. [EEC#17424][DPCA#1076]

LAUDER, CHRISTIAN, in Jamaica, testament, 10 Sep 1802. [NAS.CC8.8.133]

LAUDER, GEORGE, in Jamaica, testament, 10 Sep 1802. [NAS.CC8.8.133]

LAUDER, ROBERT SEATON, in Jamaica, testament, 10 Sep 1802. [NAS.CC8.8.133]

LAURENCE, JAMES, in St Ann's, Jamaica, a witness, 1774. [NAS.RD4.217.5]

LAURENCE, ...,from Jamaica, was admitted as a burgess of Banff, 1770.[BBR]

LAW, ROBERT, arrived at Bluefields, Westmoreland, on 23 Jan 1841 aboard the William Pirie, from Stranraer. [NA,CO.140/33]

SCOTS IN JAMAICA, 1655-1855

LAWRENCE, ALEXANDER, born 1823, a laborer, emigrated from Aberdeen aboard the Rob Roy bound for Jamaica, arrived at Kingston on 11 May 1841. [NA.CO140/33]

LAWRENCE, WILLIAM, a missionary, died at Mt. Zion, Jamaica, 17 Nov 1869. [S#8231]

LAWRIE, JAMES, in Port Antonio, Jamaica, 1740. [NAS.GD461.21]

LAWRIE, WILLIAM KENNEDY, of Redcastle, Galloway, born 1749, late of Woodhill, St Thomas in the East, Jamaica, died 28 Jan 1811. [Bath Abbey MI]

LAWSON, GEORGE, a jobber, St James, Jamaica, 1774. [BL.Add.MS22676/8]

LAWSON, GEORGE MCFARQUHAR, Jamaica, MD Edinburgh University, 1788. [EMG#21]

LAWSON, MARGARET, wife of Rev. Duncan Forbes, Hampden Church, Jamaica, died at Goodwill, Falmouth, Jamaica, 3 July 1850. [AJ#5355]

LAWSON, MARION, a Covenanter, transported from Leith to Jamaica in Aug 1685. [RPCS.XI.329]

LAWTON, EDWARD, from Leith to Jamaica on the Roselle, arrived in Kingston in Apr 1793. [JRG:27.4.1793]

LECKIE, CATHERINE, found guilty of infanticide and transported from Leith to Jamaica in Aug 1685. [RPCS.XI.136]

LECKIE, JAMES, son of William Leckie of Brioch, died in St James, Jamaica, 24 Aug 1792. [GCr#188]

LECKIE, THOMAS, born 1814, with Helen born 1819, and Sarah born 1840, arrived at Bluefields, Westmoreland, on 23 Jan 1841 aboard the William Pirie, from Stranraer. [NA.CO.140/33]

LECKIE, WILLIAM, a surgeon in Jamaica, married Janet, daughter of John Buchanan, in Edinburgh, 5 Aug 1753; 1767. [EMR] [NAS.GD1.1067.33]

LEDINGHAM, ALEXANDER, a merchant from Leith, died at Crane Wharf, Black River, Jamaica, 19 Jan 1823. [EEC#17436][DPCA#1080]

LEGG, JOHN, a merchant in Savanna la Mar, Jamaica, testament, 1776. [NAS.CC8.8.123]

LEGGAT, born 1797, son of William Leggat [1750-1840] and Jane McDowall [1761-1843], died in St Thomas in the East, Jamaica, 4 June 1816. [Glenluce MI]

LEIGHTON, JAMES, from Forfar, Angus, then in Kingston, Jamaica, died on the RMS Orinocco, 24 Nov 1852. [W#1394]

LEITH, DAVID, in Hanover, Jamaica, died 5 Sep 1841, inventory, 1843. [NAS.SC70.1.63; D1663]

LEITH, DAVID, born 1812 in Huntly, overseer at Lamblin Hall, Jamaica, died at Coal Spring, St Mary's, Jamaica, 1 Nov 1845. [AJ#5107]

LEITH, JOHN, Anotto Bay, Jamaica, grandson of John Leith of Blair, 4 Oct 1790. [NAS.RS8.910]

SCOTS IN JAMAICA, 1655-1855

LEITH, JOHN, in Kingston, Jamaica, testament, 4 Aug 1800, Comm. Edinburgh. [NAS.CC8.8.131]

LEITH, Dr JOHN, from Leith to Jamaica on the Roselle, arrived in Kingston in Apr 1793; in Jamaica, 1826. [JRG:27.4.1793][NAS.RD5.330.6]

LEITHEAD, JOHN, in Jamaica, a witness, 1770. [NAS.RD2.215.143]

LENNOX, JAMES, born 1790, son of Alexander Lennox and Helen Wilson in Helensburgh, a surgeon in Jamaica, died 15 Sep 1814. [Rhu MI]

LENNOX, or DONALDSON, JAMES, at Morant Bay, Jamaica, 1821. [NAS.SC48.49.25.17/26]

LEONARD, GEORGE, at Marischal College, 1770-1774, son of George Leonard of Salt River, Jamaica. [MCA.II.341]

LESLIE, CHARLES, a carpenter in Fraserburgh, later a gentleman in Jamaica, probate, 15 May 1782, Jamaica.

LESLIE, GEORGE, formerly in Jamaica, then in Old Aberdeen, testament, 24 May 1796, Comm. Aberdeen. [NAS.RS8.837.8]

LESLIE, JAMES, from Elgin {?}, died in Jamaica, 1783. [Elgin Town Council Minutes 15 Nov 1783]

LESLIE, THOMAS, of the brig Princess of Wales of Leith, died in Jamaica, 9 Feb 1797. [CM.11803]

LESLIE, WILLIAM, son of James Leslie in Aberdeen, died in St Lucie, Jamaica, 7 Aug 1818. [S.2.94]

LEWIS, JAMES, son of James Lewis a gentleman in Spanish Town, Jamaica, at Glasgow University, 1793. [MAGU#173]

LINDSAY, JOHN, DD, son of Rev. Harry Lindsay [died 1745] and Mary Simson in Perth, Rector of Spanish Town, Jamaica, DD Glasgow University, 12 Jan 1773. [F.4.231]

LINDSAY, JOHN, a surgeon in Jamaica, 1785-1792. [EUL.Laing ms6/96]

LITTLE, ARCHIBALD, born 22 Dec 1782, son of Rev. James Little and Elizabeth Clarke, died in Jamaica, 16 Feb 1804. [F.2.262]

LITTLE, GEORGE, MA, died in Jamaica, by Feb 1792. [GCr#70]

LITTLE, SIMON, in Hanover, Jamaica, a witness, 1796. [NAS.RD3.275.543]

LITTLE, TRISTRAM, born 1760, son of John Little and Eleanor Lowther, died at St Matthew's Bay, Jamaica, 28 Sep 1779. [Annan MI]

LITTLE, WALTER, born 1751, son of John Little and Isobel Murray in Denholm, died in Jamaica, 29 Jan 1781. [Cavers MI]

LITTLE, WILLIAM, born 1822, arrived at Bluefields, Westmoreland, on 23 Jan 1841 aboard the William Pirie, from Stranraer. [NA.CO.140/33]

LITTLEJOHN, DAVID, born 1744, sometime in Jamaica, died at 18 Duncan St., Edinburgh, 21 Aug 1833. [AJ#4467][SG#2.167]

LIVINGSTONE, HENRY, died in St Mary's, Jamaica, 1772. [Aleppo MI, Jamaica]

SCOTS IN JAMAICA, 1655-1855

LOBHAM, ELIZABETH, born 1818, a servant, emigrated from Aberdeen aboard the Rob Roy bound for Jamaica, arrived at Kingston on 11 May 1841. [NA.CO140/33]

LOCH, WILLIAM, 4th son of William Loch [1709-1779] and Margaret Brown in Hawkshaw, settled in Savanna la Mar, Jamaica, a deed, 1766. ['Family of Loch', Edinburgh, 1934, p.425][NAS.RD4.227.1187]

LOCH, WILLIAM, in Westmoreland, Jamaica, inventory, 1815. [NAS.SC70.1.14]

LOCKHART, JOHN, a doctor and a jobber, St James, Jamaica, 1774. [BL.Add.MS22676/8]

LOGAN, GEORGE, Lieutenant of the 92nd Regt., son of W. Logan a merchant in Aberdeen, died at Up Park Camp, Jamaica, 4 Oct 1819. [S.4.158]

LOGAN, JAMES, Chairman of the Quarter Sessions in Jamaica, letters, 1842/1844. [NAS.GD1.384.8/14; NRAS.Logan-Home ms11/12]

LOGAN, JEAN, in Glasgow, widow of Alexander Buchanan of Newport, St Mary's, Jamaica, testament, 1823, Comm. Glasgow. [NAS.CC9.7.81.480]

LOGAN, THOMAS, born 1772, late of Jamaica, died 13 Sept 1831. [Straiton MI]

LONGMUIR, JAMES, born 1805, second son of David Longmuir in Aberdeen, died in Fairfield, Jamaica, 30 Sep 1836. [AJ#4638]

LONGMUIR, MARY, wife of Dr George Longmuir, from Banffshire, died at Montego Bay, 1838. [AJ#4706]

LORIMER, CHARLES, in Kingston, Jamaica, dead by 1799, relict Mary Mason, a deed. [NAS.RD4.266.969]

LOTHIAN, JOHN, carpenter in Trelawney, Jamaica, grandson of Baillie John Lothian of Burntisland, 1778. [NAS.B9.315/7; 338/341]

LOVE, WILLIAM, St James, Jamaica, 1774. [BL.Add.MS22676/8]

LOWDON, ARCHIBALD, born 1750, died 4 Dec 1795. [Kingston, Jamaica,MI]

LOWDON, GEORGE, born 1754, merchant in Kingston, died 4 Dec 1795. [Kingston, Jamaica, MI]

LOUDON, JAMES, late in St Thomas in the Vale, Middlesex, Jamaica, later in London, will, 1792. [NAS.RD4.252.1397]

LOUDON, PETER, a planter in Jamaica, 1792. [NAS.RD4.252.1397]

LOWNDES, HENRY, in Wallens, Jamaica, died 24 May 1854, inventory, 1855, Comm. Edinburgh. [NAS.SC70.1.88; E4424]

LUMSDEN, ALEXANDER, born 20 June 1786 in Aberdeen, fourth son of Harry Lumsden and Catherine McVeagh, settled in St Dorothy's, Jamaica, died 1 Sep 1826. [SAA]

LUMSDEN, HENRY, son of William Lumsden in Mid Clova, Kildrummy, a cooper who emigrated to Jamaica in 1760, died in Aberdeen, Apr 1796. [TOF#628]

LUMSDEN, JAMES, born 1770, late of Jamaica, died 9 May 1834 in Aberdeen. [ANQ.3.29]

LUMSDEN, WILLIAM, born 1740, died in St Thomas in the East, Jamaica, 3 Oct 1806. [AJ#3074]
LUNAN, JOHN, born 1770, died 23 Dec 1839. [Spanish Town Cathedral MI]
LUNDIE, ARCHIBALD, in Kingston, Jamaica, a deed, 1793. [NAS.RD3.276.101]
LUNDIE, WALTER, born 28 Mar 1750 in Erskine, son of Rev. James Lundie and Christian Ballantyne, a physician in Jamaica. [F.3.193]
LYALL, JAMES GIBSON, of Gallery, late in Jamaica, only son of James Gibson Lyall, was granted Gallery, 1 June 1816. [NAS.RGS.154.17]
LYNCH, MARY A., daughter of Rev. W.H.Lynch and Sarah Skene, in Clarendon, Jamaica, 1824. [NAS.RS27.24.178; RD5.280.700]
LYON, ELIZABETH, daughter of James Lyon a wright in Jamaica, married William Turnbull, a gentleman's servant, in Edinburgh, 15 June 1785. [EMR]
LYON, GEORGE, a barrister, died in Spanish Town, Jamaica, Jan 1799. [GM.69.347]
LYON, JAMES, arrived in Falmouth, Jamaica, on the Elizabeth in June 1793. [JRG:29.6.1793]; a merchant there, a witness, 1797. [NAS.RD3.278.840]
LYON, JOHN, a surgeon, died at Montego Bay, Jamaica, 1817. [S.1.29]
LYON, WILLIAM, in Jamaica, probate, 1799, PCC.
MCALESTER, FLORENCIA, wife of Dougald McLauchlane late of Jamaica then in Blair Vochy, a sasine, 13 Aug 1768. [NAS.RS10.160]
MCANDREW, GEORGE SHIRLEY, son of James McAndrew a merchant in Elgin, at King's College, Aberdeen, 1812, settled in Jamaica. [KCA.2.414]
MCARTHUR, GILBERT, a rebel and drover from Islay, Argyll, who was transported from Leith to Jamaica in Aug 1685. [RPCS.XI.329]
MCARTHUR, JOHN, a merchant who died in Falmouth, Jamaica, 22 Jan 1813. [AJ#3452]
MCARTHUR, P., born 1780, son of Rev. P. McArthur of Torosay, died in Jamaica, 1805. [AJ#2986]
MCASKIE, MARY, a spinster in Kingston, Jamaica, 1813. [NAS.RD5.111.653]
MCAULAY, JOHN, an Anglican minister to Jamaica 22 Sep 1754. [FPA]
MCBAYNE, LACHLAN, an attorney at law in Kingston, Jamaica, an executor, 1813. [NAS.RD5.111.653]
MCBEAGH, JAMES, a physician and surgeon, St Thomas in the East, Jamaica, a witness, 1813. [NAS.RD5.44.858]
MCBEAN, ANGUS, a merchant in Kingston, Jamaica, 1778. [NAS.CS16.1.173/34]
MCBEAN, JAMES ARCHIBALD DUNCAN, staff surgeon, eldest son of Lt. Col. J. McBean of the 78th Highlanders and Elizabeth Robertson, married Harriet Isabella, only daughter of W. Duncan, Spanish Town, Jamaica, 28 Sep 1847; he died in Lucea, Jamaica, 17 Nov 1850. [AJ#5210][EEC#21577/22405][St Cuthbert's MI]

SCOTS IN JAMAICA, 1655-1855

MCBEAN, JOHN, born 1752, late of Jamaica, died in Brompton on 22 Sep.1834.[AJ#4525][GM.104.554]

MCBEAN, MARY, dau of William McBean, Roaring River Estate, Jamaica, married Charles Willis jr, Cranbrook, Kent, in Oxford, England, 22 Mar 1825. [GM.95/364]

MCBEAN, WILLIAM, at Roaring Lion River, St Anne's, Jamaica, 1789, in St John's, Middlesex, Jamaica, 1792. [NAS.RD3.290.92; RD4.252.1397]

MCCALL, JOHN, from Jamaica, died in Canonbury, Middlesex, England, on 18 May 1808. [GM.78/560]

MCCALL, JOHN, only son of John McCall formerly a merchant in Jamaica, matriculated at Glasgow University in 1813. [MAGU]

MCCALL, MARGARET, born 1813, arrived at Bluefields, Westmoreland, on 23 Jan 1841 aboard the William Pirie, from Stranraer. [NA.CO.140/33]

MCCALL, WILLIAM, born 1820, arrived at Bluefields, Westmoreland, Jamaica, on 23 Jan 1841 aboard the William Pirie, from Stranraer. [NA.CO.140/33]

MCCALLUM, ALEXANDER, and his wife Margaret, in Hanover, Jamaica, 1812. [IRO.Deeds BA12.1807]

MCCALLUM, ALEXANDER, in Lucca, Jamaica, 1818. [NAS.RS10.2860]

MCCALLUM, ARCHIBALD, a rebel from Argyll, transported from Leith to Jamaica in Aug 1685. [RPCS.XI.136]

MCCALLUM, ARCHIBALD, steerage passenger from Greenock to Jamaica aboard the Mary of Glasgow in Nov 1773. [NAS.CE60]

MCCALLUM, DUNCAN, born 1794, died in St Ann's, Jamaica, 22 Aug 1833. [Trafalgar MI, Jamaica]

MCCALLUM, Mrs MARGARET, born 1801, daughter of Robert Gardner in Irvine, wife of Duncan McCallum, died in St Ann's, Jamaica, 27 Jan 1830. [St Ann's MI]

MCCALLUM, NEIL, a Covenanter from Argyll, who was transported from Leith to Jamaica in Aug 1685. [RPCS.XI.136]

MCCALLUM, NEIL, in Hanover, Jamaica, 1828, 1836. [NAS.RS10.126; GD1.35.5.29]

MCCALMAN, DUNCAN, son of Dr McCalman in Islay, died in Jamaica, Mar 1795. [GM.65.791]

MCCANE, JOHN, died at Salt River, Old Wharf, Vere, Jamaica, 20 Apr 1799. [AJ#2693]

MCCANN, HENRY, born 1823, a laborer, arrived at Bluefields, Westmoreland, on 23 Jan 1841 aboard the William Pirie, from Stranraer. [NA.CO.140/33]

MCCARTNEY, WILLIAM, born 1822, arrived at Bluefields, Westmoreland, on 23 Jan 1841 aboard the William Pirie, from Stranraer. [NA.CO.140/33]

MCCAUL, JOHN, a merchant in Kingston, Jamaica, and co-owner of the Mercury of Glasgow, 1795. [NAS.CE60.11.4/21]

MCCHARLATIE, JOHN, a rebel from Argyll, who was transported from Leith to Jamaica in Aug 1685. [RPCS.XI.136]

MCCLELLAN, JAMES, a surgeon, died in St James, Jamaica, 20 July 1794. [EA#3213][GM.64/958]

MCCLELLAND, JOHN, born 1814, son of Robert McClelland and Christine Harvey in South Balfron, died in Jamaica, 28 May 1851. [Wigtown MI]

MCCLELLAND, ROBERT, born 1829, son of Robert McClelland and Christine Harvey in South Balfron, died in Jamaica, 28 May 1851. [Wigtown MI]

MCCLELLAND, ROBERT, died 15 Sep 1860. [Kingston MI, Jamaica]

MCCLURE, THOMAS, eldest son of William McClure a merchant in Ayr, died in Jamaica, 1817. [S.1.42]

MCCLYMONT, JAMES, son of James McClymont [1745-1825], died in Jamaica, Sep 1810. [Straiton MI]

MCCOLEMAN, Mr., from Greenock aboard the brig Jane bound for Jamaica, arrived there in July 1794. [JRG:2.8.1794]

MCCONECHY, ARCHIBALD, born 1793, son of the late Robert McConechy, died in Jamaica on 10 Feb 1824. [GrA: 30.4.1824]

MCCONECHY, ROGER GRAHAM, born 1794, son of the late Robert McConechy a merchant in Greenock, died in Jamaica on 21 Dec 1823. [GrA:24.2.1824]

MCCONOCHIE, JOHN, a Covenanter who was transported from Leith to Jamaica in Aug 1685. [RPCS.XI.136]

MCCONOCHIE, NEIL, a Covenanter from Argyll, who was transported from Leith to Jamaica in Aug 1685. [RPCS.XI.136]

MCCOOK, FRANCIS, born in Old Meldrum, Aberdeenshire, 1790, died in Kingston, Jamaica, 17 Nov 1850. [AJ.1.1.1851]

MCCOOK, JOHN, born 13 Sep 1797, son of James McCook and Isabella Kynoch in Aberdeen, at Marischal College, 1814, a planter in Jamaica, died there 20 Sep 1829. [SAA]

MCCORMACK, THOMAS, born in Dumfries 1786, manager of the Golden Grove Estate, St Thomas, Jamaica, died 13 Dec 1848. [St Andrew's MI, Jamaica]

MCCORQUODALE, ALEXANDER, a surgeon, formerly in Hanover, Jamaica, then in Inishael, Larichban, Argyll, husband of Rebecca Launce, probate 1743, London. [NA.Prob.11/724]; testament, Comm. Argyll, 1743. [NAS.CC2.10.142]

MCCORQUADALE, ARCHIBALD, a Covenanter from Argyll, who was transported from Leith to Jamaica in Aug 1685. [RPCS.XI.136]

MCCORQUODALE, DUNCAN, late of Jamaica, probate 1758, London. [NA.Prob.11/839]

SCOTS IN JAMAICA, 1655-1855

MCCORQUODALE, JOHN, of Lorn, St Elizabeth, Jamaica, owner of 1350 acres in 1754, died in Renfrewshire, testament and inventory, 25 Aug 1772, Comm. Glasgow. [NA.CO.142/31] [NAS.CC9.7.68]
MCCOURTIE, ALEXANDER, in St Thomas in the East, Jamaica, 1776, 1778. [NAS.CS228.B.6.18][NLS.Acc.8793]
MCCRACKEN, ANDREW, proprietor of Golden Grove Estate, St David's, Jamaica, 1803. [NAS.GD128.52.5]
MCCRAE, ALEXANDER, in Jamaica, 1795-1815. [NLS.ms#2944]
MCCREATH, JOHN, born 1777 in Urr, Kirkcudbrightshire, settled in Highgate, Westmoreland, Jamaica, died 15 Mar 1865. [Grange Hill MI, Jamaica]
MCCROUGH, ..., a planter in St Andrew's, Jamaica, 1754. [NA.CO137.28]
MCCULLOCH, JOHN, marshal of Jamaica, 1750. [NAS.RH15.176.8]
MCCULLOCH, JOHN, born 1819, a baker, arrived at Bluefields, Westmoreland, on 23 Jan 1841 aboard the William Pirie, from Stranraer. [NA.CO.140/33]
MCCULLOCH, JOSEPH WEIR, born 1788, son of John McCulloch and Elizabeth Murray in Lochmaben, a surgeon, died in Kingston, Jamaica, 7 Aug 1807. [Lochmaben MI, Dumfries-shire]
MCCULLOCH, ROBERT, in Jamaica, probate 1750, PCC.
MCCUNN, JAMES, 5th son of Thomas McCunn in Greenock, died in Jamaica on 13 Mar 1832. [GrA: 11.5.1832]
MCCUREITH, ARCHIBALD, was transported from Leith to Jamaica in Aug 1685. [RPCS.XI.330]
MCCURRIE, DONALD, was transported from Leith to Jamaica in Aug 1685. [RPCS.XI.330]
MCDERMEIT, ROBERT, Jamaica, a burgess and guilds-brother of Ayr, 7 Feb 1784. [AyrBR]
MCDONALD, ALEXANDER, in Jamaica, 1752. [NAS.GD201.1/4.64]
MCDONALD, ALEXANDER, late of Kingston, Jamaica, died 16 June 1840, spouse Jane Houston died Glasgow on 16 Feb 1836. [Greenock West MI]
MCDONALD, ALEXANDER, in Jamaica, 1850. [NAS.RD5.851.556]
MCDONALD, ALEXANDER, 2nd son of Rev. H.F.McDonald in Strachan, Kincardineshire, died in Jamaica, 28 Aug 1874. [EC#28091]
MCDONALD, ALLAN, 6th son of John McDonald of Dalchosnie and Mary Menzies, a planter in Jamaica, died 1825.['Clan Donald', 1904, p.437]
MCDONALD, ALLAN, late of Jamaica, died 1803. [AJ#2920]
MCDONALD, ANGUS, in Jamaica, 1850. [NAS.RD5.851.556]
MCDONALD, DONALD MACKAY, late a planter in Jamaica, died Aug 1791. [Kilmore Drumnadrochit MI]
MACDONALD, DONALD, brother of the late Col. Alexander MacDonald of Kinlochmoidart, died at Banks, St Anne, Jamaica, 19 Aug 1794.[GM.64.1054]

SCOTS IN JAMAICA, 1655-1855

MCDONALD, DONALD, in St Ann's, Jamaica, 1794-1840. [NLS.Melville ms3945/9/51]

MCDONALD, FRANCIS, born 1795, died at Morant Bay, Jamaica, 16 June 1833. [Inverawe MI]

MCDONALD, HUGH, in Jamaica, 1765. [NAS.GD201.4.90]

MCDONALD, JAMES, born 1794, late of Morant Bay, Jamaica, died in Aberlour, Banffshire, on 6 Apr 1836. [Inveraven MI]

MCDONALD, JAMES, born 1797, a millwright, emigrated from Aberdeen aboard the <u>Rob Roy</u> bound for Jamaica, arrived at Kingston on 11 May 1841. [NA.CO140/33]

MCDONALD, JOHN, born 1733, died in St Ann's, Jamaica, In June 1778. [St Ann's MI, Jamaica]

MCDONALD, JOHN, born 1820, arrived at Bluefields, Westmoreland, on 23 Jan 1841 aboard the <u>William Pirie</u>, from Stranraer. [NA.CO.140/33]

MCDONALD, JOHN, in Kingston, Jamaica, inventory, 1899. [NAS.SC70.1.383]

MCDONALD, PATRICK, in Jamaica, son of Patrick McDonald a miller in Perth, testament, 6 Sep 1772, Comm. Edinburgh. [NAS]

MCDONALD, ROBERT HENRY, born in Jamaica, second son of William Wallace MD there, matriculated at Glasgow University in 1776. [MAGU]

MACDONALD, RONALD, died in Jamaica, 1790. [GM.60.1214]

MCDONALD, WILLIAM, a surgeon in Trelawney, Jamaica, probate, 1783, PCC.

MCDONALD, WILLIAM, Lieutenant Governor of Fort Auga, Jamaica, testament, 21 Dec 1791, Comm. Edinburgh. [NAS.CC8.8.129]

MCDOUGALL, ALLAN, 6th son of Craiginch, died in Jamaica, 13 Mar 1786. [GM.IX.455.301]

MCDOUGALL, DUNCAN, a rebel from Argyll, who was transported from Leith to Jamaica in Aug 1685. [RPCS.XI.136]

MCDOUGALL, WILLIAM, planter, St Catherine's, Jamaica, died 1804, testament, 14 Sep 1807. [NAS.CC8.8.137/110]

MCDOUNIE, JOHN, a rebel, who was transported from Leith to Jamaica in Aug 1685. [RPCS.XI.136]

MCDOWALL, ALEXANDER, St Catherine's, Jamaica, 1818. [NAS.SC15.55.2]

MCDOWELL, JAMES, second son of Hay McDowell of Castle Semple, died in Belmont, Jamaica, 4 Apr 1827. [AJ#4141]

MCDOWELL, Dr WILLIAM, in Kingston, Jamaica, May 1744. [Caribbeana.6/23]

MCDUFF, ALLAN, in Kingston, Jamaica, 1746. [NAS.RD4.219.141]

MCDUFFIE, DUGALD, a merchant in Jamaica, married Janet Campbell from Argyll, in Old Cambus, 13 Apr 1765. [Haddington Episcopal Register][Argyll Court Book.xvi.]

SCOTS IN JAMAICA, 1655-1855

MCDUFFIE, JANET, from Argyll, in Kingston, Jamaica, died 1790, testament, 30 July 1799. [NAS.CC8.8.131]

MCDUSSIE, ARCHIBALD, late of Jamaica, died in Islay, Argyll, 1806. [AJ#3052]

MCEACHERN, ARCHIBALD, a planter in Bladen County, North Carolina, a Loyalist in 1776, settled in Jamaica by 1783. [NAS.AO12.35.70]

MCEWAN, ARCHIBALD, a rebel from Argyll, who was transported from Leith to Jamaica in Aug 1685. [RPCS.XI.136]

MCEWAN, DONALD, a prisoner in Edinburgh Tolbooth, who was transported from Leith to Jamaica in Aug 1685. [RPCS.XI.136][ETR#373]

MCEWAN, HENRY, born 1822, arrived at Bluefields, Westmoreland, on 23 Jan 1841 aboard the William Pirie, from Stranraer. [NA.CO.140/33]

MCFADEN, DONALD, in Jamaica, deceased by 1816. [NAS.CS40.23.11]

MCFADYEN, JAMES, born in Glasgow on 3 May 1799, 1st son of John McFadyen a merchant, at Glasgow University in 1813, MD in 1837, lecturer in Glasgow 1822-1824, the physician and island botanist of Jamaica, married Emma Tarbutt in Kingston, 15 July 1848, died there on 24 Nov 1850 . [MAGU#271][SG#1756][Caribbeana.4.80]

MCFARLANE, ALEXANDER, a merchant in Jamaica, 1737, a burgess and guildsbrother of Ayr, 4 Apr 1751. [AyrBR][JCTP.1737.595]

MACFARLANE, ANDREW, in Black Morass, Jamaica, 1774. [NAS.NRAS.934/433]

MCFARLANE, ANDREW, of Blairnairn, Rhu, in Bosnie Estate, Jamaica, 1782. [GA.T-MJ.369][NAS.NRAS.0623.TMJ365]

MCFARLANE, DUNCAN, from Buchanan, a planter in St Thomas in the East, Westmoreland, Jamaica, a deed, 1765, dead by 1771. [NAS.RD2.198/1.163]

MACFARLANE, HARRIET, daughter of Major James MacFarlane, and wife of William McKenzie, at Morant Bay, Jamaica, testament, 22 Dec 1785, Comm. Edinburgh. [NAS]

MCFARLANE, JAMES, passenger from Greenock to Jamaica aboard the Ross in Nov 1773. [NAS.CE60]; 1780. [NAS.CS16.1.179]

MCFARLANE, JAMES, at Annatto Bay, St George, Jamaica, a deed, 1813. [NAS.RD5.38.18]

MCFARLANE, JOHN, son of John McFarlane at the Water of Leven, Lennox, Scotland, husband of Alice ...., probate 16 Jan 1690, Jamaica.

MCFARLANE, JOHN, in Savannah-la-Mar, Jamaica, 1801. [NAS.AC7.75]

MCFARLANE, JOHN, born 1821, LRCE Edinburgh, a physician in Jamaica, died 5 May 1862, inventory, 1862. [Dean MI, Edinburgh][NAS.SC70.1.114; G2783]

MCFARLANE, JOHN, born 1823, arrived at Bluefields, Westmoreland, on 23 Jan 1841 aboard the William Pirie, from Stranraer. [NA.CO.140/33]

MCFARQUHAR, ALEXANDER, born in Nairn, died at Montego Bay, Jamaica, 14 Sep 1802. [AJ#2867][EA#4050]

SCOTS IN JAMAICA, 1655-1855

MCFARQUHAR, ELIZABETH, a widow, St James, Jamaica, 1774. [BL.Add.MS22676/8]

MCFARQUHAR, Dr GEORGE, born 1741, a physician in Jamaica for 22 years, died 25 Dec 1786. [St James MI, Jamaica]

MCFARQUHAR, GEORGE, a planter, Portobello Estate, St James, Jamaica, 1774. [BL.Add.MS22676/8]

MCFARQUHAR, GEORGE, born 1741, a physician, '22 years in Jamaica', died 25 Dec 1786. [St James Church MI, Montego Bay]

MCFARQUHAR, GUSTAVUS, in Coldstream, Jamaica, 2 Oct 1803, died 1803. [NAS.RD3.299.572][AJ#2900]

MCFEE, WILLIAM, born 1832, son of William McFee [1788-1869], died in Mandeville, Jamaica, 2 Jan 1870. [Mochrum MI]

MCGARRY, WILLIAM, in Jamaica in 1694. [SPAWI.1699.443]

MCGEACHY,....., son of Edward McGeachy, the Crown Surveyor of Jamaica, and his wife ..... Sellar from Elgin, was born 27 Dec 1843. [AJ#5016]

MCGEOCH, CHARLES, born 1814, with Catherine born 1814, Daniel born 1837, and Rose born 1840, arrived at Bluefields, Westmoreland, Jamaica, on 23 Jan 1841 aboard the William Pirie, from Stranraer. [NA.CO.140/33]

MCGHIE, JONATHAN, in Jamaica, a bond, 1797. [NAS.RD3.279.67]

MCGHIE, ROBERT, eldest son of the late James McGhie, late of Jamaica, a decreet, 1774. [NAS.CS16.1.400]; a merchant, St James, Jamaica, 1774. [BL.Add.MS22676/8]

MCGIBBON, ARCHIBALD, a rebel, transported from Leith to Jamaica in Aug 1685. [RPCS.XI.329]

MCGIBBON, HECTOR, a rebel, transported from Leith to Jamaica in Aug 1685. [RPCS.XI.329]

MCGIBBON, JAMES, son of James McGibbon in Jamaica, at King's College, Aberdeen, 1794. [KCA#2/377]

MCGIBBON, JOHN, a rebel from Glenowkeill, Argyll, transported from Leith to Jamaica in Aug 1685. [RPCS.XI.329]

MCGIE, PATRICK, born 1821, a basketmaker, arrived at Bluefields, Westmoreland, Jamaica, on 23 Jan 1841 aboard the William Pirie, from Stranraer. [NA.CO.140/33]

MCGIFFOG, CATHERINE, married William Duff, Jamaica, 1793. [GM.63.956]

MCGILCHRIST, DONALD, in Jamaica, probate 1783, PCC.

MCGILL, JOHN, in Clarendon, Jamaica, 1670. [SPAWI.1670/270]

MCGILLICH, JOHN, a rebel from Argyll, transported from Leith to Jamaica in Aug 1685. [RPCS.XI.329]

MCGILLVRAY, JOHN, late in West Florida, then in Jamaica, 1787. [NAS.CS17.1.16/164]

SCOTS IN JAMAICA, 1655-1855

MCGILLVRAY, WILLIAM, in Hillside Estate, Vere, Jamaica, 1816. [NAS.NRAS.392.29/1]

MCGLASHAN, CHARLES, born 1760, a former RN surgeon, MD Edinburgh 1813, then a physician and magistrate in St Andrew's, Jamaica, died 27 June 1834. [St Andrew's MI][EMG#47]

MCGOWAN, ARCHIBALD, MD, born 1800, died in Portland, Jamaica, 7 Mar 1836. [Manchioneal MI, Jamaica]

MCGOWAN, GEORGE, born 7 June 1774 in Garlieston, father of Margaret, Isabella, Elizabeth, and Caroline, died in Jamaica in June 1824. [Caribbeana#5/39]

MCGOWAN, JOHN, a rebel from Argyll, transported from Leith to Jamaica in Aug 1685. [RPCS.XI.136]

MCGOWAN, WILLIAM, jr., a merchant in Jamaica, later in Glasgow, testament, 21 Feb 1770, Comm. Glasgow. [NAS]

MCGOWN, ALEXANDER, son of bailie Alexander McGown in Rothesay, Bute, settled in Savannah, Georgia, as a merchant in 1766, a Loyalist who moved to Montego Bay, Jamaica, in 1778, died in Kingston, Jamaica, 2 June 1795. [NA.AO13.91.230][GM.65.791]

MACGREGOR, GRACE ROSS, eldest daughter of Ranald MacGregor in Banff, died at Pleasant Hill House, Jamaica, 27 Apr 1859.[Pleasant Hill MI]

MCGREGOR, JOHN WILLIAM, in Jamaica, 1791. [NAS.GD248.362.5]

MCGREGOR, NEIL, in Jamaica, testament, 19 Sep 1798. [NAS.CC8.8.131]

MCGREGOR, PATRICK, a merchant in St Thomas in the East, Jamaica, testament, 16 June 1823. [NAS.CC8.8.149; SC70.1.28]

MCGREGOR, Mr., from Greenock aboard the brig Jane bound for Jamaica, arrived there in July 1794. [JRG:2.8.1794]

MCHAFFIE, MARGARET, born 1786, widow of Jonathan Brown in Jamaica, died in Portabello, Edinburgh, 17 Aug 1852. [GM.NS38.434]

MACHENRY, CATHERINE, from Forres, Morayshire, married Robert Urquhart, at Charlton Pen, Jamaica, 22 Mar 1843. [AJ#4976]

MCICHAN, JOHN, a rebel from Baranazare, Argyll, who was transported from Leith to Jamaica in Aug 1685. [RPCS.XI.329]

MCILBRYDE, DUNCAN, a rebel from Argyll, who was transported from Leith to Jamaica in Aug 1685. [RPCS.XI.329]

MCILHOSE, JAMES, a writer in Glasgow later in Jamaica, 1796. [NAS.CS17.1.15/215]

MCILMOON, DONALD, a rebel from Argyll, who was transported from Leith to Jamaica in Aug 1685. [RPCS.XI.329]

MCILROY, GILBERT, a rebel imprisoned in Edinburgh Tolbooth, who was transported from Leith to Jamaica in Aug 1685. [RPCS.XI.329][ETR#369]

MCILROY, WILLIAM, a rebel transported from Leith to Jamaica in Aug 1685. [RPCS.XI.329]

MCILROY, WILLIAM, born 1814, a laborer, arrived at Bluefields, Westmoreland, Jamaica, on 23 Jan 1841 aboard the William Pirie, from Stranraer. [NA.CO.140/33]

MCILSHALLUM, JOHN, a rebel transported from Leith to Jamaica in Aug 1685. [RPCS.XI.330]

MCILVAIN, ARCHIBALD, a rebel from Glendaruel, Argyll, who was transported from Leith to Jamaica in Aug 1685. [RPCS.XI.329]

MCILVERRAN, DONALD, a rebel from Argyll, who was transported from Leith to Jamaica in Aug 1685. [RPCS.XI.136]

MCILVORY, DUNCAN, a rebel from Argyll, who was transported from Leith to Jamaica in Aug 1685. [RPCS.XI.136]

MCILVORY, JOHN, a rebel from Cragintyrie, Argyll, who was transported from Leith to Jamaica in Aug 1685. [RPCS.XI.126]

MCINDOE, JOHN S., of Greenfield, St Thomas in the East, Jamaica, died at 10 Kirk St., Glasgow, 28 Nov 1838. [SG#7/720]

MCINLAY, NEIL, a rebel transported from Leith to Jamaica in Aug 1685. [RPCS.XI.136]

MCINNES, ALEXANDER, born 1771, settled in Jamaica 1792, died 9 Sep 1836. [Spanish Town Cathedral MI]

MCINNES, CHARLES, eldest son of George McInnes in Old Aberdeen, died in St Thomas in the Vale, Jamaica, Dec 1828. [S#954]

MCINTOSH, ALEXANDER, in Jamaica, probate, 1748, Jamaica.

MCINTOSH, ALEXANDER, in Hanover, inventory, Jamaica, 1817. [RGD.1B.11.3.129/98-99]

MCINTOSH, CHARLES, son of Alexander McIntosh of Blirvie, married Susan Lawrence in St James, Jamaica, 25 Nov 1757, father of Susanna, Elizabeth, Susanna, John, George, Mary, and Dehany. [Caribeanna#3.160]

MCINTOSH, CHARLES, a physician in Jamaica, was admitted as a burgess of Banff in 1770. [BBR]

MACKINTOSH, DONALD, late in Jamaica, now in Greenock, 1841. [NAS.RS10.128]

MCINTOSH, DONALD, born 1779, late in Jamaica, died in Dunbarton, 28 July 1845. [SG.14.1424]

MCINTOSH, DUNCAN, from Edinburgh, a merchant in Jamaica, testament, 18 May 1744. [NAS.CC8.8.108]

MCINTOSH, JAMES, a merchant in Jamaica, then in Inverness-shire, 1780. [NAS.CS16.1.179]

SCOTS IN JAMAICA, 1655-1855

MCINTOSH, JAMES, of Westmoreland, Jamaica, inventory, 1809. [RGD.Jamaica.1b/11/3/113/185-195]

MCINTOSH, JAMES, born 1804, a carpenter, with Elspeth, born 1806, Jean, born 1827, and Isabella, born 1829, emigrated from Aberdeen aboard the Rob Roy bound for Jamaica, arrived at Kingston on 11 May 1841. [NA.CO140/33]

MACKINTOSH, JOHN, in St Thomas in the East, Jamaica, 1776. [NLS.Acc.8793]

MCINTOSH, LACHLAN, a merchant in Charleston, South Carolina, a Loyalist who settled in Kingston, Jamaica, 1778. [NAS.NRAS.0631/GDB.3]

MCINTOSH, WILLIAM, of Geddes, late in Jamaica, was granted Easter Geddes on 3 Feb 1800. [NAS.RGS.131.70]

MCINTOSH, WILLIAM, born 1814, a laborer, with Mary, born 1817, and Isabella, born 1840, emigrated from Aberdeen aboard the Rob Roy bound for Jamaica, arrived at Kingston on 11 May 1841. [NA.CO140/33]

MCINTYRE, ARCHIBALD, a rebel from Glendaruel, Argyll, who was transported from Leith to Jamaica in Aug 1685. [RPCS.XI.329]

MCINTYRE, ARCHIBALD, born 16 Aug 1774 in Glenorchy, son of Rev. Joseph McIntyre and Christian McVean, settled in Jamaica. [F.4.87]; possibly died on Kendal Estate, Hanover, Jamaica, 18 Dec 1809. [PC#69]

MCIVAR, DONALD, a rebel from Argyll, who was transported from Leith to Jamaica in Aug 1685. [RPCS.XI.136]

MCINTYRE, DONALD, born 8 Nov 1778 in Glenorchy, son of Rev. Joseph McIntyre and Christian McVean, died in Jamaica during July 1797. [F.4.87]

MCINTYRE, D., a saddler, died at Montego Bay, Jamaica, 1805. [AJ#3039]

MCINTYRE, FRANCES CHARLOTTE, third daughter of Rev, John McIntyre rector of Montego Bay, Jamaica, married John Salmon Gordon, Lieutenant of the 96th Regt., in Hackney, 22 Feb 1849. [AJ#5278]

MCINTYRE, JOHN, eldest son of Donald McIntyre a craftsman at Antigua Bay, Jamaica, at Glasgow University, 1805. [MAGU#212]

MCINTYRE, PATRICK, born 14 Feb 1773 in Glenorchy, son of Rev. Joseph McIntyre and Christian McVean, settled in Jamaica. [F.4.87]

MCINTYRE, THOMAS, Lieutenant, Adjutant of the 91st Regt., son of Major McIntyre, Edinburgh, died in Falmouth, Jamaica, 18 Oct 1828. [S#942]

MCINTYRE, WILLIAM, born 1831, died in St Andrew's, Jamaica, 1 July 1853. St Andrew's MI]

MCIVAR, DUNCAN, a rebel from Argyll, transported from Leith to Jamaica in Aug 1685. [RPCS.XI.136]

MCIVAR, JOHN, a rebel from Tulloch, Argyll, transported from Leith to Jamaica in Aug 1685. [RPCS.XI.136]

MCIVAR, MALCOLM, a rebel from Glassary, Argyll, who was transported from Leith to Jamaica in Aug 1685. [RPCS.XI.136]

SCOTS IN JAMAICA, 1655-1855

MCIVER, EDWARD, arrived at Bluefields, Westmoreland, Jamaica, on 23 Jan 1841 aboard the William Pirie, from Stranraer. [NA.CO.140/33]

MCIVER, JOHN, eldest son of Charles McIver harbour master of Greenock, died in Kingston, Jamaica, 1804. [AJ#2970]

MCKAIRNE, NEIL, a rebel from Argyll, who was transported from Leith to Jamaica in Aug 1685. [RPCS.XI.136]

MACKAY, CHARLES, died in Jamaica, 1791. [GM.61.186]

MACKAY, CHARLES, third son of James T. Mackay a hat manufacturer in Edinburgh, died on Plantain Garden River Estate, Jamaica, 27 May 1873. [EC#27686]

MCKAY, GEORGE, a planter in St Andrew's, Jamaica, 1754. [NA.CO137/28/191/6]

MCKAY, HUGH, a physician in Kingston, Jamaica, a deed, 1785. [NAS.RD4.239.1061]

MACKAY, JAMES, a physician and surgeon in St Thomas in the East, Jamaica, testament, 13 Aug 1799. [NAS.CC8.8.131]

MCKAY, MARTIN, transported from Leith to Jamaica in Aug 1685.[RPCS.XI.136]

MCKAY, THOMAS, aboard the Countess of Galloway from Creetown, Kirkcudbright, on 15 Mar 1793 bound for Jamaica, arrived in Kingston in May 1793. [RJG:1.6.1793]

MACKAY, WILLIAM PATRICK, son of James T. Mackay, 21 Danube Street, Edinburgh, died on Wheelerfield Estate, Jamaica, 1 Aug 1860. [S#1621]

MCKEAN, WILLIAM, in Jamaica, later in Dunbarton, testament, 18 Aug 1814. [NAS.CC9.78.494]

MCKEAN, WILLIAM, born in Paisley on 13 Jan 1787, first son of Alexander McKean a merchant in Jamaica, matriculated at Glasgow University in 1808, a Unitarian minister, died 28 July 1869. [MAGU]

MCKEAND, ALEXANDER, an attorney in Kingston, Jamaica, son of George McKeand, late of Jamaica, and nephew of the late Robert McKeand of Jamaica, sons of the deceased John McKeand a bailie of Wigtown, 5 July 1773. [NAS.B72.1.2]

MCKEATH, MUNGO, in St Thomas, Jamaica, probate 20 May 1669, Jamaica.

MCKECHNIE, JOHN, a millwright from Greenock, later in Westmoreland, Jamaica, dead by 1800. [GA.T-ARD#13/1]

MCKEICHAN, NEIL, a rebel from Baranazare, Argyll, transported from Leith to Jamaica in Aug 1685. [RPCS.XI.136]

MCKELLAR, ARCHIBALD, in Kingston, Jamaica, a letter, 1812. [NAS.GD1.456.79]

MCKELLO, DONALD, a rebel from Argyll, transported from Leith to Jamaica in Aug 1685. [RPCS.XI.136]

SCOTS IN JAMAICA, 1655-1855

MCKELLO, DUGALD, a rebel from Argyll, transported from Leith to Jamaica in Aug 1685. [RPCS.XI.136]

MCKELLO, JOHN, a rebel from Argyll, transported from Leith to Jamaica in Aug 1685. [RPCS.XI.136]

MCKENZIE, ALEXANDER, in St Elizabeth, Jamaica, a witness, 1823. [NAS.RD5.272.272]

MCKENZIE, CATHERINE, born 1829, emigrated from Aberdeen aboard the Rob Roy bound for Jamaica, arrived at Kingston on 11 May 1841. [NA.CO140/33]

MCKENZIE, COLIN, of Strathcathro, a merchant in Jamaica, 1767, son of Kenneth McKenzie of Dalmore. [NAS.S/H; RS35.20.335; NRAS.0771/762]

MCKENZIE, COLIN, born 1803, of Mount Gerald, Ross-shire, and of Spanish Town, Jamaica, died 1 Dec 1837. [Spanish Town Cathedral MI][AJ#4700]

MCKENZIE, D., in Kingston, Jamaica, 1809, brother-in-law of Alexander Dingwall in Caninish. [NAS,NRAS.2177/6179]

MCKENZIE, DANIEL, a Jacobite who was transported via Liverpool to Jamaica in 1748. [NA.T53/44]

MCKENZIE, FARQUHAR, a planter in Jamaica, 1715. [NAS.RD4.117.589]

MCKENZIE, GEORGE, born 1757, a book-keeper, via London to Jamaica on the Capel, in Feb 1774. [NA.T47.9/11]

MCKENZIE, GEORGE, eldest son of Colin McKenzie a writer in Dingwall, a planter in Jamaica, later by 1803 in America. [NAS.RS38.195; CS17.1.22/370]

MACKENZIE, GEORGE M., in Jamaica, deed, 1806. [NAS.RD2.305.243]

MCKENZIE, Dr JOHN, a planter in Jamaica, brother of Colin McKenzie of Strathcathro, Angus,1764. [NAS.NRAS.771/191, bundle 702]

MCKENZIE, JOHN, in Jamaica, testament, 1773, PCC.

MCKENZIE, JOHN, an attorney, son of Alexander McKenzie of Inchcoulter, died in Kingston, Jamaica, Dec 1780. [GM.IV.86]; testament, 9 Feb1785. [NAS.CC8.8.126]

MACKENZIE, JOHN, youngest son of Rev. W. Mackenzie in Tongue, a surgeon, died in Jamaica, 1809. [EA.XCI.4734]

MCKENZIE, JOHN, in Jamaica, then in Edinburgh, inventory, 24 Dec 1813. [NAS.SC780.1.9.329]

MCKENZIE, KENNETH, a schoolmaster, St James, Jamaica, 1774. [BL.Add.MS22676/8]

MACKENZIE, Mrs MARGARET, daughter of Lord Oliphant, died 6 Apr 1800, Spanish Town, Jamaica, will,1801; deed, 1819. [GM.70.797][NAS.CC8.8.132; RD5.166.556]

MCKENZIE, PETER, born 1753, a planter, via London to Jamaica on the Susanna in Jan 1774. [NA.T47.9/11]

SCOTS IN JAMAICA, 1655-1855

MACKENZIE, RODERICK, son of Kenneth MacKenzie of Redcastle, died in Jamaica, 1801. [GM.71.483]

MCKENZIE, Dr SIMON, of Mullethall, Jamaica, son of Dr McKenzie of Newton [died 1759] and Margaret McKenzie [died 1783] in Jamaica, 1773. [Avoch MI] [NAS.RS38.13.1211; RD4.237.901]

MACKENZIE, THOMAS, Jamaica, MD Edinburgh, 1814. [EMG#48]

MCKENZIE, Mr., from Kingston, Jamaica, in June 1793 aboard the Roselle bound for Leith. [JRG:29.6.1793]

MACKIE, ELIZABETH, relict of Dr Henry Miller in Jamaica, died in Kirkcaldy, Fife, 28 Oct 1853. [FH]

MACKIE, GEORGE, in Jamaica, a deed, 15 Jan 1819. [NAS.CC16.9.12.77]

MACKIE, WILLIAM, in Jamaica, later in Forres, Morayshire, testament, 11 Sep 1820. [NAS.CC16.5.3.189]

MCKINDLAY, Dr ALEXANDER, a physician in Jamaica, later died in Leith, testament, 3 Oct 1774. [NAS.CS96.1834.57; CC8.8.123]

MCKINLAY, NEIL, a rebel from Argyll, transported from Leith to Jamaica in Aug 1685. [RPCS.XI.136]

MCKINLAY, ROBERT, passenger from Greenock to Jamaica aboard the Ross in Nov 1773. [NAS.CE60]

MCKINNA, JOHN, a merchant in Edinburgh, later in Jamaica, testament, 31 Jan 1766. [NAS.CC8.8.120]

MCKINNON, JOHN, a rebel from Duppen of Kintyre, Argyll, transported from Leith to Jamaica in Aug 1685. [RPCS.XI.136]

MCKIRRECH, ARCHIBALD, a rebel from Argyll, transported from Leith to Jamaica in Aug 1685. [RPCS.XI.136]

MCKOWEN, ARCHIBALD, Jamaica, MD Edinburgh, 1818. [EMG#56]

MCLACHLAN, ALEXANDER, late of Trelawney, Jamaica, probate, 1783, PCC. [NA.Prob.11/1103]

MCLACHLAN, ARCHIBALD, a farmer from Craigintervie, Argyll, a rebel transported from Leith to Jamaica in Aug 1685. [RPCS.XI.136]

MCLACHLAN, COLIN, a surgeon and physician in Hanover, Jamaica, later in London, administration, 1754, London. [NA.Prob.11/811]

MCLACHLAN, DONALD, a rebel from Argyll, transported from Leith to Jamaica in Aug 1685. [RPCS.XI.136]

MCLACHLAN, DUGALD, sometime in Jamaica, then in Callary, Argyll, testament, 1800. [NAS.CC2.3.12]

MCLACHLAN, HUGH, of Cameron, a merchant in Kingston, Jamaica, then in Glasgow, 1756. [NAS.S/H]

MCLACHLAN, HUGH, born 1788, died in Jamaica, 22 Aug 1825. [St Andrew's MI. Jamaica]

MCLACHLAN, JOHN DOW, a rebel from Achahouse, Argyll, transported from Leith to Jamaica in Aug 1685. [RPCS.XI.329]
MCLACHLAN, JOHN, a fisherman, St James, Jamaica, 1774. [BL.Add.MS22676/8]
MCLACHLAN, ..., an overseer, Hampden, Jamaica, 1782.[NLS.ms10925/5]
MCLACHLAN, ..., son of R.S.McLachlan in Falmouth, Jamaica, married Sarah, only daughter of Mrs S.A.Bridge of Mount Edgecombe and Valley, St Ann's, Jamaica, at Brown's Town, Jamaica, on 28 Feb 1856. [CM#20755]
MCLACHLAN, ..., son of R. S. McLachlan, born in Falmouth, Jamaica, 5 Jan 1857. [EEC#23008]
MCLACHLAN, WILLIAM WALKER, son of John McLachlan a bookseller in Edinburgh, died at Dry Harbour, Jamaica, 20 Mar 1859. [EEC#23351]
MCLAGAN, ALEXANDER, died in Jamaica by Feb 1792. [GCr#70]
MCLAGAN, HECTOR, born 26 June 1768 in Melrose, son of Rev. Frederick McLagan and Christine Turnbull, died in Jamaica, 11 Sep 1808.[F.2.188]
MACLAINE, JOHN, in Kingston, Jamaica, 1788. [NAS.GD174.1418]
MACLAINE, LAUCHLAN, to Jamaica, 1789. [NAS.GD174.1431]
MCLAINE, M.H., Lt.Col.of 77th Regt., died in Spanish Town, 13 Oct 1828.[S.940]
MCLANE, Mrs MARY, in Jamaica, 1694. [SPAWI.1699.443]
MACLAREN, ALEXANDER, born 1773, son of James MacLaren, died 17 Jan 1808, buried in Jamaica. [Moulin MI, Perthshire]
MCLAREN, ANN, daughter of John McLaren a planter in Jamaica, married James MacLennan a watchmaker in Edinburgh, 22 Dec 1776. [EMR]
MACLAREN, JAMES, son of Rev. John MacLaren and his wife Magdalene Cochrane, died at Montego Bay, Jamaica, in Sep 1823. [Kilbarchan MI]
MCLAREN, JOHN, died in Jamaica, 1793. [Canongate MI, Edinburgh]
MCLAREN, JOHN, a planter, Vere, Middlesex, Jamaica, a witness, 1800. [NAS.RD2.282.784]
MCLARTY, ALEXANDER, second son of Alexander McLarty a shipmaster in Greenock, Renfrewshire, matriculated at Glasgow University in 1791, possibly died in Kingston, Jamaica, on 23 June 1794. [MAGU]
MCLARTY, ALEXANDER, a physician in Kingston, Jamaica, testament, 1821. [NAS.SC53.56.3]
MCLARTY, CHARLES, from Campbeltown, Argyll, a physician in Jamaica, died 6 Sep 1812, inventory, 31 July 1813, testament, 16 Sep 1813. [NAS.SC70.1.8.472; CC8.8.139]
MCLARTY, Dr COLIN, son of Captain McLarty in Greenock, a physician in St Thomas in the East, and Kingston, Jamaica, 1792. [NLS.Cunningham ms.Acc.7285]

SCOTS IN JAMAICA, 1655-1855

MACLARTY, ELIZA, daughter of Alexander MacLarty MD in Jamaica, 1822. [NAS.RS10.PR42/32]

MCLAUCHLAN, DANIEL, a minister in Ardnamurchan, Argyll, 1734-1737, died in Jamaica, 16 May 1745. [F.4.1060]

MCLAUGHLAN, DUGALD, in Jamaica, later in Callait, Inverness, testament, 4 July 1800, Comm. Argyll. [NAS]

MCLAUGHLAN, Captain HUGH, from Glasgow, died in Jamaica, 1755. [GJ#752]

MCLAURIN, DONALD, first son of Rev. John McLaurin in Lanarkshire, matriculated at Glasgow University in 1826, a surgeon and a Justice of the Peace in St Thomas in the Vale, Jamaica, died 1842. [MAGU]

MCLAVERTY, Rev. COLIN, married Mary Elizabeth East in Jamaica, 1 Jan 1846; '25 years the incumbent of St Peter's, Jamaica', died at Clifton Passage, Jamaica, 15 Aug 1869. [PC#2008][S#8160]

MCLAVERTY, ..., son of Mr McLaverty from Keill, Argyll, was born 27 July 1855 in Chestervale, Jamaica. [EEC#322788]

MCLEAN, ALLAN, in Kingston, Jamaica, a witness, 1776. [NAS.RD4.220.1144]

MCLEAN, ANDREW, a rebel from Argyll, who was transported from Leith to Jamaica in Aug 1685. [RPCS.XI.330]

MCLEAN, ARCHIBALD, born in Mull, a surgeon in New York, lately in Jamaica,

MCLEAN, ..., a planter, St Mary's, Middlesex, Jamaica, a deed, 1801. [NASRD2.282.787]

MCLEAN, GEORGE DUNCAN, a book-keeper in Jamaica, died 31 Jan 1859, inventory, 1859. [NAS.SC70.1.102; H721]

MCLEAN, HECTOR, third son of D. McLean WS in Edinburgh, died in Spanish Town, Jamaica, on 26 June 1818. [AJ#3698]

MCLEAN, HUGH, a rebel from Argyll, who was transported from Leith to Jamaica in Aug 1685. [RPCS.XI.136]

MCLEAN, HUGH, a merchant in Jamaica, 1788. [NAS.CS17.1.7/133]

MCLEAN, HUGH, in Spanish Town, Jamaica, dead by 1844, a sasine, an inventory, 1846. [NAS.RS38.GR2266/120; SC70.1.66]

MCLEAN, JAMES, in St Mary's, Middlesex, Jamaica, died 1824, testament, 27 May 1823. [NAS.CC8.8.149]

MCLEAN, JOHN, a rebel from Portindryan, Argyll, transported from Leith to Jamaica in Aug 1685. [RPCS.XI.330]

MCLEAN, JOHN, born 1721, Colonel of the Eastern Division of the Regiment of Horse, died 28 Nov 1764. [Kingston MI, Jamaica]

MCLEAN, JOHN, merchant in Jamaica, burgess and guildsbrother of Ayr, 4 Apr 1751. [AyrBR]

MCLEAN, JOHN, a merchant in Kingston, Jamaica, and co-owner of the ship Edinburgh, 1789. [NAS.AC.Decreet.53]

SCOTS IN JAMAICA, 1655-1855

MCLEAN, JOHN, planter, Vere, Middlesex, Jamaica, a deed, 1800. [NAS.RD2.282.784]

MCLEAN, ..., son of Rev. Daniel McLean, was born at Hampden Manse, Jamaica, 19 Dec 1861. [S#2052]

MCLEAN, ..., was born at Hampden Manse, Jamaica, 11 Apr 1863.[S#2468]

MACLEAN and MOORE, merchants in Jamaica, letters, 1778-1780. [NLS#8793/4]

MCLEHOSE, AGNES, in Jamaica, died in Edinburgh on 22 Oct 1841. [NAS.D1568]

MCLEHOSE, JAMES, an attorney at law in Jamaica, 1791,1799, died 16 Mar 1812, testament, 17 June 1817. [NAS.RD2.252.108; RD3.276,753; CS228.B.11.13; SC70.1.16]

MCLENNAN, DANIEL, in Jamaica, probate, 1776, PCC.

MCLENNAN, EWAN, born in Killilan 1802, son of John McLennan and Catherine McRae, a planter in Jamaica, died in Skye, 1850. [Kiel Duich MI]

MCLEOD, ENEAS, born 1778, son of Alexander McLeod an Excise officer in Old Deer, Aberdeenshire, a surgeon, died in Clarendon, Jamaica, 1804. [AJ#29969]

MCLEOD, HUGH, a merchant in Kingston, Jamaica, died 1818. [NAS.CS235.ui8]

MCLEOD, HUGH, a merchant in Kingston, Jamaica, 1810-1831. [NAS.CS96.2309-2316]

MCLEOD, JOHN, in Colbecks, St Dorothy, Jamaica, married Margaret McLeod in Edinburgh, 28 Nov 1773. [EMR]

MCLEOD, MALCOLM, probate 4 Feb 1681, Jamaica.

MCLERAN, Dr ALEXANDER, was drowned in Montego River, Jamaica, before Feb 1792. [GCr#70]

MCLINE, ALEXANDER, a rebel from Argyll, who was transported from Leith to Jamaica in Aug 1685. [RPCS.XI.136]

MCMASTER, ANN, born 1819, a dairymaid, arrived at Bluefields, Westmoreland, Jamaica, on 23 Jan 1841 aboard the *William Pirie*, from Stranraer. [NA.CO.140/33]

MCMEIKINE, ROBERT, a merchant in Kingston, Jamaica, son of Gilbert McMeikine, a merchant in Glen Luce, and Jean McHaffie, 1801. [NAS.RS61.623]

MCMICHAEL, DUNCAN, a rebel from Islay, Argyll, who was transported from Leith to Jamaica in Aug 1685. [RPCS.XI.136]

MCMICHAEL, ROGER, a Covenanter from Dalry, Galloway, who was transported from Leith to Jamaica in Aug 1685. [RPCS.XI.316]

MCMICHAEL, DUNCAN, a rebel from Carradale, Kintyre, Argyll, who was transported from Leith to Jamaica in Aug 1685. [RPCS.XI.329]

MCMIKIN, ROBERT, in Kingston, Jamaica, 1767. [NAS.GD180.634]

SCOTS IN JAMAICA, 1655-1855

MCMILLAN, AGNES, born 1822, arrived at Bluefields, Westmoreland, Jamaica, on 23 Jan 1841 aboard the William Pirie, from Stranraer. [NA.CO.140/33]

MCMILLAN, ALEXANDER, eldest son of Hugh McMillan a clothier in Glasgow, died in Kingston, Jamaica, 16 Sep 1842. [SG.XI.1080][GSP.779]

MCMILLAN, JOHN, a merchant planter in Jamaica, testament, 1800, Comm. Edinburgh. [NAS]

MCMILLAN, ROBERT, born 1823, arrived at Bluefields, Westmoreland, Jamaica, on 23 Jan 1841 aboard the William Pirie, from Stranraer. [NA.CO.140/33]

MCMURCHY, JOHN, a merchant in Jamaica, moved to London by 1766. [Charleston, South Carolina, Misc. Records, 1766/370]

MCNAB, ALEXANDER, in Jamaica 1800, brother of Duncan McNab in Greenock. [NAS.NRAS.0888/103/2]

MCNAB, CHARLES, from Jamaica, married Janet Buchanan, in Edinburgh, 1 Oct 1792. [EMR]

MCNAB, GILBERT, born 1814, 3rd son of William McNab of the Royal Botanical Gardens, a MD, from Edinburgh, died at St Ann's Bay, Jamaica, 1859. [Ocho Rios MI, Jamaica][S#1434]

MCNAB, JAMES, late in Jamaica, married Margaret, daughter of Malcolm McNeil of Ardelister, in Islay on 27 Feb 1804. [CM#13029]

MCNAB, ..., daughter of Dr Gilbert McNab, was born in Kingston, Jamaica, 12 Mar 1845. [EEC#21185][W#567]

MCNAB, ..., twin daughters of Dr Gilbert McNab, were born in Kingston, Jamaica, Aug 1846. [AJ#5153]

MCNAUGHT, JAMES, a witness in Jamaica, 1811. [NAS.RD5.17.657]

MACNEAL, HECTOR, born 22 Oct 1746 at Roslin, later in Kingston, Jamaica. [NAS.NRAS.0052]

MCNEIL, ARCHIBALD, a rebel from Argyll, transported from Leith to Jamaica in Aug 1685. [RPCS.XI.136]

MCNEILL, ARCHIBALD, an attorney in Kingston, Jamaica, a witness, 1791. [NAS.RD3.276.753]

MCNEIL, HECTOR, a rebel from Argyll, transported from Leith to Jamaica in Aug 1685. [RPCS.XI.136]

MCNEIL, JOHN, a rebel from Argyll, transported from Leith to Jamaica in Aug 1685. [RPCS.XI.136]

MCNEILL, JOHN, son of Neill McNeill, Hanover, Jamaica, died 1749. [NAS.PS3.11/161]

MCNEILL, LACHLAN, son of Hector and Margaret McNeill in Machrahanish, Argyll, a merchant who died in Jamaica, 1798. [SG.32.2.56]

MCNEILL, MALCOLM, in Jamaica, testament, 20 Apr 1785. [NAS.CC8.8.126]

SCOTS IN JAMAICA, 1655-1855

MCNEILL, NEILL, gentleman in Hanover, Jamaica, probate, 1749, PCC. [NA.Prob.11/774]

MCNEILL, NEILL, in Hanover, Jamaica, later in Glasgow, testament, 8 May 1749, Comm. Glasgow. [NAS]

MCNEILL, NEIL, of Ardylamie, a planter and merchant in Hanover, Jamaica, then died in Glasgow during 1749, testament, 16 Dec 1785. [NAS.CC9.7.60/73]

MCNEIL, ..., daughter of Thomas McNeil, was born in Caledonia, Westmoreland, Jamaica, 25 Aug 1844. [AJ#5050]

MCNEILLIE, JOHN, in Newmilns Estate, Hanover, Jamaica, a deed, 1824. [NAS.RD5.280.525]

MCNEISH, CHARLES, a merchant in Savanna la Mar, Jamaica, a witness, 1808. [NAS.RD3.325.1180]

MCNICOL, JOHN, a skipper in Kingston, Jamaica, inventory, 7 Jan1814, testament, 9 Jan1816. [NAS.SC70.1.9.355; CC8.8.142]

MCPHADZEAN, ANGUS, from Argyll, a planter in Westmoreland, Jamaica, 1785. [NAS.CC2.8.88.6]

MCPHERSON, ANGUS, a prisoner in Edinburgh Tolbooth, transported to Jamaica in 1726. [NAS.HH.11.15]

MACPHERSON, CAROLINA EVINA, eldest daughter of John MacPherson-McNiel in Kingston, Jamaica, married James Hay Campbell, Major of the Highland Light Infantry in Kilburn on 17 Oct1867. [S#7558]

MCPHERSON, DONALD, settled in Unity Valley, Jamaica, by 1774. [NAS.NRAS.771, bundle 166]; possibly later in Strathdearn, dead by 1805. [NAS.GD128.52.5]

MCPHERSON, DUGALL, in Kingston, Jamaica, 1780. [NAS.NRAS.771,bundle700]

MCPHERSON, EWAN, born in Kingussie, Inverness-shire, died in Clarendon, Jamaica, 3 Jan 1840. [AJ#4813]

MCPHERSON, JOHN, from Dalwhinnie, then in Jamaica, 1779. [NAS.CS16.1.175]

MCPHERSON, JOHN, in St Thomas in the East, Jamaica, died in Aug1800, testament, 15 Dec 1801. [NAS.CC8.8.132]

MCPHERSON, JOHN, in Jamaica, died in Loanhead on 19 Nov 1838. [NAS.C2416]

MCPHERSON, JOHN, died on Cluny Estate, St Thomas in the East, Jamaica, 1833. [AJ.4474][DPCA.11 Oct1833]

MCPHERSON, ROBERT, born 1772, son of Angus McPherson and Ann Grant in Rothiemurcus, died in Jamaica, 1839. [Old Rothiemurcus MI]

MCPHERSON, WILLIAM, in Vere, Middlesex, Jamaica, died 25 May 1798, testament, 20 Sep.1820. [NAS.CC8.8.145]

MCQUEEN, DANIEL, born 1715, a planter in St Andrew's, 1754, died 8 July 1758. [NA.CO137/28/191-196][Kingston MI, Jamaica]

MCQUEEN, DONALD, born 1795, a surgeon, son of Rev. Edmund McQueen in Barra, died in Jamaica, 7 Jan 1819. [EEC#16854][S.3.126]

MCQUEEN, DUNCAN, a rebel from Argyll, transported from Leith to Jamaica in Aug 1685. [RPCS.XI.136]

MCQUEEN, HUGH, a rebel from Argyll, transported from Leith to Jamaica in Aug 1685. [RPCS.XI.136]

MCQUEEN, JAMES, born 1716, a merchant in Kingston, Jamaica, died 19 Feb 1765. [Kingston MI]

MCQUEEN, JANET, a Covenanter, transported from Leith to Jamaica in Aug 1685. [RPCS.XI.136]

MCQUEEN, WILLIAM, a physician in Jamaica, testament, 21 Apr 1804. [NAS.CC8.8.135]

MCQUHAE, RICHARD, born 21 Dec 1766 in St Quivox, son of Rev. William McQuhae and Elizabeth Park, died in Jamaica, 9 Mar 1805. [F.3.66]

MCRAE, ALEXANDER, son of Alexander McRae in Kingston, Jamaica, at King's College, Aberdeen, 1793. [KCA.2/375]

MCRAE, ALEXANDER, born 1735, died in Jamaica, 3 Mar 1796. [Canongate MI]

MCRAE, JOHN, in Lottery, Trelawney, Jamaica, died 25 Oct 1837, inventory, 1838. [NAS.SC70.1.56]

MCRAE, WILLIAM GORDON, son of Alexander McRae in Kingston, Jamaica, at King's College, Aberdeen, 1784. [KCA.2.362]

MCROBBIE, FRANCES, daughter of William McRobbie in Smailwood, Jamaica, married George Outram an advocate, in Edinburgh, 28 Nov 1837.[AJ#4691]

MCROBBIE, THOMAS, died in Kingston, Jamaica, 19 July 1845. [W#601]

MCSHERRY, RICHARD, overseer at Greencastle, St Mary's, Jamaica, a witness, 1786. [NAS.RD3.246.892]

MCTAILLIOR, DONALD, a Covenanter from Fordie, Perthshire, transported from Leith to Jamaica in Aug 1685. [RPCS.XI.329]

MCVERRAN, DONALD, transported from Leith to Jamaica in Aug 1685. [RPCS.XI.136]

MCVICAR, ALEXANDER, born 1770, son of John McVicar and Mary Murray in Lochmaben, Renfrewshire, died in Port Royal, Jamaica, 23 Jan1796. [Lochmaben MI][GA-AGN.321]

MCVICAR, ARCHIBALD, an overseer at Sixteen Mile Walk, Jamaica, testament, 3 Dec 1763. [NAS.CC8.8.119]

MACVICAR, DAVID, Master in Chancery in Jamaica, son of Neil MacVicar of Fergushill a writer, died in Spanish Town, Jamaica, on 13 Jan 1825.[EEC#17713]

SCOTS IN JAMAICA, 1655-1855

MCVICAR, or AFFLECK, JAMES, in St Thomas in the East, Jamaica, eldest son of Robert McVicar an Exciseman in Stranraer, and his wife Mary, only child of James Affleck of Edingham, 1773. [NAS.CS16.1.154/77]

MCVICAR, JOHN, from Argyll, emigrated via Bristol to Jamaica in 1793, settled on Good Hope Estate, Trelawney. [GA.AGN.321]

MCVICAR, MARJORY, in Kingston, Jamaica, died 23 Oct 1827, testament and inventory, 28 May 1829. [NAS.CC8.8.153]

MCVIG, DUNCAN, a rebel from Argyll, transported from Leith to Jamaica in Aug 1685. [RPCS.XI.329]

MCWALTER, DUNCAN, a merchant in Jamaica, dead by 1771. [Argyll Sheriff Court book #XVII, 13.6.1771]

MCWHINNIE, WILLIAM, eldest son of David McWhinnie in Ayr, a planter who died on Whitehall Estate, St Mary's, Jamaica, 1806. [AJ#3094]

MCWILLIAM, ANNA ELIZA, daughter of Alexander McWilliam late of Jamaica, died in Elgin, Morayshire, 26 Feb1840. [AJ#4809]

MCWILLIAM, FRANCES, wife of Alexander McWilliam, died in Kelleta, Clarendon, Jamaica, 29 Jan1832. [AJ#4397]

MCWILLIAM, JAMES, born 1791, died in St Thomas in the East, Jamaica, 17 Dec 1843. [AJ#5012]

MCWILLIE, JOHN, a Covenanter imprisoned in Edinburgh Tolbooth, who was transported from Leith to Jamaica in Aug 1685. [ETR#369][RPCS.XI.329]

MACK, THOMAS, in Kingston, Jamaica, 1786-1795, later a tenant in Gordon Mains, Berwickshire, 1800. [NAS.CS26.912.14; CS29/912]

MAIN, JAMES, born 1819, a surgeon, emigrated from Aberdeen aboard the Rob Roy bound for Jamaica, arrived at Kingston on 11 May 1841. [NA.CO140/33]

MAIN, ..., daughter of Rev. Andrew Main, was born in Comfort, Jamaica, 22 Jan 1848. [SG#1704]

MAIN, ..., daughter of Rev. A. Main, was born at Ebenezer Manse, Jamaica, on 20 Apr 1856. [CM#20805]

MAIN, ..., son of Rev. A. Main, a United Presbyterian minister, was born at Ebenezer Manse, Jamaica, on 5 Sep. 1859. [CM#21850]

MAITLAND, RICHARD, in Jamaica, probate 1763, PCC.

MALCOLM, DONALD, son of John McCallum of Knockalva, a planter in Hanover, Jamaica, administration, 1812, London. [NA.Prob.11/1535]

MALCOLM, DUGALD, of Pell River, Hanover, Jamaica, 1774, 1778; probate, 1785, PCC. [NAS.CS16.1.173/50][NA.Prob.11/1126][Argyll Sheriff Court Book.XVII.13.5.1774]

MALCOLM, G., died on Argyle Estate, Hanover, Jamaica, 1813. [AJ#3409]

MALCOLM, GEORGE, son of John McCallum of Knockalva, father of John Malcolm a barrister in law in St Catherine, Jamaica, probate 1813. [RGD.Jamaica.LOS.87/152]

MALCOLM, HUGH, son of John Malcolm and Catherine Campbell, formerly a Customs Clerk in Port Glasgow, then a merchant in Jamaica, probate, 1764, PCC. [NA.Prob.11/897][Argyll Sheriff Court Book, xvii, 13 May 1774]

MALCOLM, HUGH, sometime in Jamaica, died in Glasgow, testament, 16 Mar 1795. [NAS.CC9.7.75]

MALCOLM, JAMES, a merchant in Jamaica, deceased, father of Amelia and James, 1756. [CRP.I.7/256]

MALCOLM, NEIL, a merchant in Jamaica, 1774. [Argyll Sheriff Court Book, xvii, 13 May 1774]

MALCOLM, NEILL, son of John McCallum of Knockalva, planter in Hanover, Jamaica, will, 1802, London. [NA.Prob.11.1376]

MALCOLM, WILLIAM, a wheelwright and carpenter in Kingston, Jamaica, later in Dunmore, Stirlingshire, testament, 29 Jan 1814. [NAS.CC9.21.6/W183]

MALLOCH, DAVID, born 1785, fourth son of William Malloch a cabinet maker in Leith Walk, Edinburgh, died in Kingston, Jamaica, 19 Dec 1830.[AJ#4336]

MANN, JOHN, a planter on Bellisle, Westmoreland, Jamaica, 1830. [NAS.SC48.49.25.28/110]

MANSON, ALEXANDER, a prisoner in Edinburgh Tolbooth, transported from Leith to Jamaica in Aug 1685. [ETR#369][RPCS.XI.329]

MANSON, DAVID, born 1783, son of John Manson a merchant in Perth and Elizabeth Keay, died in Jamaica, 2 July 1821. [Perth, Greyfriars, MI]

MARNOCH, JOHN, born in Findhorn, Morayshire, in 1758, settled on Garredu Estate, Trelawney, Jamaica, died 1 Feb1815. [Falmouth MI, Jamaica]

MARQUIS, ALEXANDER, born 1759, a carpenter, died 22 July 1799. [Palisades MI, Port Royal, Jamaica]

MARSHALL, JOHN, late in Jamaica, later in Angus, 1776. [NAS.RS35.26.181]

MARSHALL, THOMAS, born in Glasgow, fourth son of Robert Marshall a merchant, at Glasgow University in 1791, manager of Frome Estate, Jamaica, died 15 July 1802. [MAGU#165][AJ#2857][Caribbeanna.4.17]

MARSHALL, WILLIAM, a smith from Edinburgh, transported from Leith to Jamaica in Aug 1685, landed at Port Royal, Jamaica, in Nov 1685. [RPCS.XI.329][LJ#157]

MARSHALL, WILLIAM, from Falkirk, Stirlingshire, a merchant in Jamaica, testament, 10 Oct 1796. [NAS.CC8.8.130]

MARTIN, JOHN, from Dumfries, emigrated via London to Jamaica in Mar 1684. [CLRO/AIA]

SCOTS IN JAMAICA, 1655-1855

MARTIN, PETER, second son of Peter Martin, Belleville, Edinburgh, died in Richmond, Jamaica, Nov 1808. [EA#4705][SM.71.158]
MARTIN, RACHEL, a sick-nurse in Jamaica, died 15 Nov 1844. [NAS.E287]
MARTINE, JAMES, in Clarendon, Jamaica, letters, 1727. [NAS.GD24.3.318]
MASON, WILLIAM, born 1764, a merchant in Jamaica, died 1 Dec 1841. [St Andrews MI, Fife]
MASSON, ROBERT, in Clarendon, Jamaica, married Janet Lillie, Forres, Morayshire, there on 18 Dec 1830. [AJ#4331]
MATHER, JOHN, a merchant in Jamaica, 1779, later in Hamilton, Lanarkshire. [NAS.CS16.1.174/177; SC37.59.3/192]
MATTHEWS, MATTHEW, a Jacobite, transported via Liverpool to Jamaica, 1748. [NA.T53.44]
MATHIESON, GILBERT, a planter, Castle Wemyss Estate, St James, Jamaica, 1774. [BL.Add.MS22676/8]
MAXWELL, JOHN, from Glasgow, educated at Edinburgh University around 1658, emigrated to Jamaica in 1662, a physician and cleric in Port Royal, husband of Mary ....., father of John, died in Jamaica during 1673, probate 17 Nov 1673, Jamaica. [LSS.fo.74][SRA.TPM.113.562][MMP.i.435]
MAXWELL, JOHN, aboard the Countess of Galloway from Creetown, Kirkcudbright, on 15 Mar 1793 bound for Jamaica, arrived in Kingston in May 1793. [RJG:1.6.1793]
MAXWELL, JOHN, late in Jamaica, son of William Maxwell, a burgess of Dundee, 1818. [DBR]
MAXWELL, JOSEPH, born 1684, Secretary of Jamaica, died 9 July 1735. [Spanish Town Cathedral MI]
MAXWELL, PATRICK, born 1754, a physician, died in Hanover, Jamaica, 28 Aug1811. [Hanover MI]
MAXWELL, WILLIAM, born 1760, an attorney in Kingston, Jamaica, died 20 May 1802. [Kingston MI][NAS.RD2.282.787]
MEEK, JAMES, born 1820, a baker, arrived at Bluefields, Westmoreland, Jamaica, on 23 Jan 1841 aboard the William Pirie, from Stranraer. [NA.CO.140/33]
MEIKLE, JOHN, a surgeon-physician in St Dorothy's, Jamaica, son of John and Mary Meikle in Paisley, Renfrewshire, 1779, dead by 1822. [NAS.CS15.1.179; CS17.1.35/508; 42/18]
MEIN, JAMES, late in Jamaica, then in Newstead, 1820. [NAS.RS57.5629]
MELDRUM, URQUHART, born in Old Meldrum, Aberdeenshire, a physician, educated at Aberdeen and Edinburgh universities, died in Trelawney, Jamaica, 2 Mar 1822. [AJ#3835]

SCOTS IN JAMAICA, 1655-1855

MELVILLE, ROBERT, late Govenor General of Jamaica, 1772. [NAS.RS27.200.240]

MENZIES, ALEXANDER, a planter in St Andrew's, Jamaica, 1754. [NA.CO137/28/191-196]

MENZIES, ALEXANDER, born 1802, died 20 July 1815. [Kingston MI, Jamaica]

MENZIES, ARCHIBALD, in Kingston, Jamaica, was granted Pitnacree, 2 June 1809. [NAS.RGS.140.16.24; SC48.49.25.2/196; RD3.333.921]

MENZIES, EDWARD, born 1787, late Kingston, Jamaica, died New Scone, Perth, 12 Aug 1852. [GM.NS38.434]

MENZIES, JEAN, daughter of William Menzies in Jamaica, married Alexander Fraser of Moremount, 11 Mar 1764. [EMR]

MENZIES, JOHN, from Edinburgh, a merchant in Jamaica, died 1768, testament, 21 Feb 1769. [NAS.CC8.8.121]

MENZIES, MARIA ELIZABETH, eldest daughter of Edward Menzies of Paradise Pen, Kingston, Jamaica, married James Menzies of Pitnacree, in Perth, 2 July 1833. [AJ#4461][SG#155]

MERCER, ALEXANDER, a merchant in Edinburgh, later in Jamaica, testament, 16 May 1788, Comm. Edinburgh. [NAS]

MERCER, COLIN, born 15 June 1731, son of Rev. James Mercer and Elizabeth Logan in Perth, an army surgeon who died in Jamaica, 1754. [F.4.194]

MERCER, Lieutenant LAWRENCE, born in Gask, son of Rev. Lawrence Mercer and Jean Lindsay, died in Jamaica, Aug 1742. [F.4.274]

MERCER, ROBERT, born 1656, a baker from Loudoun, Ayrshire, emigrated via London to Jamaica in the Richard and Sarah in 1683. [CLRO/AIA]

METHVEN, CHARLES CAITHNESS, an agent in Dundee, later in Jamaica, died 19 Apr1845, inventory, 1853. [NAS.SC70.1.80; F1710]

MIDDLETON, GEORGE, born 1810, son of Rev. George Middleton in Midmar, Aberdeenshire, died in Jamaica, 28 Sep 1852. [AJ.24.11.1852]

MIDDLETON, THOMAS, born 1800, a ploughman, with Mary Ann born 1799, a laborer, William born 1818, a blacksmith, Ann born 1830, and Jane born 1775, arrived at Bluefields, Westmoreland, Jamaica, on 23 Jan 1841 aboard the William Pirie, from Stranraer. [NA.CO.140/33]

MILBURN, WILLIAM OGILVY, from Brechin, Angus, died in Kingston, Jamaica, 18 June 1835. [AJ#4573]

MILL, JAMES, from Carnoustie, Angus, son of William Mill, a writer in Arbroath later a merchant at St Ann's Bay, Jamaica, 1853. [NAS.CS313.38]

MILL, WILLIAM, eldest son of .... Mill of Millfield, provost of Arbroath, died at St Ann's Bay, Jamaica, 9 Nov 1850, also his wife who died there on 2 Dec 1850. [FJ#941][W#1183][EEC#22068]

SCOTS IN JAMAICA, 1655-1855

MILLER, ANDREW, born 1788, died in St Elizabeth's, Jamaica, 27 Aug1830. [Black River MI][NAS.CS46.1845.12.85]

MILLER, DAVID, a surgeon in Bristol, formerly in Westmoreland, Jamaica, 1750. [NAS.RD4.176/1.142; RS35.17.546]

MILLER, GEORGE, born 1802, for 25 years a master at Montego Bay Academy, Jamaica, died in Kilbarchan, Renfrewshire, 21 Nov 1873. [Kilbarchan East MI]

MILLER, HENRY, from Kirkcaldy, Fife, then in St Thomas in the East, Jamaica, 1839. [NAS.SC20.34.20.279/282]

MILLER, JAMES, in Jamaica, married Elizabeth Fordyce from Aberdeen, in Edinburgh, 20 June 1781. [EMR]

MILLER, JAMES, in Harmony Hall, Jamaica, died 4 Aug 1836, inventory, 1837. [NAS.SC70.1..54; D959]

MILLER, JAMES, late of Halfwaytree, Jamaica, died in Edinburgh, 24 Sep 1840. [EEC#20115]

MILLER, JOHN, a merchant in Glasgow then in Jamaica, 1800, later in Glasgow, 1821. [NAS.CS18.710.15; CS17.1.40/269]

MILLER, JOHN, in Jamaica, later in Breadiesholm, 1813. [NAS.RS10.2266]

MILLER, JOHN, a merchant in Kingston, Jamaica, later in Muirsheal, died 1854. [NAS.NRAS.0623. JMT, bundle 2]

MILLER, MARGARET, widow of Walter Miller a merchant in Jamaica, died in Granton, Edinburgh, 18 Dec 1847, inventory, 1852. [NAS.SC70.1.77]

MILLER, ROBERT, in Jamaica, then in Glasgow, testament, 8 Feb 1821. [NAS.CC9.81.134]

MILLER, THOMAS, in Jamaica, 1785. [NAS.B41.7.8.325]

MILLER, WILLIAM, born 7 Mar 1767, son of Rev. Thomas Miller and Beatrix Colquhoun in Lerwick, Shetland Islands, died in Spanish Town, Jamaica, 24 Oct 1791. [GC.57] [F.7.286]

MILLER, WILLIAM, born 1802, son of David Miller and Isabella Gilchrist, died in Jamaica, 1817. [Dundee, Howff, MI]

MILLER, WILLIAM, first son of John Miller a merchant in Jamaica, matriculated at Glasgow University in 1817. [MAGU]

MILNE, ALEXANDER, of Castle Gordon, died in Bath, Jamaica, 1823. [EEC#17517]

MILNE, ALEXANDER, born in Skene, Aberdeenshire, 1803, a mason, died on Content Estate, Hanover, Jamaica, 3 Oct 1837. [AJ#4705]

MILNE, ANDREW JAMIESON, minister in Kingston, Jamaica, 1855-1874, Principal of the Collegiate School in Kingston, 1858. [F.7.670]

MILNE, FRANCIS, late a merchant in Glasgow, died in Jamaica 14 Nov 1814. [Kingston MI]

SCOTS IN JAMAICA, 1655-1855

MILNE, JOHN, born 1822, from Aberdeen aboard the Rob Roy bound for Jamaica, arrived at Kingston on 11 May 1841. [NA.CO140/33]; possibly born 1813, youngest son of Alexander Milne in Mains of Skene, Aberdeenshire, who died on Hopewell Estate, Hanover, Jamaica, 1 Sep 1841. [AJ#4901]

MILNE, PETER, born 1755, a tailor who emigrated via London to Jamaica on the Charming Nancy in Jan 1774. [NA.T47.9/11]

MILNE, WALTER, in Jamaica, 1849. [NAS.RD5.835.504]

MILNE, WILLIAM, in Jamaica, probate 1770, PCC.

MILNE, WILLIAM, born 1815, son of John Milne in Mill of Boyndie, Customs officer, died at Old Harbour, Jamaica, 7 May 1850, inventory, 1853. [AJ#5346][NAS.SC70.1.78; F1601]

MINTO, ELIZABETH, wife of Robert Minto, died 17 Apr 1783, also their daughter Isabella, born 10 July 1781, died 7 July 1802. [St James MI, Montego Bay, Jamaica]

MINTO, ROBERT, born 1740, a jobber and overseer, St James, Jamaica, 1774, died in Trelawney on 3 May 1803. [BL.Add.MS22676/8][Lottery MI]

MINTO, WALTER, born 1779, died in Trelawney, Jamaica, 18 Dec 1830. [Lottery MI, Jamaica]

MITCHELL, ALEXANDER, in St Andrew's, Jamaica, testament, 11 July 1799. [NAS.CC8.8.131]

MITCHELL, ALEXANDER, from Glasgow, married Elizabeth Gordon Cater MacFadyen, eldest daughter of James MacFadyen, MD in Kingston, Jamaica, in East Barnet 29 Apr1857. [EEC#21091]

MITCHELL, HUGH, formerly a surgeon in Jamaica, died in Edinburgh, 22 July 1799. [SM.61.496]

MITCHELL, JAMES, a merchant, a deed, 1791, died in Kingston, Jamaica, 1805.[NAS.RD2.252.108][AJ#3015]

MITCHELL, JAMES, youngest son of John Mitchell, Pitt Street, Edinburgh, died in Spanish Town, Jamaica, 1816. [S.1.10]

MITCHELL, JOHN, transported from Leith to Jamaica in Aug 1685. [RPCS.XI.136]

MITCHELL, JOHN, in Clarendon, Middlesex, Jamaica, a deed, 1791. [NAS.RD2.252.108]

MITCHELL, JOHN, in Jamaica, inventory, 1824. [NAS.SC70.1.32]

MITCHELL, JOHN, born 1824, arrived at Bluefields, Westmoreland, Jamaica, on 23 Jan 1841 aboard the William Pirie, from Stranraer. [NA.CO.140/33]

MITCHELL, WILLIAM, in Bushy Park, Jamaica, a burgess of Edinburgh, 23 July 1794. [EBR]

MITCHELL, Mrs, and family, from Kingston, Jamaica, in June 1793 aboard the Roselle bound for Leith. [JRG:29.6.1793]

SCOTS IN JAMAICA, 1655-1855

MOFFAT, ALEXANDER, a prisoner in Edinburgh Tolbooth, transported to Jamaica, Sep 1726. [NAS.HH.11.15]

MOIR, ALEXANDER, in Jamaica, 1845. [NAS.GD171.1301]

MOIR, GEORGE, a merchant in Jamaica, co-owner of the Magnet of Glasgow, 1800. [NAS.CE60.11.6/18]

MONCREIFF, DAVID, born 13 Jan1691 in Kirkwall, Orkney Islands, son of merchant Harry Moncreiff and Barbara Erberie, settled in St Catherine's, Jamaica, 1730, Provost Marshal of Jamaica, dead by 1739. [NAS.GD237.2.2.21/2] ['Moncreiff and the Moncreiffes', Edinburgh 1929, p.271]

MONTEATH, ANDREW, a carpenter, died in Falmouth, Jamaica, 11 June 1797. [GM.67.800]

MONTEATH, THOMAS, and AMELIA, in Jamaica, a deed, 1795. [NAS.RD3.273.11]

MONTEATH, WILLIAM, a merchant on Green Island, Jamaica, son of Walter Monteath of Kepp and Jean Douglas, a deed, 1777. [NAS.RD4.237.607]

MONTEATH, WILLIAM, born 1807, died in Kingston, Jamaica, 26 Apr1841. [GSP.668]

MORNOCH, JOHN, in Cornwall, Jamaica, inventory, 1818. [NAS.SC70.1.17]

MOUAT, HECTOR, in Jamaica, 1790. [NLS.ms5028/40]

MOUAT, JOHN, from Kirkwall, in Jamaica, 1764. [NAS.GD31.300]

MOFFAT, JAMES, in Jamaica, 1811. [NAS.CS42.4.2]

MOFFAT, ..., born 1766 in Glasgow, died at Montego Bay, Jamaica, on 18 Mar1814. [Montego Bay MI]

MOIR, ALEXANDER WILSON, of HM Customs, son of James Moir a surgeon RN, Edinburgh, married Isabella Watson, youngest daughter of Rev. James Watson of St Andrew's United Presbyterian Church, Kingston, Jamaica, there on 12 Dec 1851. [W#1295]

MOIR, JAMES, formerly a writer in Alloa, Clackmannanshire, later in Kingston, Jamaica, 1881. [NAS.CS284.191]

MOIR, JANE, born 1758, via London to Jamaica on the Reward, Dec 1773. [NA.T47.9/11]

MONCRIEFF, BENJAMIN SCOTT, born 1782, died in St Ann's, Jamaica, 22 Mar1849. [Ochios Rios MI, Jamaica]

MONCRIEFF, DAVID, in Spanish Town, Jamaica, 1731. [NAS.GD24.3.344]

MONCRIEFF, PETER, born 1813, died in St Ann's, Jamaica, 6 Feb1876. [Ochios Rios MI, Jamaica]

MONCRIEFF, ROBERT LAIDLAW, born 1797, son of Rev. William Moncrieff and Jean Laidlaw in Annan, Dumfries-shire, died at Harker's Hall, Jamaica, 8 Sep 1836.[Annan MI]

SCOTS IN JAMAICA, 1655-1855

MONCRIEFF, ..., a jobber, St James, Jamaica, 1774. [BL.Add.MS22676/8]

MONKE, WILLIAM, a soldier who was shipped to Jamaica on the Grantham in 1659. [SPAWI.1659.126]

MONTIER, ALEXANDER, in Kingston, Jamaica, letter, 1729-1736. [NAS.RH15.54.9]

MONTEITH, ALEXANDER, a carpenter in Kingston, Jamaica, 1749; died in Falmouth, Jamaica, on 11 June 1797. [NAS.GD30.1586][GM.67.800]

MONTEITH, JAMES, son of Walter Monteith of Kepp, died in Jamaica, 18 Sep 1798; his widow Amelia, born 1767, died in Lympstone, Devon, 20 Apr 1833. [AJ#2661][GM.103.476]

MONTGOMERY, CHARLES, on Rozelle Estate, St Thomas, Jamaica, 1764. [NAS.NRAS#3572.2.18]

MONTGOMERY, Colonel CHARLES, "after 35 years in Jamaica returned home on the Garthland and died in the Buck's Head Inn, Greenock, Feb 1804", testament, 9 Oct1805. [NAS.CC8.8.136] [AJ#2928]

MONTGOMERIE, ROBERT, born 1785, eldest son of Hugh Montgomerie and Elizabeth Barclay in Dalry, died in Jamaica. [HAF]

MOODIE, JEAN, daughter of James Moodie in Jamaica, married William, son of Dr William Keith in South Carolina, in Edinburgh, 12 Mar1769. [EMR]

MOORE, DONALD, a rebel from Argyll, who was transported from Leith to Jamaica in Aug 1685. [RPCS.XI.136]

MOORE, JOHN MITCHELL, in Jamaica, died Jan 1794, testament, 25 May 1794. [NAS.CC8.8.129]

MOORE, ROBERT, from Carluke, Lanarkshire, transported from Leith to Jamaica in Aug 1685, landed at Port Royal in Nov 1685. [RPCS.XI.329][LJ#169]

MORGAN, GEORGE THOMSON, MA, son of James Morgan a merchant in Jamaica, at King's College, Aberdeen, 1821-1825, LRCS Edinburgh, 1831.[KCA.2.443]

MORGAN, JAMES, of Bonnymuir, born 1756, son of George Morgan [1722-1783] and Elspit Morgan [1714-1792], '25 years in Jamaica', died 15 July 1823. [St Nicholas MI, Aberdeen]

MORGAN, Dr WILLIAM, late Rector of Kingston, Jamaica, then Professor of Philosophy at Marischal College, Aberdeen, testament, 12 Feb 1789, Comm. Aberdeen. [NAS]

MORGAN, WILLIAM, a merchant in Jamaica, co-owner of the Favourite of Greenock, 1800. [NAS.CE60.11.6/22]

MORISON, DANIEL, born 1797, son of Daniel Morison, 5 St Mary's Place, Edinburgh, died on Bybrook Estate, St Thomas in the Vale, Jamaica, 11 Nov 1831. [AJ#4385]

SCOTS IN JAMAICA, 1655-1855

MORISON, J., a surgeon from Dalkeith, Midlothian, died in Kingston, Jamaica, 6 Aug 1819. [S.3.144]

MORRICE, DAVID, born 1773, fourth son of Rev. William Morrice in Kincardine O'Neil, Aberdeenshire, died on Elim Estate, St Elizabeth's, Jamaica, 7 Sep 1826. [AJ#4117] [Black River MI]

MORRICE, JAMES, second son of Rev. William Morrice in Kincardine O'Neil, Aberdeenshire, died on Green Island, Jamaica, 19 Jan 1816. [AJ#3560]

MORRICE, ROBERT, son of Rev. William Morrice and Helen Paterson in Kincardine O'Neil, Aberdeenshire, at Marischal College, Aberdeen, 1779-1783, later a planter in Jamaica. [MCA.II.355]

MORRIS, ALEXANDER, a planter in Cornwall, Jamaica, dead by 1796. [NAS.CS16.1.201/440]

MORRIS, DAVID, born 1824, youngest son of Robert Morris in Pittenweem, Fife, an engineer who died in Jamaica, 5 Nov 1849. [PR.29.12.1849]

MORRIS, LOUDEN, eldest son of Andrew Morris a surgeon in Glasgow, at Glasgow University, 1768, later a surgeon on Green Island, Jamaica, 1788. [MAGU#87].

MORRISON, ALEXANDER, a planter in Cornwall, Jamaica, 1793. [NAS.CS17.1.12/253]

MORRISON, ARCHIBALD, a merchant in Jamaica, dead by 1804. [NAS.AC7.77]

MORRISON, DONALD, a rebel from Argyll, transported from Leith to Jamaica in Aug 1685. [RPCS.XI.136]

MORRISON, GEORGE, late in Jamaica, then in Aberdeen, 1796. [NAS.GD105.51]

MORRISON, JAMES, a physician in Jamaica, graduated MD from Marischal College, Aberdeen, in 1760s. [MCA]

MORRISON, JAMES, merchant in Jamaica, deceased, widow Mary Allan, 1791. [NAS.RS61.283]

MORRISON, Mrs JOSEPH, eldest daughter of William Wilson, George Street, Edinburgh, died in Spanish Town, Jamaica, 31 Dec 1843.[EEC#20995][W.5.437]

MORRISON, LEWIS, of Springfield, born 1814, died at Morant Bay, Jamaica, 24 Sep 1838. [AJ#4743]

MORRISON, WILLIAM, surgeon in Banff, to Jamaica 1784. [PSAS.114.495]

MORRISON, WILLIAM, eldest son of John Morrison factor at Craigievar, Aberdeenshire, a baker in Aberdeen, later in Port Morant, Jamaica, 1799. [NAS.CS26.909.29]

MORRISON, WILLIAM, born 1817, emigrated from Aberdeen aboard the Rob Roy bound for Jamaica, arrived at Kingston on 11 May 1841. [NA.CO140/33]

MORRISON, WILLIAM, a planter in Jamaica, died 1 Sep 1850, inventory, 1854, Comm. Edinburgh. [NAS.SC70.1.8; E3965]

MORTON, ALICE BISHOP, born 1843, wife of Charles Goldie of HM Customs late of Greenock, Renfrewshire, died in Kingston, Jamaica, 16 Nov 1869. [S#8232]

MOWAT, JOHN, a planter, Dumfries Estate, St James, Jamaica, 1774. [BL.Add.MS22676/8]

MOWAT, JOHN, son of Rev. Hugh Mowat and Elizabeth Baikie in Orkney, a planter at Orkney Hall, Jamaica, died 1800. [F.7.216]

MOWAT, SARAH, in St James, Jamaica, 1774. [BL.Add.MS22676/8]

MOWAT, WILLIAM, a planter, Dumfries Estate, St James, Jamaica, 1774. [BL.Add.MS22676/8]

MOWRAS, GEORGE, steerage passenger from Greenock to Jamaica aboard the Mary of Glasgow in Nov 1773. [NAS.CE60]

MOYES, JAMES, planter, St Elizabeth's, Cornwall, Jamaica, a deed, 1816. [NAS.RD5.108.372]

MUDIE, ALEXANDER, born 1763, late a physician in Jamaica, died 17 Feb 1844 at 35 Albany Street, Edinburgh. [New Calton MI, Edinburgh][NAS.E187]

MUIR, EBENEZER, fourth son of Dr George Muir a minister in Paisley, Renfrewshire, in Savannah la Mar, Jamaica, 1784. [NAS.SC58.61.15]

MUIR, JAMES, jr., a merchant in Liverpool, died in Kingston, Jamaica, 23 Mar 1850, an inventory, 1850. [NAS.SC70.1.71; E2430][W#1104]

MUIR, JOHN, a physician and surgeon in Trelawney, Jamaica, died 21 Nov 1816, testament, 1817. [NAS.CC8.8.143; SC70.1.16]

MUIR, JOHN, eldest son of Rev. John Muir in St Vigeans, Angus, died in Kingston, Jamaica, 19 Mar 1848, inventory, 1852. [NAS.SC70.1.74; E2879] [AJ#5287]

MUIR, ROBERT ALEXANDER, in Fiar Prospect, Jamaica, died in Bull Pen, Jamaica, 4 Sep 1827. [AJ#4166]

MUIR, THOMAS, son of John Muir of Greenhall, Blantyre, Lanarkshire, died in Jamaica, Apr 1819. [AJ#3731]

MUIR, ..., from Leith to Jamaica on the Roselle, arrived in Kingston in Apr 1793. [JRG:27.4.1793]

MUIRHEAD, AGNES, widow of Dougald Stewart a merchant in Jamaica, testament, 8 Mar 1793, Comm. Stirling. [NAS]

MUIRHEAD, THOMAS F., a deed, 1880. [NAS.RD5.1799.214.269]

MUNDELL, JOSEPH, born 1765, son of Peter Mundell and Ann Little in Dumfries, died in Clarendon, Jamaica, Mar 1810. [Mouswald MI]

MUNDELL, PETER, son of Peter Mundell and Ann Little in Dumfries, a merchant, died in Kingston, Jamaica, 30 Sep 1801. [Mouswald MI]

MUNRO, CHARLES, born 1755, a book-keeper, via London to Jamaica on the Capel, Feb 1774. [NA.T47.9/11]

SCOTS IN JAMAICA, 1655-1855

MUNRO, COLIN, a planter in St Thomas in the East, Middlesex, Jamaica, died 1800, testament, 18 July 1810. [NAS.CC8.8.136]

MUNRO, DUNCAN, via Portsmouth to Jamaica on the Richmond Sep 1775. [NA.T47.9/11]

MUNRO, GEORGE, a Customs Officer in Jamaica, second son of Sir Harry Munro of Foulis, died in Kingston, Jamaica, 22 Apr 1802. [GM.72.686]

MUNRO, HUGH, a surgeon in St Thomas in the Vale, Jamaica, died in Spanish Town, Jamaica, 1797. [EWJ#1]

MUNRO, HUGH, born 1750, '45 years resident', died 23 Apr 1829. [Trinity Chapel MI, Green Island, Jamaica][NAS.242/70/4/11]

MUNRO, J., in Savanna-la-Mar, Jamaica, 1780. [NA.CO137.1-35]

MUNRO, JAMES, died in Jamaica before Feb 1792. [GCr#70]

MUNRO, JOHN, in Savanna-la-Mar, Jamaica, 1780. [NA.CO137.1-35]

MUNRO, JOHN, late of Passage Fort, Kingston, Jamaica, was granted Kirkton Alves, 20 Dec 1787. [NAS.RGS.124.201]

MUNRO, JOHN, from Jamaica, married Elizabeth, youngest daughter of Alexander McKinlay of HM Customs in Greenock, there on 10 Nov 1806. [GrA: 14.11.1806]

MUNRO, ROBERT HUGH, Knockpatrick Estate, St Elizabeth's, Jamaica, a deed, 1793, died 1798. [NAS.RD3.263.659][Black River MI]

MUNRO, ROBERT, in Jamaica, died Feb 1829, inventory, 1831. [NAS.SC70.1.44; C266]

MUNRO, WILLIAM, in Jamaica, then in Forres, Morayshire, died 10 Jan1809, testament, 9 Nov1809. [NAS.CC16.4.1.172; CC16.9.10/237][SM.71.158]

MUNROE, WILLIAM, a cordiner in Port Royal, Jamaica, probate 1 Dec 1697, Jamaica.

MURCHISON, ALEXANDER, graduated MD from Marischal College, Aberdeen, 7 July 1813, a physician in Jamaica, late of Springfield, Vere, a member of the Jamaican House of Assembly, died in Elgin, 10 Oct 1845.[MCA][W#618]

MURDOCH, ARCHIBALD, son of James Murdoch and Beatrix Campbell in Doune, Stirlingshire, died in Jamaica Dec 1800. [Kilmadock MI]

MURDOCH, Mr., from Glasgow aboard the Betsy and Brothers bound for Jamaica, arrived in Kingston in May 1793. [JRG:25.5.1794]

MURE, THOMAS, late in Jamaica, then in Warriston, a burgess of Edinburgh, 3 Nov1790. [EBR]

MURRAY, ALEXANDER, born 1797, son of Rev. Andrew Murray and Janet Mackie in Aucherderran, Fife, died in Jamaica, 22 Oct 1821. [Auchterderran MI] [AJ#3861][F.5.77]

MURRAY, AMELIA, daughter of William Murray a merchant in Edinburgh, wife of Thomas Monteith, Green Island, Hanover, Jamaica, a deed, 1796. [NAS.RD3.275.543]

MURRAY, ANDREW, in St David's, Jamaica, inventory, 1844. [NAS.SC70.1.66]

MURRAY, ANNA, imprisoned in Edinburgh Tolbooth on a charge of infanticide, transported from Leith to Jamaica in Aug 1685. [ETR#369][RPCS.XI.330]

MURRAY, ARCHIBALD, from Kincardine, a divinity student in 1826, a teacher in Jamaica, died there 1844. [AUPC]

MURRAY, EDWARD, born 9 June 1714, son of John Murray, Marquis of Atholl, died in Port Royal, Jamaica, 2 Feb 1737, probate 16 June 1737, PCC.

MURRAY, GEORGE, born 1729, in Savanna-la-Mar, 1780, died 14 Apr 1804. [NA.CO137.1-35][Savanna la Mar MI, Jamaica][NAS.CS16.1.154/177]

MURRAY, GEORGE, Custos of Westmoreland, Jamaica, 1780. [NA.CO137/79]

MURRAY, GEORGE HOME, died 9 May 1810. [Kingston, MI, Jamaica.]

MURRAY, Mrs ISABEL, a resident of Port Royal, Jamaica, in 1700. [DD#324]

MURRAY, JAMES, of Airy Castle, St Thomas in the East, Jamaica, a bond, 1766. [NAS.RD2.236/2.634]

MURRAY, JAMES, married Anne, eldest daughter of Patrick Waugh, Arbuthnott Cottage, Stirlingshire, and Dromilly Estate, Trelawney, Jamaica, on Georgia Estate, Trelawney, 24 Sep 1840. [AJ#4848]

MURRAY, JEAN, in Charleston, South Carolina, and in Jamaica, died 1783, testament, 8 July 1796. [NAS.CC8.8.130]

MURRAY, JOHN, in Port Royal, Jamaica, 1733. [NAS.NRAS.0682;GD267.3/21]

MURRAY, JOHN, of Philiphaugh, died on Hopewell Estate, Jamaica, 28 Feb1800. [AJ#2727]

MURRAY, JOHN, born 1812, a shoemaker, emigrated from Aberdeen aboard the Rob Roy bound for Jamaica, arrived at Kingston on 11 May 1841. [NA.CO140/33]

MURRAY, LEWIS, a planter in St Thomas, Jamaica, probate 9 Oct 1692, Jamaica.

MURRAY, Dr PATRICK, born 1744, a physician and Grand Court judge in Jamaica, died in Kirkcudbright in 1829. [GM.99.477]

MURRAY, PETER, Jamaica, graduated MD from Edinburgh University, 1802. [EMG.33]

MURRAY, ROBERT, in Jamaica, son of Robert Murray in Canongate, Edinburgh, a deed, 1798. [NAS.RD4.265.256]

MURRAY, ROBERT, of Knapdale, Jamaica, died at sea 21 June 1820. [GM.90.639]

MURRAY, WALTER, of Golden Grove Plantation, Jamaica, 1767. [NAS.NRAS.2177/6083]

MURRAY, Hon. WALTER, a planter, Latium Estate, St James, Jamaica, 1774. [BL.Add.MS22676/8]
MURRAY, WILLIAM, a mariner on the Josiah, probate 24 Oct 1693, Jamaica.
MURRAY, WILLIAM, born 1772, Dundee, Jamaica, died in Brighton, May 1826. [GM.96.573]
MURRAY, WILLIAM, in Latuine, Jamaica, a burgess of Banff, 1799. [BBR]
MURRAY, WILLIAM, born 1784, son of Alexander Murray and Catherine McGuffie, died in Jamaica, 22 Aug 1800. [Wigtown MI]
MURRAY, WILLIAM, surgeon in Old Monkland, Lanarkshire, then in Jamaica, died in Scotland, testament, 12 Oct 1809. [NAS.CC10.1.211]
MURRAY, WILLIAM, of Hyde Estate, St Thomas in the Vale, Jamaica, deceased, brother of James Murray an innkeeper in Perth, 1813. [NAS.B59.38.6.257]
MURRAY, Dr, from Leith to Jamaica on the Roselle, arrived in Kingston in Apr 1793. [JRG:27.4.1793]
MUSCHET, ROBERT, a merchant in Jamaica, a deed, 1774. [NAS.RD2.218.1162]
MUSCHETT, ..., a planter, Great River Estate, St James, Jamaica, 1774. [BL.Add.MS22676/8]
MUSCHET, ROBERT, of Green, a merchant in Jamaica, 1778. [NAS.CS16.1.173/400]
MUSHET, ROBERT, in St Elizabeth, Jamaica, only son and heir to the late Robert Mushet in Greenock, a decreet, 1773.[NAS.CS16.1.189]
NAPIER, GEORGE, died at Whitehall, Clarendon, Jamaica, 1806.[AJ#3064]
NAPIER, JOHN, son of MacVey Napier WS, died in Kingston, Jamaica, 8 June 1822. [AJ#3839]
NASMYTH, JAMES, born 1719, proprietor of Water Valley Estate, St Mary's, Jamaica, died 9 Sep 1794. [Rosend MI, Jamaica]
NASMYTH, Dr JAMES, a physician in Jamaica, 1778. [NAS.CS16.1.174]
NASMYTH, ROBERT, eldest son of Thomas Nasmyth of Jamaica, 1811. [NAS.GD1.906.10; RGS.143.39.70]
NASMYTH, THOMAS, of Rhodes Hall, MD, died in Water Valley, Jamaica, 1806. [AJ#3060][NAS.RD5.117.341]
NEILL, WILLIAM HENRY, born 9 Mar 1816 in Edinburgh, son of John Neill, died in Jamaica, 1838. [Calton MI, Edinburgh]
NEILSON, GEORGE, a jobber, St James, Jamaica, 1774. [BL.Add.MS22676/8]
NEILSON, THOMAS, sometime a merchant in St Mary's, Jamaica, son of Thomas Neilson a merchant in Falkirk, Stirlingshire, died in Glasgow Feb 1800, testament, 1800. [NAS.CC9.7.77]
NEISH, DAVID, born 1804, son of John Neish and Susan Robertson, died in Jamaica, 17 Feb1828. [Trottick, Angus, MI]

SCOTS IN JAMAICA, 1655-1855

NEISH, JOHN, son of John Neish and Susan Robertson, died in Jamaica, 27 Sep 1831. [Trottick, Angus, MI]

NELSON, ELIZABETH, born 1822, a servant, arrived at Bluefields, Westmoreland, Jamaica, on 23 Jan 1841 aboard the William Pirie, from Stranraer. [NA.CO.140/33]

NEWAL, ANDREW, a merchant in Westmoreland, Jamaica, 1780. [NAS.CS16.1.179]

NEWHAM, COLIN, born 1784, son of Daniel Newham in Templeton, died in Clarendon, Jamaica, 10 Jan1804. [CM.12887]

NEWLANDS, DAVID, born 1822, from Glasgow, died at Linstead, St Thomas in the Vale, Jamaica, 28 May 1844. [SG#1314]

NICHOLSON, THOMAS, a joiner in Clarendon, Jamaica, died 10 July 1822, testament, 8 Aug 1826. [NAS.CC8.8.151]

NICOL, GEORGE, in Jamaica, a bond, 1783. [NAS.RD2.235/1.275]

NICOL, JOHN, born 14 Oct 1763 in Aberdeen, owner and master of the Lucia of London, died Kingston, Jamaica, 2 Apr 1807. [St Andrew's Church MI, Jamaica]

NICOL, JOHN, an attorneys' clerk in Kingston, Jamaica, 1818. [NAS.RD5.146.1]

NICOL, JOHN, born 10 Sep 1799 in Edinburgh, settled in St David's, Jamaica, by 1830, died 29 Apr1864. [St Cuthbert's MI, Edinburgh]

NICOL, ROBERT, born Inverness 1797, late in Jamaica, died Inverness on 27 Feb 1844. [Chapel Yard MI, Inverness]

NICOL, WILLIAM, in Elgin Plantation, died in Clarendon, Jamaica, 16 Feb 1818. [AJ#3669][S.2.67]

NICOLL, GEORGE, late in Jamaica, was granted Arthurstone, 3 July 1789. [NAS.RGS.125.158]

NICOLL, JAMES, son of James Nicoll a mason in Dundee, settled in Kingston, Jamaica, burgess of Dundee, 15 Nov 1823. [DBR]

NICOLL, JOHN, who was transported from Leith to Jamaica on 7 Aug 1685. [RPCS.XI.136]

NICOLSON, RICHARD, of Mount Pleasant, died in Kingston, Jamaica, 1802. [AJ#2839]

NIMMO, THOMAS, died in Jamaica, 8 Feb 1774. [St Andrew's MI, Jamaica]

NISBET, GEORGE, second son of George Nisbet of Cairnhill, Old Monkland, at Glasgow University in 1782, died in Westmoreland, Jamaica, on 30 Jan 1811. [MAGU#132][Caribbeana#4.17]

NISBET, GEORGE, from Edinburgh, in Jamaica, inventory, 1895. [NAS.SC70.1.338]

NISBET, JAMES, of Letham, born 1737, died in Jamaica, 4 Oct 1780. ['Nisbet of that Ilk', London, 1941, p.208]

SCOTS IN JAMAICA, 1655-1855

NISBET, JOHN, eldest son of George Nisbet of Cairnhill, in Bellisle Estate, Westmoreland, Jamaica, a deed, 1784. [NAS.RD2.238/1.940]

NISBET, Dr JOHN, died in Westmoreland, Jamaica, Aug 1825. [AJ#4062]

NISBET, ROBERT, of Greenholm, born 1730, died in Jamaica, 5 July 1787, probate, 1788, PCC. ['Nisbet of that Ilk', London, 1941, p.208]

NIVEN, ANDREW, from Alyth, Perthshire, a divinity student 1828, then a minister in Stirling and in Jamaica, died 1846. [AUPC]

NIXON, JAMES, born 1812, a blacksmith, with Mary Ann born 1818, a laborer, arrived at Bluefields, Westmoreland, Jamaica, on 23 Jan 1841 aboard the William Pirie, from Stranraer. [NA.CO.140/33]

NOBLE, JOHN, from Jamaica, died in Greenock on 4 Oct 1808. [GrA:12.10.1808]

NOCKELLS, CHARLES, Mount Pleasant, St Thomas in the East, Jamaica, died in Edinburgh, 8 Sep 1850. [EEC#22015]

NORTON, DAVID, in Spanish Town, Jamaica, graduated MD from King's College, Aberdeen, 1 Sep 1768. [KCA#132]

OCHILTREE, DAVID, a Covenanter who was transported from Leith to Jamaica on 7 Aug 1685. [RPCS.XI.329]

OGILVIE, Dr DAVID, late of Kingston, Jamaica, then in Old Aberdeen, 1782. [NAS.CS17.1.1/142]

OGILVIE, Dr GEORGE, a surgeon, late of Kingston, Jamaica, then in Aberdeen, 1782. [NAS.CS17.1.1/78]

OGILVIE, GEORGE, Langley Park, Jamaica, married Barbara, 3rd daughter of James Dundas of that Ilk, in Edinburgh, 10 Sep 1785. [EMR]

OGILVIE, GEORGE, in St Mary's, Jamaica, a will, 1780, [NAS.RD4.249.742]; probate 1791, PCC.

OGILVIE, GEORGE, late of Jamaica, then in Dundee, 1800. [DCA.H187]

OGILVIE, JAMES, born 1747, son of Sir William Ogilvie and Helen Baird in Banff, died in Jamaica on 6 June 1774. [Banff MI]

OGILVIE, JOHN, in St Mary's, Jamaica, 3 July 1802. [NAS.RD3.300.1112]

OGILVIE, JOHN, eldest son of John Ogilvie a glass merchant in Glasgow, died in Kingston, Jamaica, 19 Dec 1830. [EEC#18608]

OGILVY, ALEXANDER, in Jamaica, dead by 1811. [NAS.GD16.43.60]

OGLE, JOHN, born 1810, with Mary born 1816, William born 1837, Isabell and Margaret both born 1839, arrived at Bluefields, Westmoreland, Jamaica, on 23 Jan 1841 aboard the William Pirie, from Stranraer. [NA.CO.140/33]

OLIPHANT, DAVID, in Clarendon, Jamaica, 1738. [NAS.GD34.3.384]

OLIPHANT, DAVID, a physician in South Carolina, later in Jamaica, a deed, 1772. [NAS.RD3.235.265]

SCOTS IN JAMAICA, 1655-1855

OLIPHANT, DAVID, in Tremolesworth, St Mary's, Jamaica, eldest son of David Oliphant a merchant in Edinburgh, deeds, 1809. [NAS.RD3.334.1050; RD3.346.35]

OLIPHANT, JOHN, of Bachilton, in Jamaica, a decreet, 1773/1774. [NAS.CS16.1.80/398]

OLIPHANT, JOHN MORRISON, in Clarendon, Jamaica, dead by 1791. [NAS.RD2.252.108]

OLIPHANT, MARGARET, wife of Alexander Cumming in St Catherine, Middlesex, Jamaica, eldest daughter of Lord Oliphant, a deed, 1784, died 1800, testament, 11 Feb 1801. [NAS.RD4.255.417; CC8.8.132]

OLIVER, JAMES, a Covenanter from Jedburgh Forest, Roxburghshire, transported from Leith to Jamaica on 7 Aug 1685, landed at Port Royal in Nov 1685. [RPCS.XI.329][LJ#175]

OMAN, CHARLES, son of Charles Oman in Edinburgh, died on Trinity Estate, St Mary's, Jamaica, 18 Nov 1818. [S.3.108]

ORR, JAMES, from Ayr, a merchant in Jamaica, died 1750, testament, 11 Feb 1758. [NAS.CC8.8.117]

ORD, JAMES, a planter in St Andrew's, Jamaica, 1754. [NA.CO137/28]

ORR, JOHN, in Bybrook, St Elizabeth's, Jamaica, 1778. [NLS.ms.5329/85; ms5332/236]

ORR, JOSEPH, in Jamaica, probate, 1798, PCC.

ORR, Captain SAMUEL, son of James Orr a merchant in Leith, died in Kingston, Jamaica, 9 July 1815. [SM..75.959]

ORR, Mr., from Glasgow aboard the Mary bound for Jamaica, arrived in Kingston in May 1793. [JRG:18.5.1793]

ORROCK, Captain, JOHN, late of the 33rd Regt., died in Kingston, Jamaica, 14 Feb 1838. [AJ#4712]!

PATERSON, WILLIAM, born Kilmarnock, Ayrshire,1755, settled in Jamaica, died at Wellington Square, Ayr, 9 June 1832. [Kilmarnock Laigh MI]

PATERSON, ..., born 15 Apr1839 in Monklands, St Thomas in the East, Jamaica, son of Robert Paterson. [EEC#19888910]

PATON, JOHN, born 1798, a merchant from Greenock, died at Orangehill, Montego Bay, Jamaica, on 21 May 1841. [GrA:13.7.1841][Montego Bay MI]

PATON, JOSEPH, a gentleman in Jamaica, a burgess and guilds-brother of Ayr, 4 Apr 1751. [AyrBR]

PATTEN, ARCHIBALD, a Jacobite transported via Liverpool to Jamaica in 1748. [NA.T53/44]

PATTERSON, JAMES, in Jamaica, probate 1731, PCC.

PATTERSON, JOHN, in St Andrew's, Jamaica, probate 3 Oct 1692, Jamaica.

SCOTS IN JAMAICA, 1655-1855

PATTERSON, WILLIAM, born 1755, late in Jamaica, died Wellington Square, Ayr, 9 Sep 1832. [AJ.4407]; a witness in Kingston, Jamaica, 1793. [NAS.RD3.276.101]

PATTIE, JOHN, in Lucea, Hanover, Jamaica, then in Park of Troquier, testament, 24 Aug 1816. [NAS.CC5.19.163]

PATTON, ANDREW, in St Andrew's, Jamaica, probate 28 Apr 1685, Jamaica.

PAUL, ARCHIBALD, son of Andrew Paul in Linlithgow, West Lothian, died in St Ann's, Jamaica, 30 Sep 1822. [EEC#17375]

PAUL, GEORGE, in Panton, Jamaica, died 29 Mar 1834, inventory, 1845, Comm. Edinburgh. [NAS]

PAUL, ROBERT, born 1821, with Margery, born 1821, emigrated from Aberdeen aboard the Rob Roy bound for Jamaica, arrived at Kingston on 11 May 1841. [NA.CO140/33]

PEARSON, MICHAEL, in Jamaica, 1820. [NAS.RD5.193.513]

PEARSON, ROBERT, died in Kingston, Jamaica, on 1 July 1700. [DP#352]

PEEBLES, JAMES, 1st son of Rev. William Peebles in Newtown of Ayr, at Glasgow University in 1796, graduated MA in 1801, settled in Kingston, Jamaica, a witness, 1806; died there on 23 June 1822. [MAGU][EEC#17347][RGG#494][NAS.RD3.313.88]

PENMAN, EDWARD, in Jamaica, 1792. [NAS.CS228.B.8.27]

PENNYCOOK, ROBERT, in Flowerhill, Westmoreland, Cornwall, Jamaica, deeds, 1820s; died 13 Sep 1826, testament/inventory, 1 June 1827. [NAS.RD5.340/102; 354/465; 268/103; CC8.8.151; B1001]

PETERKIN, ALEXANDER, of Greeshop, Moray, and Chatham, Jamaica, died in Cheltenham, England, on 26 Dec 1817. [AJ#3652]

PETERSWALD, WILLIAM, in St Mary, Jamaica, 19 Apr 1836. [NAS.RS27.45.228]

PEW, ALEXANDER, son of Alexander Pew in Leith, died at Anetto Bay, Jamaica, 1820. [EEC#17070]

PHILLIPS, CHARLES H., late of Jamaica, 24 Dec 1826. [NAS.B2.2.4.60]

PIERSON, Captain, of the Anne, died in Jamaica, by Feb 1792. [GCr.70]

PITBLADDO, THOMAS, born 18 Apr 1847, son of James and Margaret Pitbladdo in Edinburgh, died in Jamaica, 23 Feb 1877. [Montego Bay MI]

PITCAIRN, DAVID, a merchant in Jamaica, died Oct 1730, probate 1731, PCC, testament, 28 Dec 1733. [NAS.CC8.8.95]

PITCAIRN, ROBERT, a planter in St Catherine's, Jamaica, 1770, testament, 28 July 1778. [NAS.GD1.675.31/61/63]

PITCAIRN, ROBERT, born 1737, from Newburgh, Fife, a tavern keeper in Spanish Town, Jamaica, letters 1780-1803, and 1792-1823; died 22 July 1799. [NAS.GD1.675.113/135/143] [Spanish Town MI]

POLLOCK, HUGH, a saddler in Charleston, South Carolina, a Loyalist who moved to Jamaica, died there in 1782. [NA.AO12.99.336; AO13.133.437]
POLLOCK, WALTER, of Braemar, St Mary's, Jamaica, 1803, died 22 Oct 1820. [NAS.B59.38.6.242][EEC#17101]
POLLOCK, WILLIAM, born 1822, arrived at Bluefields, Westmoreland, Jamaica, on 23 Jan 1841 aboard the William Pirie, from Stranraer. [NA.CO.140/33]
POLSON, HUGH, son of John Polson and Janet Mackay in Navidale, Provost of the Vice Admiralty Court of Jamaica, 1774; a deed, 8 Aug 1779; probate, 1794, PCC. [BM#295][NAS.RD4.737.908]
PORTEOUS, GEORGE, born 11 July 1766 in Glasgow, son of Rev. William Porteous and Grizel Lindsay, died in Spring Valley, Jamaica, 6 Dec 1793. [F.3.443]
PORTEOUS, GEORGE, a currier from Haddington, married Frances, daughter of Alexander McDonald, in Kingston, Jamaica, 8 July 1842. [EEC#20500]
PORTEOUS, JAMES, born 25 June 1761 in Glasgow, son of Rev. William Porteous and Grizel Lindsay, husband of Catherine, a letter,1817, died in Bonhill, Jamaica. [NAS.RD5.119.63][F.3.443]
POTTS, JOHN, from Dumfries, died at Ballard's River, Clarendon, Jamaica, 15 Feb 1798. [AJ#2635]
POUSTIE, JOHN, a Jacobite transported via Liverpool to Jamaica, 1748. [NA.T53.44]
PRINGLE, JAMES, in Jamaica, 1765. [NAS.GD18.4206]
PRINGLE, JAMES, born 1758, via London to Jamaica on the Dawes, Nov 1774. [NA.T47.9/11]
PRINGLE, JOHN ALEXANDER GORDON, born 1832, Ensign of the 3rd West Indian Regiment, died in Kingston, Jamaica, 31 July 1853. [Kingston MI]
PURDIE, ROBERT, from Lanark, died on Leogan Estate, Cornwall, Jamaica, Aug 1843. [EEC#20669][SG.XI.1228]
RADCLIFF, JAMES, indented in Edinburgh on 18 Mar 1741 for service in Jamaica. [CM#3273]
RADCLIFFE, Rev. J., of the Church of Scotland in Kingston, Jamaica, married Isabella, eldest daughter of A. D. Cooke, MD, Custos of St Mary's, in Green Park, St Ann's, Jamaica, 29 Jan1862. [S#2106]
RAE, WILLIAM, a merchant in Kingston, Jamaica, died 7 May 1837, inventory, 1837. [NAS.SC70.1.55; C1759]
RAINY, WILLIAM, in Jamaica, died 1836, inventory, 1847. [NAS.SC70.1.68]
RAIT, JOHN, a merchant in Jamaica, 1813, grandson of Duncan Clyde a cooper in Campbeltown, Argyll. [NAS. RS10.2329]
RAITT, ANDREW, a planter in St Andrew's, Jamaica, 1754. [NA.CO137/28/191]
RAMSAY, EBENEZER, born 1815, son of Ebenezer Ramsay and Margaret Flint in

Alloa, died in Jamaica, 3 Dec 1858. [Alloa MI]
RAMSAY, GEORGE, in Jamaica, 1759. [NLS.ms5078/5080]
RAMSAY, JOHN, an Anglican minister sent to Jamaica, 23 Sep 1759. [FPA]
RAMSAY, MARY, in Jamaica by 1738. [IRO.Attorney, 29.2-7/204]
RANKIN, ALEXANDER JOHNSTON, 2nd son of the late John Rankin in Greenock, died in Jamaica on 3 Oct 1833. [GrA: 9.12.1833]
RANKIN, HUGH, steerage passenger from Greenock to Jamaica aboard the Mary of Glasgow in Nov 1773. [NAS.CE60]
RANKIN, JAMES, in Hopetoun, St James, Jamaica, son of Alexander Rankin of Couston, a deed, 1813. [NAS.RD5.27.45]
RANKIN, JANE, eldest daughter of John Rankin a merchant in Greenock, married Hinton Spalding of Jamaica, in Greenock on 2 Apr 1811. [GrA:3.4.1811]
RANKIN, Mr., from Glasgow aboard the Mary bound for Jamaica, arrived in Kingston in May 1793. [JRG:18.5.1793]
RANKINE, JAMES, a planter and merchant in Jamaica 1788-1814, later in Dundee. [NAS.CS230.Sed.Bk.4/2]
RATTRAY, JAMES, of Chesterfield, St Andrew's, Jamaica, dead by 1812, father of Isabella and Jane. [NAS.CS97.107.38]
RATTRAY, JOHN, eldest son of Thomas Rattray, a merchant, and Janet Marshall, a merchant in Jamaica, from 1763. [GA.B10.15.7056]
RATTRAY, Mrs, of St Andrews, Jamaica, died on 2 Nov 1806, days after surviving the shipwreck of The Lily of Greenock . [GrA: 7.11.1806]
REDDIE, ANDREW, a gentleman in Hanover, Jamaica, died in Lucea, 15 Feb 1820, probate, 1820. [NA.Prob.11/1667][GkAd#2393]
REID, ALEXANDER, in Jamaica, probate, 1742, PCC.
REID, ALEXANDER, youngest son of James Reid in Ardoch, an overseer, Tryall Estate, Jamaica, died 3 Nov 1827, Orchard Estate, Jamaica. [AJ#4180]
REID, ANDREW, a rebel from Argyll, imprisoned in Edinburgh Tolbooth, who was transported from Leith to Jamaica on 7 Aug 1685. [ETR#369][RPCS.XI.328]
REID, COLIN, a jobber, St James, Jamaica, 1774. [BL.Add.MS22676/8]
REID, EBENEZER, born 1777, 'a schoolmaster...43 years in Kingston, Jamaica,' died on 25 May 1843, inventory, 1846. [Kingston Church MI][NAS.SC70.1.67; E897]
REID, EDWARD, in St David's, Jamaica, 1670. [SPAWI.1670/270]
REID, GEORGE, a planter in Jamaica, formerly a factor of the Royal African Company in Barbados, 1684. [SPAWI.1684/2030]; a petitioner in Jamaica, 19 Nov 1691. [ActsPCCol]
REID, ISABELLA, widow of Commander John Reid RN, died at Bunker's Hill, Jamaica, 20 Jan1878. [EC#29151]

SCOTS IN JAMAICA, 1655-1855

REID, JAMES, son of David Reid the Customs Collector in Edinburgh, to Jamaica, 1808. [NAS.GD51.1.195.50/52]

REID, JAMES, second son of Alexander Reid, South Castle Street, Edinburgh, died in St Dorothy's, Jamaica, 14 Jan 1822. [EEC#17275]

REID, JAMES, born 1815, arrived at Bluefields, Westmoreland, Jamaica, on 23 Jan 1841 aboard the William Pirie, from Stranraer. [NA.CO.140/33]

REID, Mrs JEAN, widow of William Henderson, Annotto River Plantation, died in St George's, Jamaica, 27 May 1829, inventory, 1854. [S.996][NAS.SC70.1.85; F1958]

REID, JOHN, born 1663, a groom, emigrated via London to Jamaica in Mar 1684. [CLRO/AIA]

REID, JOHN, born 1757, son of Mathew Reid and Mary Irving in Dornock, died in Jamaica, 25 Dec 1816. [Dornock MI, Dumfries-shire]

REID, JOHN LYNCH, died at John's Hall, Jamaica, 29 July 1856. [CM#20911]

REID, ROBERT, a merchant in Falmouth, Jamaica, died 28 Feb 1835, inventory, 1844. [NAS.SC70.1.66; E890][F.134]

REID, THOMAS, jr., a planter, New Canaan Estate, St James's, Jamaica, 1774. [BL.Add.MS22676/8]

REID, THOMAS, a merchant in Jamaica, 1779. [NAS.CS16.1.75]

REID, Dr THOMAS, eldest son of Robert Reid a land surveyor in Perth, died in Port Antonio, Jamaica, 11 Dec 1819. [S.4.164]

REID, WILLIAM, probate 26 May 1675, Jamaica.

REID, WILLIAM, 'late of Jamaica', died 11 Oct 1837. [Kilspindie, Perth, MI]

REID, WILLIAM, son of Dr Andrew Reid, 95 South Portland Street, Glasgow, died at Montego Bay, Jamaica, on 15 Dec 1841. [GSP#705]

REID, WILLIAM, born in Paisley 27 Mar 1811, son of Robert Reid a merchant, matriculated at Glasgow University in 1828, at Glasgow University in 1828, minister of Borgue 1843-1866, married Anna, third daughter of John Robert Tomlinson in Huntly, Manchester, Jamaica, 16 June 1849, and died in Huntly, Mandeville, Jamaica, on 25 Oct 1866. [MAGU][F.3.397][SG#18/1832]

RENNY, ALEXANDER, eldest son of Robert Renny a merchant in Jamaica, was granted Borrowfield, Montrose, 21 Dec 1795. [NAS.RGS.128.148]

RENNY, JAMES, a planter in Jamaica, 1780, a deed, 1783, died at Morant Bay, Jamaica, 22 Dec 1798, probate, 20 Mar 1800, PCC. [NLS#8794][AJ#2669][NAS.RD3.242.1202/67]

RENNY, ROBERT, late of Jamaica, then Montrose, Angus, 1787. [GA.TD219/6]

RENWICK, ALEXANDER, first son of William Renwick a merchant in Jamaica, matriculated at Glasgow University in 1811. [MAGU#258]

RENWICK, JOHN, second son of William Renwick a merchant in Jamaica, matriculated at Glasgow University in 1819. [MAGU]

SCOTS IN JAMAICA, 1655-1855

REYNALLS, EDWARD, from Jamaica, an apprentice surgeon, died in Edinburgh, 6 Sep 1751. [AJ#194]

RHIND, JOHN, a cooper in Jamaica, testament, 5 May 1789. [NAS.CC8.8.128]

RICCALTOUN, ADAM ALEXANDER, sixth son of Rev. John Riccaltoun in Hobkirk, Roxburghshire, died at Florence Hall, Jamaica, 18 Nov 1825. [EEC#17845]

RICHARD, THOMAS, a Covenanter from Greenock Mains, Muirkirk, Ayrshire, imprisoned in Edinburgh Tolbooth, who was transported from Leith to Jamaica on 7 Aug 1685. [RPCS.XI.329][ETR#369]

RICHARDS, ROBERT, in Kingston, Jamaica, a bond, 1767. [NAS.RD4.265.1001]

RICHARDSON, WILLIAM, born 1817, with Martha born 1817, and Catherine born 1831, arrived at Bluefields, Westmoreland, Jamaica, on 23 Jan 1841 aboard the William Pirie, from Stranraer. [NA.CO.140/33]

RICHMOND, WALTER, a merchant in Kingston, Jamaica, 1770. [NAS.RD4.211.55]

RICHMOND, WILLIAM, born 16 July 1780 in Irvine, Ayrshire, son of Rev. James Richmond and Margaret Cunningham, died in Jamaica, 25 June 1796. [F.3.100]

RIDDOCH, ALEXANDER, a witness in St James, Jamaica, 1787. [NAS.RD3.249.423]

RIDDOCK, JAMES, a carpenter, St James parish, Jamaica, 1774. [BL.Add.MS22676/8]

RITCHIE, ALEXANDER, settled in Jamaica 1763, an attorney and JP, died in Kingston on 3 Apr1807, probate 17 Sep 1807, PCC. [AJ#3101] [Kingston MI]

RITCHIE, EWING, a merchant in Kingston, Jamaica, 1806. [NAS.CS96/CS235.Seqn.2/2]

RITCHIE, JAMES, born 1819, son of John Ritchie and Margaret Henderson in Logie, died in Jamaica, 11 Nov 1861. [Logie MI, Stirlingshire]

RITCHIE, JOHN, in Molynes, Virgin Valley, St James, Jamaica, around 1770-1800. [NAS.B59.37.4.13/29]

ROBB, ALEXANDER, from Old Machar, Aberdeenshire, graduated MA from King's College, Aberdeen, 1848, a minister in Jamaica. [KCA#300]

ROBB, HENRY, in Kingston, Jamaica, inventory, 1873. [NAS.SC70.1.162]

ROBB, JOHN, of Brownberry, died in Jamaica 1802. [AJ#2853]

ROBB, JOHN, born 1817, second son of Alexander Robb jr of Bruckter, died in New Monklands, Jamaica, 7 June 1842. [AJ#4939]

ROBB, WILLIAM, in Jamaica, a deed, 1808; eldest son of John Robb the sheriff of Dunblane, was granted Duthieston, 2 June 1818. [NAS.RD3.325.1180; RGS.157.46.102]

ROBB, Miss, died in Brownberry, St Elizabeth's, Jamaica, 31 Mar1805. [CM#13073]

SCOTS IN JAMAICA, 1655-1855

ROBERTON, ROBERT, in St Thomas in the East, Surrey, Jamaica, died 1812, testament, 14 May 1817. [NAS.CC8.8.143]

ROBERTS, ABRAHAM, in Jamaica, a deed, 17 Apr 1791. [NAS.RD3.298.139]

ROBERTSON, ALEXANDER, in Jamaica, probate 1764, PCC.

ROBERTSON, ALEXANDER, in Jamaica, son of James Robertson of Bishopmill, 1768. [NAS.RS29.8.87]

ROBERTSON, ALEXANDER, late in Jamaica, then in Strathardle, Kirkmichael, Perthshire, a decreet, 1774, [NAS.CS16.1.285]; husband of Margaret Farquharson of Alrick, a sasine, 1788. [NAS.GD16.11.32]

ROBERTSON, ALEXANDER, an Anglican minister in Clarendon, Jamaica, from 1775. [FPA]

ROBERTSON, ALEXANDER, Naval Officer of Jamaica, died there 1791. [GM.61/1235]

ROBERTSON, ALEXANDER, a surgeon, late in Jamaica, married Lilias, dau of Alexander Wilson a merchant in Inverness, 25 Oct 1802. [GM.72/1224]

ROBERTSON, ALEXANDER, born 1793 in Old Meldrum, Aberdeenshire, '28 years in Jamaica', died at Hillside Pen, St David's, Jamaica, 1837. [AJ#4662]

ROBERTSON. ALEXANDER HAMILTON, born 1813, son of Rev. J. M. Robertson in Livingstone, died in St David's, Jamaica, 5 Aug 1832. [EEC#18858]

ROBERTSON, ALLAN, former Sheriff Clerk of Caithness, Paymaster of the 2nd West Indian Regiment, died in Spanish Town, Jamaica, 1 Aug 1849.[AJ#5307]

ROBERTSON, ARCHIBALD, in St Andrew's, Surrey, Jamaica, died Aug 1800, testament, 1801. [NAS.CC8.8.132]

ROBERTSON, ARCHIBALD, a physician and surgeon in Bellemont, St Elizabeth, Jamaica, died 11 Sep 1820, inventory, 1861. [NAS.SC70.1.110; G2359]

ROBERTSON, CHARLES, died in Jamaica before Feb 1792. [GCr#70]

ROBERTSON, Mrs CAROLINE, widow of John Robertson of Bellmont, Jamaica, a bond, 1821. [NAS.RD5.239.54]

ROBERTSON, DANIEL, eldest son of Captain Daniel Robertson in Calcutta, died in Fourpaths, Clarendon, Jamaica, 27 Mar 1849. [SG#18/1819]

ROBERTSON, DAVID, a saddler in Jamaica, died 1800, inventory, 1835. [NAS.SC70.1.50/333; D601]

ROBERTSON, DAVID, a seaman, died in the Old Calabar River, Jamaica, on 7 May 1856, inventory, 1857. [NAS.SC70.1.93; H246]

ROBERTSON, DONALD, an attorney in Jamaica, 1806. [NAS.RD3.313.88]

ROBERTSON, DUNCAN, a surgeon-physician in Jamaica, a witness, 1793. [NAS.RD3.263.659]

ROBERTSON, DUNCAN, born 21 Oct 1781, son of Rev. James Robertson and Isabella Graham in Callendar, to Jamaica. [F.4.340]

ROBERTSON, DUNCAN, of Carron Vale and Friendship Estate, Jamaica, a deed, 1821. [NAS.RD5.239.54]
ROBERTSON, DUNCAN, a councillor, died at Gilnock Hall, Jamaica, 9 May 1850. [GM.NS34/230]
ROBERTSON, FRANCIS, attorney at law, Kingston, Jamaica, 1792; 1805. [NAS.CS17.1.11/7][AUL.ms3175/206]
ROBERTSON, HENRY, a planter in Jamaica, 1780. [NLS.ms8794]
ROBERTSON, J., from Leith to Jamaica on the Roselle, arrived in Kingston in Apr 1793. [JRG:27.4.1793]
ROBERTSON, JAMES, a merchant in Jamaica, son of James Robertson of Bishopmills, 1740. [NAS.RS29.6.449]
ROBERTSON, JAMES, in Jamaica, probate 1763, PCC.
ROBERTSON, JAMES, born 11 Mar 1769, son of George Robertson and Ann Allan in Aberdeen, at King's College, Aberdeen, 1786-1790, later a surgeon in Jamaica. [KCA.2.366]
ROBERTSON, JAMES, in Savanna-la-Mar, Jamaica, 1780. [NA.CO137.1-35]
ROBERTSON, JAMES, in Jamaica, a burgess of Banff, 1783. [BanffBR]
ROBERTSON, JAMES, formerly in Georgia, then in Jamaica, a deed, 1787. [NAS.RD3.247.402]
ROBERTSON, JAMES, in Jamaica, 24 Apr 1784, 7 Mar 1788, 24 Feb 1789, [NAS.RS29.88.211; RS8.757]
ROBERTSON, JAMES, in Jamaica, married Maria, youngest daughter of Alexander Innes of Cathlaw, 4 Mar1789. [AJ]
ROBERTSON, JAMES, Clerk Signet, died Kingston, Jamaica, 1794. [GM.64/768]
ROBERTSON, JAMES, in Jamaica, 1807. [NAS.CS228.B.14.28]
ROBERTSON, JAMES, son of James Robertson MD in Jamaica, at King's College, Aberdeen, 1810-1814, graduated MA, MRCS, settled St Ann's, Jamaica. [KCA#2/409]
ROBERTSON, JAMES, born 1770, MA, died 12 Jan 1812. [Kingston MI, Jamaica]
ROBERTSON, JAMES, late in Jamaica, testament, 31 Aug 1816. [NAS.CC16.9.11,283]
ROBERTSON, JAMES, born 1800, son of James Robertson, died in Jamaica, 20 July 1819. [Duns MI]
ROBERTSON, JAMES, a civil engineer in Jamaica, died 14 Jan 1829, inventory/testament, 2 July 1829. [NAS.CC8.8.152; D54]
ROBERTSON, JOHN, a prisoner in Edinburgh Tolbooth, transported to Jamaica, 13 Sep 1726. [NAS.HH11.15]
ROBERTSON, JOHN, in Jamaica, letter, 1760. [NAS.RH1/2.977]
ROBERTSON, JOHN, a gentleman on Green Island, Jamaica, 1783. [NAS.CS17.1.2/217]

SCOTS IN JAMAICA, 1655-1855

ROBERTSON, JOHN, from Leith to Jamaica on the Roselle, arrived in Kingston in Apr 1793. [JRG:27.4.1793]
ROBERTSON, JOHN, a surgeon-physician in Jamaica, a witness, 1793. [NAS.RD3.263.659]
ROBERTSON, JOHN, late in Jamaica, then in Kelso, 1821. [NAS.CC18.4.5.82/108]
ROBERTSON, JOHN, in Bellemont, Jamaica, inventory, 1823. [NAS.SC70.1.26]
ROBERTSON, JOHN, in Kingston, Jamaica, died 1807, testament, 1836. [NAS.CC8.11.7.116]
ROBERTSON, JOHN, from Portobello, Lothian, in Jamaica, died 24 Sep 1833, inventory, 1834. [NAS.SC70.1.51; D663]
ROBERTSON, MARY MARGARET ADAM, dau of the late John Robertson, Belmont, Jamaica, married Chevalier Francis Sargent, chamberlain to the Duke of Lucca, in Paris, 29 May 1841. [GM.NS16/199]
ROBERTSON, PATRICK, in Jamaica, probate 1791, PCC.
ROBERTSON, PETER, in St Thomas in the East, Jamaica, 1821; deeds, 22 Aug1826, 1836. [NAS.RD5.330.159; 543.23; SC49.48.25.16/252; GD132.158]
ROBERTSON, ROBERT, a wharfinger, St James parish, Jamaica, 1774. [BL.Add.MS22676/8]
ROBERTSON, ROBERT, in St Thomas in the East, Jamaica, inventory, 1817. [NAS.SC70.1.15]
ROBERTSON, WILLIAM, a surgeon in Jamaica, spouse to Agnes Norie, possibly from Dundee, a decreet, 1773. [NAS.CS16.1.121]
ROBERTSON, WILLIAM, in St Ann's, Jamaica, was admitted as a burgess of Nairn on 8 Aug 1774. [NAS.GD1.1429.6.5; GD2.132]
ROBERTSON, WILLIAM, born 1737, late in St Ann, Jamaica, died 14 Sep 1825 in Brighton, England. [GM.95/286]
ROBERTSON, Captain, a planter in Northside, Jamaica, before 1700. [DP#305/313]
ROBINSON, ALEXANDER, Naval Officer of Kingston, 3rd son of James Robinson, Bishopmill, Moray, died in Port Royal, Jamaica, 19 Sep 1791. [GM.61/1062]
ROBINSON, ROBERT, born 1829, fourth son of Archibald Robinson a farrier in Greenock, died in Jamaica on 8 June 1843. [GrA:21.7.1843]
ROBINSON, ..., from Leith to Jamaica on the Roselle, arrived in Kingston in Apr 1793. [JRG:27.4.1793]
ROBISON, Dr GEORGE, of the Hospital Staff, died at Fort Charlotte, Lucea, Jamaica, 7 Jan 1804. [CM#121875]
ROBISON, WALTER, in Clarendon, Jamaica, 1773. [NAS.CS16.1.154/186]
ROCHEAD, JOHN, a merchant in Jamaica, burgess of Glasgow, 1719.[GBR]

SCOTS IN JAMAICA, 1655-1855

ROLLAND, ALEXANDER, second son of Patrick Rolland in Montrose, died in Jamaica, 22 Jan 1820. [EEC#17004]
ROLLAND, JAMES DAVID, died in Jamaica, 8 Apr 1820. [EEC#17006]
ROLLAND, PATRICK, born 1798, son of Patrick Rolland in Montrose, died in Jamaica, 22 Jan 1820. [MC#28]
ROME, JOHN, in Jamaica, eldest son of Peter Rome in Redkirk, 1782. [NAS.CS17.1.40/32]
RONALDSON, WILLIAM, son of William Ronaldson [1739-1817] and Marion Cleghorn [1734-1825] in Colinton, died at Martha Bay, Jamaica by 1840. [Colinton MI, Edinburgh]
RONEY, ALEXANDER, born 1827, son of John Roney and Mary Law, died in Kingston, Jamaica, 11 June 1853. [Dundee, Western, MI]
ROSE, ALEXANDER, born 1752, died in Westmoreland, Jamaica, 1807. [AJ#3099][Crosspath MI, Jamaica]
ROSE, ALEXANDER, MD, 40 years in Jamaica, died in St Elizabeth's, Jamaica, 24 Dec 1822. [DPCA#1074]
ROSE, HUGH, son of John Rose in Jamaica, at King's College, Aberdeen, 1789. [KCA#2.370]
ROSE, Dr JAMES, in St Ann's, Jamaica, a witness, 1774. [NAS.RD4.217.5]
ROSE, JOHN, from Aberdeenshire, in Jamaica, died 1 Aug 1775, testament, 27 Mar 1776. [NAS.CC8.8.123]
ROSE, JOHN, born 1810, son of Alexander Rose [1767-1846] and Mary Clark [1773-1850] in Summerfield, died 15 Nov 1838 on Treadways Estate, St Thomas in the Vale, Jamaica. [Alloway MI]
ROSE, WILLIAM, from Glasgow, died on Unity Valley Estate, Portland, Jamaica, 27 Apr 1844. [SG#1310]
ROSE, Mr, from Jamaica, was buried in St Nicholas kirkyard, Aberdeen, 25 Dec 1788. [ACA]
ROSE, Dr...., from Nairn, a physician in Jamaica, 1808. [NAS.GD171.914]
ROSS, ALEXANDER, son of John Ross, late from Jamaica, was buried in St Nicholas kirkyard, Aberdeen, 1 July 1778. [ACA]
ROSS, COLIN, a merchant in Jamaica, died 1779, testament, 4 May 1802. [NAS.CC8.8.133]
ROSS, GEORGE, a planter in St Thomas in the Vale, Jamaica, 1792-1794. [NAS.GD248.977.2; RD4.252.1397]
ROSS, HERCULES, in Jamaica, a burgess of Glasgow, 9 Oct 1782; was granted the lands of Rossie, 3 July 1784. [GBR][NAS.RGS.122.138]
ROSS, JAMES, second son of William Ross tacksman of Duochorly, died in Jamaica, 14 Nov 1822. [DPCA#1074]

ROSS, JAMES AMOSS, a merchant in Kingston, Jamaica, 1799. [see Thomas Gillespie's will, probate 16 Aug 1799, PCC]

ROSS, JOHN, a prisoner in Edinburgh Tolbooth, transported to Jamaica, Sep 1726. [NAS.HH11.15]

ROSS, JOHN, in Jamaica, 1760. [NAS.RH1.2.977]

ROSS, JOHN, born 2 May 1757, in Ross Isle, St Thomas in the East, Jamaica, died 13 Aug 1825. [St Andrew's MI, Jamaica]

ROSS, JOHN, MD, a physician at Montego Bay, died Sep 1863, testament, 1854, inventory, 1869, Comm. Edinburgh. [NAS.SC70.1.120; G3404][S#2588]

ROSS, Mrs MARGARET, in St Mary's, Jamaica, 1807. [NAS.GD417.211]

ROSS, PATRICK, a hairdresser in Kingston, Jamaica, 1829. [NAS.SC48.25.27/74]

ROSS, ROBERT, born 12 May 1769, a merchant, died 5 Oct 1824. [St Andrew's MI, Jamaica]; 1813, [NAS.RD5.111.653]

ROSS, STEWART, a witness in Kingston, Jamaica, 1783. [NAS.RD2.236/2.612]

ROSS, THOMAS, clerk to Thomas Gally an attorney at law in Kingston, Jamaica, 1789. [NAS.RD4.246.447]

ROSS, WILLIAM, a cooper in Port Royal, Jamaica, probate 7 Jan 1694, Jamaica.

ROSS, WILLIAM, born 1741, son of James Ross and Agnes Dunn in Mill of Towtie, died in Jamaica, 1798. [Fetteresso MI]

ROSS, WILLIAM, only son of Alexander Ross a doctor in Jamaica, at Glasgow University in 1778. [MAGU]

ROSS, WILLIAM, a merchant at Port Maria Bay, Jamaica, 1780. [NAS.CS16.1.179]

ROSS, WILLIAM, a merchant in Jamaica, son of David Ross in Roslin, 1783. [NAS.CS17.1.2/257]

ROSS, WILLIAM, in St Mary's, Jamaica, died 1802, testament, 1823. [NAS.CC8.8.149]

ROSS, WILLIAM, born 28 Apr 1753, died in Kingston, Jamaica, 19 July 1815. [Kingston MI]

ROSS, WILLIAM, late Attorney General of Jamaica, died in Bath, 16 Sep 1845. [AJ#5099]

ROSS, Dr, in Jamaica, 1760. [NAS.RH1.2.977]

ROSS, Mr., from Glasgow aboard the Mary bound for Jamaica, arrived in Kingston in May 1793. [JRG:18.5.1793]

ROUGHEAD, JAMES, a merchant in Port Royal, Jamaica, eldest son of Thomas Roughead of Whitsomehill, 1715. [NAS.RD3.144.151; RD4.117.295]

ROWAND, ANDREW, from Glasgow, died in Kingston, Jamaica, 1806. [AJ#3052]

RUDDACH, CHARLES, a plantation overseer in Jamaica, 1790. [NLS.ms5028/40]

SCOTS IN JAMAICA, 1655-1855

RUDDACH, JOHN, a physician at Montego Bay, Jamaica,eldest son of George Ruddach a vintner in Portsoy, Banffshire, a deed, 1787, a burgess of Banff, 1800. [NAS.RD3.249.423] [BBR]

RUPERT, Mr., from Glasgow aboard the Betsy and Brothers bound for Jamaica, arrived in Kingston in May 1793. [JRG:25.5.1794]

RUSSELL, CHARLES, gentleman in Kingston, Jamaica, 1783. [NAS.RD2.235/2.215]

RUSSELL, DAVID, a merchant who died at Black River, Jamaica, 10 Feb 1800. [AJ#2731]

RUSSELL, DAVID, JP, second son of David Russell and Mary Black in St Andrews, died on Mesopotamia Estate, Jamaica, on 24 Apr 1867. [St Andrews, Fife, MI] [S#7485]

RUSSELL, ROBERT, JP, eldest son of David Russell and Mary Black in St Andrews, Fife, died on Dry River Estate, Jamaica, 5 Aug 1867. [St Andrews MI] [S#7514]

RUSSELL, WILLIAM G., a book-keeper in Jamaica, 1883. [NAS.RS.Kirkcaldy.22.57]

RUTHERFORD, EBENEZER, a carpenter in Jamaica, died June 1804, testament, 15 May 1806. [NAS.CC8.8.136]

RUTHERFORD, JAMES, born 1732, died in Jamaica, 29 May 1791. [St Andrew's MI, Jamaica]

RUTHERFORD, JOHN, a gentleman in Port Royal, probate 18 Oct 1692, Jamaica.

RUTHERFORD, THOMAS, St James, Jamaica, 1774. [BL.Add.MS22676/8]

RUTHERFORD, ..., a planter, Equity Estate, St James, Jamaica, 1774. [BL.Add.MS22676/8]

RUTHVEN, JANE MIDDLETON, from Cults, Galloway, died on Good Intent, Westmoreland, Jamaica, 1853. [S.9.4.1853]

RUTHVEN DUGALD MALCOLM, born 1752, of the Cottage, Trelawney, Jamaica, died 3 Dec 1814, will, probate, Jamaica, 1815. [NA.Prob.11/1790][Cambridge MI, Jamaica]

RUTHVEN, JAMES VIRGO, a planter in Jamaica, died 12 Oct 1830, inventory, 1856. [NAS.SC70.1.92]

RYBURN, THOMAS, in Jamaica, co-owner of Glasgow ships, 1798, died in Kingston, Jamaica, 3 Sep 1799. [NAS.CE60.11.5/71/108] [AJ#2707]

SAMUELLS, PAUL STEVENS, born 1774, MD, in Edinburgh late in Negril Spots, Jamaica, died18 Nov 1850, inventory, 1851. [NAS.SC70.1.72; E2498][DeanMI]

SAUNDERS, JAMES, born 1795, son of Alexander Saunders in Banff, died in Jamaica, 3 Sep 1811. [Banff MI]

SAUNDERS, ROBERT, a ship carpenter, late of Jamaica, then in Dunfermline, will and testament, 20 July 1786. [NAS.B20.6.10.355/360]

SCOTS IN JAMAICA, 1655-1855

SAWERS, ALEXANDER, in Jamaica, 1773. [NAS.CS16.1.154]
SAWYERS, WILLIAM, from Stirling, '43 years in Jamaica', died there 1819. [S.3.145]
SCARLETT, Sir WILLIAM, Chief Justice of Jamaica, died 10 Oct 1831. [PA#124]
SCHANKS, ROBERT, a midshipman on HMS Iphigenia, youngest son of John Schanks, Eden Grove, Fife, died at Port Royal, Jamaica, 31 Jan 1820.[S.4.169]
SCHAW, JAMES ATKIN, in Jamaica, probate, 1769, PCC.
SCHAW, JAMES, born 1774, died Montego Bay, Jamaica, 30 Sep 1798. [Montego Bay MI]
SCOLLAY, JOHN, from Orkney, a merchant in Jamaica, 1788, 1800. [NAS.NRAS.0627, box 23, bundle 14; CS17.1.19/179]
SCORGIE, JOHN, born 1812, emigrated from Aberdeen aboard the Rob Roy bound for Jamaica, arrived at Kingston 11 May 1841. [NA.CO140.33]
SCOTT, ADAM, a millwright in St James, Jamaica, 1774. [BLAddms22676/8]
SCOTT, ANDREW, born in Penicuik, 25 Mar 1804, merchant in Kingston, Jamaica for 37 years, died in London 10 May 1857, buried in Glasgow Necropolis. [St Andrews MI, Jamaica]
SCOTT, ANDREW, jr, married Louisa, dau of Henry Mitchell in Kingston, Jamaica, on 29 May 1851. [W.1238]
SCOTT, ANDREW, born 1824, a merchant and magistrate in Kingston, Jamaica, died in Rothesay 29 Jan 1866. [St Andrew's MI, Jamaica]
SCOTT, ARCHIBALD, a merchant in Jamaica, died 21 Jan 1855, inventory, 1855. [NAS.SC70.1.88; F2137]
SCOTT, CHARLES, third son of Francis Scott of Harden, died in Jamaica, 1805. [AJ#3029]
SCOTT, EBENEZER, MD, surgeon on HMS Cornwallis, died in Port Royal, Jamaica, 30 Dec 1838. [AJ#4755]
SCOTT, Mrs ELIZABETH, born 1828, wife of Rev. John Scott, died at Montego Bay, Jamaica, 15 Nov 1848. [West Linton MI]
SCOTT, FRANCIS CARTERET, at Montego Bay, Jamaica, 1787; Customs Collector at Montego Bay, married Charlotte Elizabeth Cunningham, eldest daughter of Col. Cunningham of the Scots Brigade, 1801. [NAS.GD237.9.4.9][GM.71.11051]
SCOTT, GEORGE, son of Thomas Scott a merchant in Glasgow, died at Roaring River, Jamaica, 15 Aug 1798. [EA#3639]
SCOTT, GEORGE, Kinloss, Jamaica, was granted Woodend, Roxburghshire, on 20 Dec 1836. [NAS.RGS.212.5]
SCOTT, JAMES, in St Thomas's, Jamaica, 1670. [SPAWI.1670/270]
SCOTT, JAMES, from Comieston, died in Jamaica, 14 Oct 1801. [GM.72.83]
SCOTT, JAMES, born 6 June 1786 in Dundee, third son of Rev. James Scott and Margaret Munro in Auchterhouse, Angus, a planter at Leogane, St James, a

witness, 1818, died in Falmouth, Jamaica, 12 Dec 1824.
[NAS.RD5.144.504][EEC#17695][AJ#4024][F.5.310]
SCOTT, JOAN, daughter of George Scott and Isobel Pott, in Jamaica, 1779.
[NAS.CS16.1.175]
SCOTT, JOHN, a planter in St Andrew's, Jamaica, 1754. [NA.CO137/28/191-6]
SCOTT, JOHN, in Jamaica, probate 1792, PCC.
SCOTT, JOHN, born 1811, with Elizabeth Scott, born 1817, arrived at Bluefields, Westmoreland, Jamaica, on 23 Jan 1841 aboard the William Pirie, from Stranraer. [NA.CO.140/33]
SCOTT, Rev. JOHN, born 1820, son of Andrew Scott and Janet Penman, minister of the United Presbyterian Congregation of Montego Bay, Jamaica, died there 4 Dec 1848, his wife Elizabeth Snell died there 15 Nov 1848. [AJ#5271] [West Linton MI]
SCOTT, JOHN, from Glasgow, died at the Cottage, Falmouth, Jamaica, 1 Jan 1851. [W#1191]
SCOTT, LOUISA, wife of Archibald Scott, Falmouth, Jamaica, formerly in Greenock, died in Bath, St Thomas in the East, Jamaica, 22 Nov 1843. [GEP#839]
SCOTT, MARY, daughter of George Scott, late of Jamaica, died in Edinburgh, 22 Feb1789. [GM.XII.578.38]
SCOTT, MICHAEL, born at Cowlairs House on 30 Aug 1789, fifth son of Allan Scott a merchant in Glasgow, matriculated at Glasgow University in 1801, a merchant in Jamaica from 1806 to 1822, died in Glasgow on 7 Nov 1835. [MAGU][NAS.RD5.193.513]
SCOTT, THOMAS, in St Elizabeth's, Jamaica, probate 12 Aug 1684, Jamaica.
SCOTT, THOMAS, a surgeon in Port Royal, Jamaica, probate 25 Apr 1695, Jamaica.
SCOTT, THOMAS, born 25 Sep 1763, son of Rev. James Scott and Beatrix Mercer in Perth, died in Jamaica, 17 Aug 1814. [F.4.232]
SCOTT, Mr., cabin passenger from Greenock to Jamaica aboard the Mary of Glasgow in Nov 1773. [NAS.CE60.1.17
SCROGGIE, JOHN, in Jamaica, father of John, Alexander, Elizabeth, and Murdoch, a deed, 1776. [NAS.RD4.220.1144]
SCRYMGEOUR, HENRY, late in Jamaica, youngest son of David Scrymgeour of Birkhill, 1793; married Mary, daughter of Captain Frederick Maitland of Rankeillor, in Edinburgh, 3 Apr 1793. [NAS.NRAS#783/9][EMR]
SELBY, THOMAS, from Edinburgh, died in Jamaica, testament, 1829. [NAS.SC70.1.41]
SEMPLE, WILLIAM, a witness in Jamaica, 1806. [NAS.RD3.313.88]

SCOTS IN JAMAICA, 1655-1855

SETON, JOHN, in Collessie, Fife, late of Jamaica, a deed, 1777, a sasine, 1782. [NAS.RDD2.227.237; RS32.268]

SETON, JOHN, in Jamaica, testament, 7 Nov 1797. [NAS.CC8.8.130]

SHAND, FRANCIS, born in Kemnay, 2 Aug 1786, 2nd son of Rev. John Shand and Margaret Dauney, at King's College, Aberdeen, 1799-1803, a witness, 1816, an advocate who died in Spanish Town, Jamaica, 10 Mar 1827. [KCA.II.385][SAA]

SHAND, JOHN, in Spanish Town, Jamaica, was granted Arnhall, 2 June 1815; a deed, 1816. [NAS.RGS.151.6; RD5.92.619]

SHAND, WILLIAM, an estate manager in Jamaica, 1791-1823, later a merchant in Scotland, was granted Balmakewan, 2 June 1824. [NAS.CS46.1852; RGS.151.6]

SHAND,......, daughter of William Shand of Balmakewan, was born on Hopewell Plantation, St Ann's, Jamaica, 5 Sep 1825. [BM.XVIII.779]

SHANNAN, ARCHIBALD, born 1835, son of Archibald Campbell Shannan, a merchant in Jamaica, died in Maxwell Valley, Falmouth, Jamaica, 26 Dec 1838. [SG#8.745]

SHARP, JOHN, in Trelawney, Jamaica, 12 Oct 1860. [NAS.RS.Nairn.7/63]

SHAW, ALEXANDER, a bookseller, late of Turnbull and Shaw in Virginia, later in Kingston, Jamaica, Feb 1789. [NAS.CS17.1.7/90]

SHAW, ALEXANDER, in Jamaica, a witness, 1816. [NAS.RD5.97.266]

SHAW, ALEXANDER, first son of Rev. John Shaw in Greenock, at Glasgow University in 1766, died in Jamaica on 10 Aug 1804. [MAGU][GM.74.1071] [Caribbeana.4.15]

SHAW, ALEXANDER, in Jamaica, inventory, 1869. [NAS.SC70.1.145/356]

SHAW, DAVID, in St Mary's, Jamaica, testament, 17 Mar 1812. [NAS.CC8.11.VI/345]

SHAW, JAMES, Jamaica, a burgess of Edinburgh, 1763. [EBR]

SHAW, JAMES, in Jamaica, 1842. [NAS.NRAS#0050/43]

SHAW, JOSEPH, Drax Hall Estate, Jamaica, married Elizabeth, eldest daughter of Peter Stuart, at Birchbank, Craigellachie, Banffshire, 5 Jan 1876. [AJ#6679]

SHAW, LACHLAN, a planter in Hanover, Jamaica, probate, 1766, PCC. [NA.Prob.11/922]

SHAW, LACHLAN, born 27 Jan 1729, son of Rev. Lachlan Shaw and Anne Grant in Elgin, Morayshire, settled in Jamaica, died in London. [F.6.390]

SHAW, SUSAN GORDON, daughter of Captain A. Shaw of Dalnavert, married George Kinghorn Prince, MD, Agulto Vale, St Mary's, Jamaica, son of Thomas Prince in Jamaica, at Port Antonio on 23 Apr 1826; she died there on 9 Dec 1826. [EEC#17914][AJ#4128]

SHAW, SARAH, daughter of David Shaw of St Mary's, Jamaica, died 1 July 1835. [NAS.E859.16]

SCOTS IN JAMAICA, 1655-1855

SHAWE, ROBERT, in Kingston, Jamaica, died in London, 15 Oct 1818. [NAS.C430]

SHEARER, JAMES, born 1813, with Mary born 1811, Alexander born 1834, Jane born 1836, and Elizabeth born 1840, arrived at Bluefields, Westmoreland, Jamaica, on 23 Jan 1841 aboard the William Pirie, from Stranraer. [NA.CO.140/33]

SHEARER, JOSEPH, of Drax Hall Estate, Jamaica, married Elizabeth Jane, eldest daughter of Peter Stuart at Birchbank, Craigellachie, 5 Jan 1876. [AJ#6679]

SHERIFF, ALEXANDER, master of Elgin Grammar School, settled in Jamaica, 1765. [Elgin Town Council Minutes, 24.10.1765]

SHERIFF, ALEXANDER, possibly from Aberdeen, a surveyor in St Mary's, Jamaica, probate, 10 Mar 1802.[PCC.]

SHERIFF, DAVID, born 1751, son of David Sheriff in Aberdeen, Custos and representative in Assembly for St George's, Colonel of Foot Militia, died in Kingston, Jamaica, 4 Sep 1805. [St Andrew's MI, Jamaica]

SHIRIFF, JOHN DAVID, surgeon, son of Alexander Shireff advocate in Aberdeen, died in Port Antonio, Jamaica, 28 Nov 1824. [AJ#4022]

SHIRIFF, ROBERT P., to Jamaica, 1803. [NAS.NRAS.8.23.15]

SHIELDS, ALEXANDER, born 1661, son of James Shields, a miller, and his wife Helen Brown in Heughhead, Earlston, Berwickshire, educated at Edinburgh University around 1675, and at Utrecht University in the Netherlands, ordained as a Puritan minister in London during 1685, imprisoned in Newgate Gaol, London, Edinburgh Tolbooth, and on the Bass Rock, chaplain to the Cameronian Regiment in the Netherlands, a minister in St Andrews in 1697, appointed chaplain to the Second Expedition to Darien in 1699, emigrated from Greenock to Darien aboard the Rising Sun on 21 July 1699, at Caledonia Bay, Darien, on 2 Feb 1700, died in the house of Isobel Murray in Port Royal, Jamaica, on 14 June 1700. [F.7.655; F.5.239][Erskine's Journal#240/244]

SHIELDS, JOHN, born 1813, a bricklayer, arrived at Bluefields, Westmoreland, Jamaica, on 23 Jan 1841 aboard the William Pirie, from Stranraer. [NA.CO.140/33]

SHIELDS, MICHAEL, son of James Shields, a miller, and Helen Brown in Heughhead, Earlston, Berwickshire, emigrated to Darien in 1699, later settled in Jamaica. [F.5.239]

SHORTRIDGE, JOHN, born 1786, first son of William Shortridge a merchant in Glasgow, matriculated at Glasgow University in 1799, sometime in Jamaica, died in London on 22 Nov 1878. [MAGU]

SIBBALD, DAVID, planter, Trelawney, Cornwall, Jamaica, testament, 1772. [NAS.RD2.232/1.795]

SILVER, ALEXANDER, sometime in Jamaica, dead by 1797. [NAS.GD70.220]

SCOTS IN JAMAICA, 1655-1855

SIMPSON, ALEXANDER FRASER, second son of Rev. Alexander Simpson in Fraserburgh or New Machar, Aberdeenshire, at King's College, Aberdeen, 1812-1820, died in Vere, Jamaica, 24 July 1834. [AJ#4540][KCA.II.426]

SIMPSON, ALEXANDER, born 1780, died in Trelawney, Jamaica, 3 Oct 1844. [Falmouth MI, Jamaica]

SIMPSON, DAVID, son of William Simpson, schoolmaster, and Ann Hamilton in Dalkeith, a merchant in Jamaica, later in London, will and inventory, 1746, probate 1747, PCC, testament, 19 July 1756. [NA.Prob.11/753][NAS.CC8.8.116]

SIMPSON, GEORGE, in St Andrew's, Jamaica, probate 13 Sep 1693, Jamaica.

SIMPSON, GEORGE, a clerk in Kingston, Jamaica, son of George Simpson a merchant in Elgin, and Elizabeth Russell, a deed, 1788. [NAS.RD4.244.318]

SIMPSON, JOHN, a Covenanter from Garieside, Roxburghshire, imprisoned in Edinburgh Tolbooth, transported from Leith to Jamaica in Aug 1685, landed at Port Royal in Nov 1685. [RPCS.XI.330][ETR#369][LJ#15]

SIMPSON, SIMON, youngest son of Rev. Alexander Simpson in Fraserburgh, Aberdeenshire, died in Spanish Town, Jamaica, 5 Jan 1825. [AJ#4029]

SIMPSON, WILLIAM, a carpenter in St Catherine's, Middlesex, Jamaica, son of George Simpson a merchant in Elgin, a deed,1788. [NAS.RD4.318]

SIMS, ANDREW, sometime in Jamaica, died in Peterhead, Aberdeenshire, 9 Feb 1803. [Peterhead MI]

SINCLAIR, ARCHIBALD, a merchant and attorney in Spanish Town, an executor in 1750, [see NA PROB 11/778][EUL. Laing MS II.498]; in Jamaica, a decreet, 1773, possibly from Caithness; a bill of exchange, 1781; a deed, 1783. [NAS.CS16.1.129; RD2.235/1.39; RD2.236/1.651]

SINCLAIR, DANIEL, late a distiller in Jamaica, then in Stirling, testament, 4 June 1763, Comm. Stirling. [NAS]

SINCLAIR, DAVID, in Jamaica, 1719. [NAS.GD164.545]

SINCLAIR, DAVID, a mariner in Jamaica, testament, 10 July 1733. [NAS.CC8.8.95]

SINCLAIR, DIANA, born 1752, via London to Jamaica on the Fanny, Dec 1773. [NA.T47.9/11]

SINCLAIR, DUNCAN, a Covenanter, transported from Leith to Jamaica in Aug 1685. [RPCS.XI.136]

SINCLAIR, EDWARD, SSC, from Edinburgh, died at Mount Pleasant, Jamaica, the home of David Cooper, 22 Mar 1840. [EEC#20055]

SINCLAIR, JAMES, in Jamaica, possibly from Canisby, 1808. [NAS.GD139.390.2]

SINCLAIR, JOHN, a baker from Glasgow, died at Montego Bay, Jamaica, 31 Aug 1843. [SG.XI.1239]

SINCLAIR, JOHN, born 1817, arrived at Bluefields, Westmoreland, Jamaica, on 23 Jan 1841 aboard the William Pirie, from Stranraer. [NA.CO.140/33]

SCOTS IN JAMAICA, 1655-1855

SINCLAIR, KENNEDY, in Jamaica, 1772. [NAS.CS16.1.148/340]
SINCLAIR, MATTHEW, born 1808, second son of Lord Charles Sinclair and Mary Agnes Chisholm, late of the 84th Regiment, died at Fort Auga, Clarendon, Jamaica, 12 Aug 1827. [Clarendon MI]
SINCLAIR, ROBERT, an attorney, son of Robert Manson Sinclair of Bridgend, a deed, 1800; died in Spanish Town, Jamaica, 1801. [AJ#2779][NAS.RD4.289.454]
SINCLAIR, WILLIAM, born 1759, died in Hanover, Jamaica, 15 July 1795. [Winchester MI, Jamaica]
SINCLAIR, WILLIAM, at Martha Brae, Jamaica, 1812. [NAS.SC48.49.25.5/200]
SIVEWRIGHT, DAVID, in St Thomas, Jamaica, died 15 Nov 1847, inventory, 1852. [NAS.SC70.1.74; E2924]
SIVEWRIGHT, JOHN HENRY, born 1847, third son of C. K. Sivewright in Burntisland, died in Orange Valley, Jamaica, 23 Aug 1865. [Falmouth MI, Jamaica]
SKEEN, ANDREW, in Clarendon, Jamaica, probate 15 Nov 1692, Jamaica.
SKEEN, ROBERT, in Jamaica, probate 1760, PCC.
SKENE, ANDREW, Lieutenant of the 60th Regt., son of Captain Skene in Aberdeen, died in Jamaica, 6 Oct 1808. [SM.71.158]
SKENE, Dr JAMES, son of Professor Francis Skene in Aberdeen, MD 1766, a physician in South Carolina from 1767 to 1778, a Loyalist who settled in Kingston, Jamaica, by 1784. [NA.AO12.52.163; AO12.109.274][MCA]
SKINNER, FREDERICK NAPEAU, barrack-master, Maroon Town, Jamaica, died 10 July 1850, inventory, 1854, Comm. Edinburgh. [NAS]
SMAIL, JAMES, late in Jamaica, was granted Overmains, 3 Feb 1786. [NAS.RGS.123.162]
SMALL, JAMES, 3rd son of James Small in Montrose, died at Montego Bay, Jamaica, on 24 Nov 1821. [EEC#17257][AJ#3867]
SMALL, MARY, daughter of James Small, married John Linnell of Burret Pen, Hanover, Jamaica, at Montego Bay, Jamaica, 25 Mar 1841. [AJ#4871]
SMALL, ROBERT, eldest son of James Small in Montrose, died in Flamstead, Montego Bay, Jamaica, on 16 Oct 1821. [EEC#17257][AJ#3867]
SMART, ALEXANDER, son of .... Smart in Inchgrundie, died at Greenhill, St Ann's, Jamaica, 23 Dec 1833. [AJ#4501]
SMART, ROBERT, in Vere, Jamaica, probate 17 Sep 1694, Jamaica.
SMELLIE, JOHN, of Plotfield, Jamaica, at Torbanehill, Bathgate, by 1810. [NAS.NRAS.0623.137]
SMELLIE, THOMAS, of Dublin Castle, Jamaica, died in New York, 1801. [AJ#2822]
SMITH, ALEXANDER, in Jamaica, 1757. [NAS.CS16.1.99/122[

SMITH, ANDREW COVENTRY, born 1808, son of Joseph Smith and Margaret Clegg in Ruthwell, died in Jamaica, 25 Mar 1831. [Ruthwell MI, Dumfries-shire]
SMITH, ARCHIBALD, born 1810, Christian, born 1811, Craig, born 1833, and John, born 1835, emigrated from Aberdeen aboard the Rob Roy bound for Jamaica, arrived at Kingston on 11 May 1841. [NA.CO140/33]
SMITH, DAVID, died at Hampstead Park, Kingston, Jamaica, 6 Feb 1869. [S#7985]
SMITH, FRANCIS, born 1768, son of William Smith and Jean Currie in Gallhills, Kirkpatrick-Fleming, died in Jamaica, 22 Sep 1796. [Kirkconnel MI]
SMITH, J., at Stony Hill, Jamaica, 1785. [NAS.GD190.3.332]
SMITH, JAMES, son of George Smith a cotton manufacturer in Glasgow, died in Munce, St David's, Jamaica, 1804. [AJ#2970]
SMITH, JOHN, son of .... Smith and Elspet Strachan [1729-1797], settled in Jamaica. [Huntly, Aberdeenshire, MI]
SMITH, JOHN, born 1793, son of David Smith and Euphame Ramsay, died in Jamaica, 1820. [Dunnikier, Fife, MI]
SMITH, JOHN, a planter in Jamaica, inventory, 1872. [NAS.SC70.1.158]
SMITH, JOHN BAIRD, youngest son of Adam Smith, late of Stockbridge, died on passage from Jamaica to America, Feb 1823. [EEC#17501]
SMITH, PATRICK, a merchant, son of Patrick Smith, a merchant in Glasgow, and Janet Maxwell, to Jamaica, 1763. [NAS.B10.15.7085]
SMITH, ROBERT, formerly a mason in Jamaica, late portioner of Torryburn, testament, 12 Dec 1763, Comm. Stirling. [NAS]
SMITH, ROBERT, son of William Smith an agent in Jamaica, at Glasgow University in 1762. [MAGU]
SMITH, ROBERT, in Kingston, Jamaica, co-owner of the Nancy of Glasgow, 1805. [NAS.CE60.11.8/63]
SMITH, ROBERT, a planter at New Montbleau, Jamaica, later in Glasgow, testament, 29 Nov 1821. [NAS.CC9.7.81.243]
SMITH, Mr., from Glasgow aboard the Betsy and Brothers bound for Jamaica, arrived in Kingston in May 1793. [JRG:25.5.1794]
SMITH, ..., from Greenock aboard the brig Jane bound for Jamaica, arrived there in July 1794. [JRG:2.8.1794]
SNELL, ELIZABETH, wife of Rev. John Scott, died at Montego Bay, Jamaica, on 15 Nov 1848. [SG.18.1784]
SNODGRASS, ARCHIBALD, son of Hew Snodgrass [1747-1807] and Henrietta Somerville [1747-1798] in Paisley, a merchant in Jamaica. [Paisley MI]; lately in Glasgow, now in Jamaica, 1822. [NAS.CS228A.9.17]
SNODGRASS, HEW, first son of Hew Snodgrass a magistrate's clerk in Paisley, at Glasgow University in 1784, a merchant in Glasgow, settled in Blue

SCOTS IN JAMAICA, 1655-1855

Mountain Valley, 1815 then at Morant Bay, Jamaica, died at Port Royal, Jamaica, on 24 Oct 1819. [MAGU#140][S.4.155][AJ#3756][NAS.SC58.42.6.94; RD5.97.266; NRAS.2654.1.10] [Caribeanna.4.17]

SNODGRASS, NEIL, born 1774, son of Hew Snodgrass [1747-1807] and Henrietta Somerville [1747-1798], in Paisley, died in Jamaica, 1817. [S.I.48] [Paisley MI]

SOMERVELL, JAMES, son of David Somervell formerly in Glasgow then in Jamaica, matriculated at Glasgow University in 1745. [MAGU]

SOMERVILLE, JAMES, a planter on Forest Estate, Westmoreland, Jamaica, first son of John Somerville of Jenlaw and Marion Shiells, Process of Divorce, 1794, Comm. Edinburgh; a witness, 1766. [NAS.RD4.227.1187]

SPALDING, CHARLES ANTHONY, born 1825, fourth son of Hinton Spalding, MD, Custos Rotulorum of St Andrew's, Jamaica, Commissioner of Stamps for Jamaica, died at Nether Arthurlie the home of Henry Dunlop his uncle, 29 Aug1861. [S#1939]

SPALDING, COLIN ALEXANDER, fifth son of Hinton Spalding, MD, in Kingston, Jamaica, died at The Pen, Halfway Tree, Jamaica, 28 May 1863. [S#25101]

SPALDING, HELEN, second daughter of Hinton Spalding MD, Kingston, Jamaica, wife of William R. Myers, died in Westfield, Spanish Town, 22 Oct 1863. [S#2627]

SPALDING, HINTON, born 1790, MD in Kingston, Jamaica, died in Bremen, Germany, 2 June 1853. [EEC#22463]

SPALDING, STEWART, a planter in Jamaica, married Ann, daughter of Charles Spaldinf a confectioner in Edinburgh, 28 July 1796. [EMR]

SPALDING, WILLIAM SHAND, born 1821, third son of Hinton Spalding MD, died at Mount Atlas, Jamaica, 10 July 1839. [EEC#19943][SG#8/799]

SPALDING, ..., from Greenock aboard the Friends, Captain Dunlop, bound for Jamaica, arrived there in Oct 1794. [JRG:25.10.1794]

SPARK, WILLIAM, in St Thomas, Surrey, Jamaica, will, subscribed 1 Jan 1764, probate, 25 Aug 1767, Westmoreland County, Virginia.

SPEARS, JOHN, son of Henry Spears, died at Green River, Jamaica, 30 Sep 1837. [FH.4.1.1838]

SPENCE, GEORGE, Jamaica, MD, Edinburgh University, 1790. [EMG#22]

SPENCE, JAMES, a schoolmaster and minister, son of George Spence and his wife Christian Thorn in Inch, Aberdeenshire, emigrated in 1698, settled in St Mary's, Jamaica, died 1737. [APB.3.57][EBR.162/6294]

SPENCE, JOHN, a bricklayer, Clarendon, Jamaica, a witness, 1776. [NAS.RD2.220.656]

SPENCE, THOMAS, a surgeon, son of James Spence a perfumer in Edinburgh, died in Jamaica, Jan 1803. [AJ#2691][EEC#14269]

SCOTS IN JAMAICA, 1655-1855

SPENCER, THOMAS, second son of John Spencer a merchant in Jamaica, at Glasgow University, 1793. [MAGU#173]

SPIMMEN, JOHN, from Creetown, Kirkcudbright, aboard the Countess of Galloway on 15 Mar 1793 bound for Jamaica, arrived in Kingston in May 1793. [RJG:1.6.1793]

SPITTAL, WILLIAM, in St Thomas, Jamaica, died 21 Nov 1837, inventory, 1841. [NAS.SC70.1.60; C2562]

SPOTTISWOOD, JAMES, a merchant in Jamaica, married Barbara, daughter of James Syme a merchant or writer in Edinburgh, 25 Feb 1753; was granted Dunnipace, 6 Aug 1756 . [EMR][NAS.RGS.103/161; GD1.529.200/254/255/273]

STEEDMAN, ALEXANDER, son of Rev. John Steedman and Jean Kinnaird in Edinburgh, died in Jamaica, Oct 1735. [F.1.140]

STEEL, ALEXANDER, in Jamaica, 1850. [NAS.RD5.868.518]

STEEL, JOHN, eldest son of Mrs Steel in Cupar, died in Westmoreland, Jamaica, 27 Aug 1857. [FJ]

STEEL, MARY, daughter of Dr John Steel in Jamaica, married Louis Ruffen a manufacturer in Edinburgh, 16 Apr 1790. [EMR]

STEELE, JAMES, born 1794, eldest son of William Steele a schoolmaster in Dunbartonshire, MA Glasgow 1814, a minister in Kingston, Jamaica, 1821, died Sep 1822. [F.7.670]

STEELE, THOMAS, in Jamaica, a letter, 1694, 1699. [NAS.GD3.5.812]

STEELE, Mrs, and family, from Kingston, Jamaica, in June 1793 aboard the Roselle bound for Leith. [JRG:29.6.1793]

STEINSON, WILLIAM, born 1797, second son of James Steinson in Elgin, died on Quebec Estate, St Mary's, Jamaica, 22 Nov 1821. [AJ#3867]

STEPHEN, JOSEPH, born 1 Jan 1797, youngest son of Alexander Stephen farmer in Mains of Glenfarquhar and Isobel Robertson, died in Jamaica, 15 Jan 1821. [S.5.224][Fordoun MI]

STEPHENSON, ALEXANDER, born 1805, son of Richard Stephenson and Agnes Armstrong, died in Jamaica, 22 June 1826. [Graitney MI]

STEPHENSON, GEORGE, a planter in Jamaica, a deed, 1810. [NAS.RD3.336.235]

STEPHENSON, MARY FENTON, wife of William Turner, died in Wallingford, St Elizabeth's, Jamaica, 17 June 1838. [SG.7.716]

STEPHENSON, ROBERT, a carpenter in Kingston, Jamaica, will, 1792, father of George Stephenson, [NAS.RD2.305.110]

STEPHENSON, THOMAS, born 1797, son of Richard Stephenson and Agnes Armstrong, died in Jamaica, 3 Oct 1818. [Graitney MI]

STEPHENSON, WILLIAM, born 1795, son of Richard Stephenson and Agnes Armstrong, died in Newmills, St James, Jamaica, 18 June 1835, inventory, 1848, Comm. Edinburgh. [NAS.F692] [Graitney MI]

STEUART, ADAM, from Kilmarnock, in Kingston, Jamaica, will, 1783. [NAS.RD2.237.825]
STEUART, DONALD, from Kilmarnock, in Kingston, Jamaica, a witness, 1783. [NAS.RD2.237.825]
STEUART, PETER, born 1773, son of Robert Steuart and Janet Robertson, died in Jamaica, 1815. [Eccles MI]
STEVEN, WILLIAM, from Aberdeenshire, in Jamaica, testament, 24 Jan 1740. [NAS.CC8.8.103]
STEVENSON, Rev. ANDREW, MD, minister of the Presbyterian Church at Montego Bay, Jamaica, died there 14 Apr 1848. [SG#1724]
STEVENSON, ELIZABETH, daughter of Hamilton Stevenson in Jamaica, married John Stirling a grocer, in Edinburgh, 15 Jan 1796. [EMR]
STEVENSON, HAMILTON, in Jamaica, a deed, 20 Feb 1781. [NAS.RD2.231.892]
STEVENSON, HENRY, in Jamaica, died 7 July 1845. [NAS.F699]
STEVENSON, JAMES, born 29 Mar 1767 in Glasgow, first son of Nathaniel Ross a merchant, at Glasgow University in 1779, died in Jamaica. [MAGU#126] [Caribeanna.4.15]
STEVENSON, JAMES, a planter in Jamaica, died 24 May 1844, inventory, 1847. [NAS.SC70.1.67; E1165]
STEVENSON, JOHN, in Kingston, Jamaica, a deed, 1783. [NAS.RD2.234.1440]
STEVENSON, THOMAS, first son of Thomas Stevenson in Jamaica, at Glasgow University in 1821. [MAGU]
STEWART, ADAM, a planter in St David's, Jamaica, probate 11 Nov 1696, Jamaica.
STEWART, AGNES, late of Kingston, Jamaica, widow of Dougall Stewart a merchant in Kingston, Jamaica, a deed, 1777. [NAS.RD3.237/1.36]
STEWART, ALEXANDER, in Jamaica, probate, 1781, PCC.
STEWART, ALEXANDER, born 1818, and Ellen, born 1823, arrived at Bluefields, Westmoreland, Jamaica, on 23 Jan 1841 aboard the William Pirie, from Stranraer. [NA.CO.140/33]
STEWART, ANGUS, a prisoner in Edinburgh Tolbooth, transported to Jamaica, 1726. [NAS.HH11.15]
STEWART, ARCHIBALD, HM Hospital in Jamaica, 1704. [NLS.Melville MS163.13]
STEWART, ARCHIBALD, died in Jamaica before Feb 1792. [GCr.70]
STEWART, CHARLES, fifth son of Charles Stewart of Redshieland and Isabel Haldane, died in Jamaica, 1767. ['Stewarts of Appin']
STEWART, DANIEL, in St Elizabeth's, Jamaica, 1771. [NLS.ms5320]
STEWART, DAVID ROBERTSON, died in Jamaica, 10 May 1834. [SG#262]
STEWART, DOUGALD, a merchant in Jamaica, relict of Agnes Muirhead in Falkirk, testament, 8 Mar 1795, Comm. Stirling. [NAS]

SCOTS IN JAMAICA, 1655-1855

STEWART, DUNCAN, born 1737, died at Ramble Pen, Clarendon, Jamaica, 28 Apr 1798. [AJ#2638][NAS.NRAS.0630, dr.2, bundle 29; NRAS.2654.2.6]

STEWART, DUNCAN, of Flowerhill, St Thomas in the East, Jamaica, a witness, 1792. [NAS.RD3.256.777]

STEWART, FRANCIS, in St David's, Jamaica, died 10 July 1864, inventory, 1865. [NAS.SC70.1.125; H1860]

STEWART, GEORGE, born 1722, died 23 Mar 1755. [Kingston, Jamaica, MI]

STEWART, GEORGE, born 1821, a laborer, with Ann, born 1822, emigrated from Aberdeen aboard the Rob Roy bound for Jamaica, arrived at Kingston on 11 May 1841. [NA.CO140/33]

STEWART, ISABELLA, fourth daughter of Dr James Stewart, Mayday Hill, Jamaica, married John William McDonald a writer in Edinburgh, 26 Mar 1832.[FH.526]

STEWART, JAMES, in Jamaica, 1694. [SPAWI.1699.443]

STEWART, JAMES, a millwright in Flowerhill, St Thomas in the East, Surry, Jamaica, a deed, 1792. [NAS.RD3.256.777]

STEWART, JAMES, in St Mary's, Jamaica, a witness, 1798. [NAS.RD3.281.13]

STEWART, JAMES, in St Catherine's, Middlesex, Jamaica, a deed, 1813. [NAS.RD5.55.275]

STEWART, JAMES, in Spanish Town, Jamaica, 1815. [NAS.SC49.48.25.9.143]

STEWART, JAMES, late in Jamaica, died in Perth, 2 Feb 1823. [DPCA#1076]

STEWART, Hon. JAMES, died in Islington Pen, St Andrew's, Jamaica, 25 Mar 1824. [FH#120][EEC#17593]

STEWART, JAMES GILLESPIE, born 29 Sep 1813 in Blair Atholl, son of Rev. John Stewart and Ann Wight, died in Greenpark, Falmouth, Jamaica, 23 Aug 1851. [F.4.145][Green Park MI, Jamaica]

STEWART, JOHN, at Montego Bay, Jamaica, and Jean Buchan from Edinburgh, a marriage contract, 1807. [NAS.RD5.265.753; RD5.266.23]

STEWART, JOHN, a clerk in Kingston, Jamaica, 1824. [NAS.NRAS.0623.JMT/2]

STEWART, MALCOLM, in Jamaica, died 13 Nov 1840 in Edinburgh. [NAS.C2489]

STEWART, MARGARET, born 1810, arrived at Bluefields, Westmoreland, Jamaica, on 23 Jan 1841 aboard the William Pirie, from Stranraer. [NA.CO.140/33]

STEWART, ROBERT, youngest son of James Stewart of Tar, died in Land Rumney, St Mary's, Jamaica, 1801. [AJ#2822]

STEWART, ROBERT, born 1799, died in Jamaica, 1824. [Kirkmichael, MI, Banff]

STEWART, THOMAS, late of Jamaica, will, 28 July 1706. [NAS.RH15.14.100]

STEWART, Rev. THOMAS, born 1766, son of James Stewart of Rothesay, an Anglican minister to Jamaica, 19 Aug 1792, died in Westmoreland, Jamaica, 19 May 1820. [FPA][Savanna-la-Mar MI]

SCOTS IN JAMAICA, 1655-1855

STEWART, WALTER GEORGE, born 1801, died 1 June 1864. [Spanish Town Cathedral MI]
STEWART, WILLIAM, via Portsmouth to Jamaica on the Richmond Sep 1775. [NA.T47.9/11]
STEWART, WILLIAM, at Crawl River, Clarendon, Jamaica, a deed, 1776. [NAS.RD2.220.656]
STEWART, WILLIAM, a merchant in Ayr, then in Jamaica, 1779. [NAS.CS16.1.175]
STEWART, WILLIAM, Jamaica, married Maria Odelia van Hoogment, daughter of Gerevid van Hoogmert a merchant in La Rochelle, France, 3 Jan 1780.[EMR]
STEWART, WILLIAM, in Jamaica, son of James Stewart a farmer in Hazlehead. [NAS.RS54.PR38/27]
STEWART, Dr, settled in Port Morant, Jamaica, before 1700. [DP#305]
STEWART, Mr., cabin passenger from Greenock to Jamaica aboard the Mary of Glasgow in Nov 1773. [NAS.CE60]
STEWART, Mr., from Kingston, Jamaica, in June 1793 aboard the Roselle bound for Leith. [JRG:29.6.1793]
STEWART, ..., from Greenock to Jamaica on the Bell, arrived in Kingston in Jan 1793. [JRG:19.1.1793]
STEWART, Mr., from Glasgow aboard the Betsy and Brothers bound for Jamaica, arrived in Kingston in May 1793. [JRG:25.5.1794]
STIRLING, ARCHIBALD, a planter, Hampden Estate, St James, Jamaica, 1774. [BL.Add.MS22676/8]
STIRLING, CHARLES, a planter in Jamaica, 1763-1797. [NAS.GD24.1.459/461]
STIRLING, GEORGE, born 20 Aug 1768, seventh son of William Stirling a merchant in Glasgow and Mary Buchanan, died in Jamaica, 15 Aug 1790. ['Stirlings of Cadder', St Andrews, 1933, p.56]
STIRLING, HENRY, born 8 Dec1719, third son of Dr William Stirling and Janet Smith in Glasgow, died in Jamaica, 9 June 1745. ['Stirlings of Cadder', p.52]
STIRLING, ISABELLA, daughter of Robert Stirling in Jamaica, married William Trotter a merchant in Edinburgh, 17 June 1781. [EMR]
STIRLING, JAMES, a merchant in Kingston, Jamaica, 1765. [NAS.GD201.5.130]
STIRLING, JOHN, born 23 Feb1768, second son of William Stirling of Cadder, at Glasgow University 1789, settled in Hampden Estate, St James, Jamaica, died 24 Mar 1795. [Hampden MI, Jamaica][MAGU#128]
STIRLING, JOHN, owner of Content Plantation, St James, Jamaica, 1789. [GA.T-SK11/3/147]
STIRLING, PATRICK, in Port Royal, Jamaica, around 1710. [NAS.B59.38.1]

SCOTS IN JAMAICA, 1655-1855

STIRLING, PATRICK, a planter, Content Estate, Hampden, St James, Jamaica, 1774; at Montego Bay, 1775. [BL.Add.MS22676/8][NAS.GD24.1.459; NRAS.8.24.9]

STIRLING, ROBERT, son of James Stirling of Keir, a planter in Jamaica, 1742, a merchant in Kingston, Jamaica, 1746, a burgess and guildsbrother of Ayr, 4 Apr 1751. [GA.T-SK.11.2.38]['Stirlings of Keir', Edinburgh, 1858, p.539][AyrBR]

STIRLING, ROBERT, a merchant in Jamaica, co-owner of the Jane of Glasgow, 1806. [NAS.CE60.11.8/1]

STIRLING, WILLIAM, of Auchyle, a surgeon in Jamaica, 1732. [NAS.GD171.4209]

STITT, EDWARD, a Covenanter from Durisdeer, Dumfries-shire, imprisoned in Edinburgh Tolbooth, transported from Leith to Jamaica in Aug 1685. [RPCS.XI.145][ETR#372]

STORRAR, LAWRENCE, late of Lucea, Hanover, Jamaica, died in Auchtermuchty, Fife, 3 Jan 1848. [FJ][FH]

STOTHART, JAMES, born 1774, son of Andrew Stothart and Mary Little in Gretna, settled at Montego Bay, Jamaica, died 6 Feb 1818. [Montego Bay MI]

STRACHAN, CHARLES, son of Charles Strachan and Elizabeth Smart [1750-1831] in Edzell, settled on Southampton Island, Jamaica. [Edzell MI, Angus]

STRACHAN, DAVID, a barber in Port Royal, Jamaica, administration, 2 Aug 1722, New York.

STRACHAN, JAMES, son of William Strachan and Ann Tyler, died in Jamaica, 4 Mar 1841. [Arbroath Abbey MI]

STRACHAN, WILLIAM R., son of Dr J M Strachan in Dollar, died in St Elizabeth's, Jamaica, 16 Aug 1860. [S#1638]

STRAITON, WILLIAM, a merchant in Jamaica, dead by 1743. [NAS.GD170.3353]

STRATTON, THOMAS, a merchant in Kingston, and an executor in 1750. [see NA PROB 11/778]; a burgess and guildsbrother of Ayr, 4 Apr1751. [AyrBR]; a planter, St Andrew's. Jamaica, 1754. [NA.CO137.28]

STRATTON, THOMAS, in Kingston, Jamaica, sister of Ann Stratton wife of Patrick Cushnie in Stonehaven, 1821. [NAS.RD5.214.245]

STUART, ARTHUR, died in Jamaica, probate 1658, PCC.

STUART, DANIEL, in St Elizabeth's, Jamaica, dead by 1771.[NLS.ms5320.80/4]

STUART, JAMES COULTER, youngest son of Captain Stuart of Dullatur, died at Ardoch Pen, St Ann's, Jamaica, 19 Apr 1826. [AJ#4099]

STUART, JOHN, a merchant in Kingston, Jamaica, later in Glasgow, 1852. [NAS.CS313.858]; possibly died at 9 Roseberry Terrace, Glasgow, 2 Mar 1877. [EC#28838]

STUART, ROBERT, a schoolmaster who emigrated to Jamaica on 3 Jan 1689. [Rawlinson MS#A306/93]

SCOTS IN JAMAICA, 1655-1855

STUART, WILLIAM MILLER, MD, son of John Stuart a tobacconist in Glasgow, died in Kingston, Jamaica, 6 May 1832. [AJ#4408]
STUART, ..., in Jamaica, 1709. [BM.Sloane#4042/65]
SURGEON, JOHN, a gentleman in Jamaica, a burgess and guildsbrother of Ayr, 4 Apr 1751. [AyrBR]
SUTHERLAND, ANNE, died 1 Dec 1791. [Kingston MI, Jamaica]
SUTHERLAND, ARTHUR, in Jamaica, father of James Cubbiston Sutherland who was apprenticed as a writer, and later admitted to the Society of Writers to the Signet, 3 July 1820. ['History of the Society of Writers to H M Signet', Edinburgh, 1890]
SUTHERLAND, DONALD, a planter, St George, Surry, Jamaica, son of Rev. John Sutherland and Ann.... in Tain, a deed, 1780; testament, 27 Nov 1801. [NAS.RD2.228/2.652; CC8.8.132]
SUTHERLAND, JAMES, born 1734, a merchant in Jamaica, died 12 Feb 1796. [Kingston MI, Jamaica] [NAS.RD2.264.402]
SUTHERLAND, ROBERT, of Dunrobin, Jamaica, 1775. [NAS.CS16.1.185/187]
SUTHERLAND, THOMAS, a cooper in Kingston, Jamaica, a witness, 1783. [NAS.RD2.234.1440]
SUTHERLAND, WILLIAM, of Greenwall, died in Jamaica, 1817. [S.I.29]
SUTHERLAND, WILLIAM, in Jamaica, 25 July 1826. [NAS.RD5.328.502]
SUTHERLAND, ..., a merchant, emigrated via Greenock to Jamaica, 1757. [AUL.ms1160.5.12]
SWINTON, JOHN, a joiner in Port Royal, Jamaica, probate 26 Feb 1678, Jamaica.
SYLVESTER, GEORGE F., died on Content Estate, Hanover, Jamaica, 24 Jan 1862. [S#2095]
SYMONS, JAMES, born 1820, a carpenter, emigrated from Aberdeen aboard the Rob Roy bound for Jamaica, arrived at Kingston on 11 May 1841. [NA.CO140/33]
SYMPSON, ALEXANDER, in Jamaica, probate 1798, PCC.
TAIT, ROBERT, born in Jamaica, only son of Robert Tait a merchant, at Glasgow University in 1790. [MAGU]
TAIT, WILLIAM, third son of Charles Tait and Mary Erskine in Chapel of Garioch, settled in Jamaica, died at Annetto Bay, 5 June 1826. [SAA]
TARBAT, JAMES, a writer in Jamaica, 1793. [NAS.RD4.254.934]
TATE, JOHN, clerk to Cruickshank, Finlayson, and Haldane, attornies at law in Spanish Town, Jamaica, 1808. [NAS.RD3.326.769]
TAYLOR, ALEXANDER, a witness in Jamaica, 1775. [NAS.RD4.718.871]
TAYLOR, ALEXANDER, born 1840, MD, from Invergordon, died at Annetto Bay, Jamaica, 23 Dec 1872, [Annotto Bay MI]

TAYLOR, ANN HELEN, second daughter of Alexander Taylor in Glasgow, married James Paterson, Monklands, St Thomas-in-the-East, Jamaica, in St Andrew's church, Jamaica, 8 Jan 1846. [AJ#5122]
TAYLOR, CHARLES JOHNSTONE, fourth son of Robert Taylor lately a merchant in Jamaica, at Glasgow University in 1842. [MAGU]
TAYLOR, JAMES, in Jamaica, formerly a writer in Cupar, eldest son of William Taylor a feuar in Pitlessie, 1800. [NAS.CS26.916.54]
TAYLOR, JOHN, a merchant in Jamaica, co-owner of the Mercury of Glasgow, 1795. [NAS.CE60.11.4/21]
TAYLOR, JOHN, in Bardowie, Jamaica, died 1800, inventory, 1831. [NAS.SC70.1.45; D279]
TAYLOR, JOHN, in Jamaica, a deed, 8 July 1825. [NAS.RD4.20.281]
TAYLOR, JOHN, of Ballochneck, eldest son of Rev. Dr William Taylor in Glasgow, died in Bardowie, St Andrew's, Jamaica, 17 Aug1829. [S#1029]
TAYLOR, SIMON, in Kingston, Jamaica, 1773, 1776, 1787-1795. [NLS.Acc.8793] [NAS.RD4.249.742; GD22.1.314-316]
TAYLOR, SIMON, in Pleasant Hill, Jamaica, second son of John Taylor of Kirktonhill, died in Kingston, Jamaica, 1 Nov 1838. [AJ#4746]
TAYLOR, ..., from Greenock to Jamaica on the Bell, arrived in Kingston in Jan 1793. [JRG:19.1.1793]
TELFER, JAMES, in Jamaica, 1779. [NAS.CS16.1.175]
TELFER, ROBERT, born 1796, son of Robert Telfer and Elizabeth Dykes in Dunning, Perthshire, died in Oldbury, Jamaica, 21 Oct 1839. [Dunning MI]
TEMPLETON, JAMES, in Jamaica, testament, 4 Nov 1829. [NAS.CC8.8.132/242]
TENNANT, AGNES, wife of David Fraser a merchant in Jamaica, 1771. [NAS.RS27.192.342]
TENNANT, JAMES, a wharfinger, St Thomas in the East, Jamaica, a witness, 1813. [NAS.RD5.44.858]
THOM, JOHN, born 1800, third son of John Thom a merchant in Glasgow, and brother of Robert Thom the British Consul in Ningpo, China, a land surveyor, died at Middleton College, Clarendon, Jamaica, 15 Apr 1851. [W#1224][AJ#5396]
THOMAS, JOHN, second son of George Thomas a surgeon in Jamaica, at Glasgow University, 1813. [MAGU#271]
THOMPSON, ROBERT, from Creetown, Kirkcudbright, aboard the Countess of Galloway on 15 Mar 1793 bound for Jamaica, arrived in Kingston in May 1793. [RJG:1.6.1793]
THOMSON, ADAM, born 1 Oct 1820 in Paisley, died at Prospect Hill, Montego Bay, Jamaica, 9 Dec 1897. [Montego Bay MI]

SCOTS IN JAMAICA, 1655-1855

THOMSON, ADAM, a missionary in Jamaica, married Agnes, youngest daughter of the late Captain William Currie, at Seafield Cottage, Greenock, on 22 Jan 1850. [GrA:22.1.1850]

THOMSON, AGNES, in Jamaica, died 19 Dec 1850, inventory, 1852. [NAS.SC70.1.77; F1553]

THOMSON, ALEXANDER, an attorney in Jamaica, a burgess of guildsbrother of Ayr, 4 Apr 1751. [AyrBR]

THOMSON, ALEXANDER, a surgeon, St Thomas in the Vale, Middlesex, Jamaica, a deed, 1772. [NAS.RD2.771/1.170]

THOMSON, ALEXANDER, Jamaica, married Rachel Pattullo, 10 Feb 1789.[EMR]

THOMSON, ARCHIBALD, a Covenanter who was transported from Leith to Jamaica in Aug 1685. [RPCS.XI.329]

THOMSON, ARCHIBALD, steerage passenger from Greenock to Jamaica aboard the Mary of Glasgow in Nov 1773. [NAS.CE60]

THOMSON, ARCHIBALD, of Hillhead, Jamaica, from Hillhead, Glasgow, a decreet, 1820; died 9 Mar 1821. [NAS.CS42.27.47][S.4.226]

THOMSON, ARCHIBALD, in Jamaica, 3 May 1833. [NAS.RS10.318]

THOMSON, ARCHIBALD, born 1840 in Moray, died in New Orleans during Mar 1872, buried at Port Antonio, Jamaica, 3 May 1872. [Port Antonio MI]

THOMSON, DAVID, a merchant in Kingston, Jamaica, 1761. [NAS.GD180.418]

THOMSON, DONALD, a Covenanter from Argyll who was transported from Leith to Jamaica in Aug 1685. [RPCS.XI.329]

THOMSON, DUGALD, from Cardross, a merchant in Jamaica, 1802, testament, 6 Dec1823. [NAS.RS10.1341; CC9.7.81]

THOMSON, DUNCAN, a rebel from Argyll who was transported from Leith to Jamaica in Aug 1685. [RPCS.XI.130]

THOMSON, Hon. EDWARD, died in Spanish Town, Jamaica, 20 Jan 1860. [S#1438]

THOMSON, GEORGE, son of James Thomson, a mason and wright in Kirkton of Blantyre then an indentured servant for 3 years in Jamaica, 1742-1745. [NAS.GD1.1732.17]

THOMSON, JAMES, a mason and wright in Kirkton of Blantyre, later in Jamaica, 1742. [NAS.GD1.732.17]

THOMSON, JAMES, a planter, Coffee Vale Plantation, Surry, Jamaica, only son of William Thomson and Christian Laidlaw in Linton, Tweedale, a deed, 1811. [NAS.RD5.17.657]

THOMSON, JAMES, in Cornwall, Jamaica, died 1 Jan 1829, inventory, 1831. [NAS.SC70.1.43; C334]

SCOTS IN JAMAICA, 1655-1855

THOMSON, JAMES, born 1765, son of John Thomson a merchant in Dumfries, and a nephew of bailie Robert Thomson, '44 years in Rio Bueno, Jamaica', died there 29 May 1831. [PA#106]

THOMSON, JOHN, in Jamaica, 1782. [NAS.CS17.1.1/61, 123]

THOMSON, JOHN, born 1793, son of John Thomson a shoemaker in Aberdeen and Margaret Mitchell, died in Jamaica, Dec 1830. [Banchory-Devenick MI]

THOMSON, JOHN, of Whitefield Hall, Jamaica, natural son of George Thomson in Aberdeen, died May 1839. [NAS.P3.16/59]

THOMSON, JOHN, in Jamaica, later in Montrose, testament, 2 Mar 1814. [NAS.CC3.126]

THOMSON, JONATHAN, born 1730 in Kirkhill, son of Rev. Robert Thomson and Mary Calder, died in Jamaica, 2 Dec 1748. [F.5.473]

THOMSON, KENNETH, born 29 Dec1766 in Durness, son of Rev. John Thomson and Mary Robertson, died in Kingston, Jamaica, 24 July 1794. [F.7.102]

THOMSON, MACKAY, born 11 Dec 1784 in Durness, son of Rev. John Thomson and Mary Robertson, died in Kingston, Jamaica, 1803. [F.7.102]

THOMSON, NEIL, a Covenanter from Argyll who was transported from Leith to Jamaica in Aug 1685. [RPCS.XI.136]

THOMSON, PETER, son of John Thomson in Burntisland, Fife, died in Kingston, Jamaica, 1803. [GM.72.374]

THOMSON, ROBERT, Jamaica, married Jean, daughter of Robert Kennedy of Daljarrock, Maybole, Ayrshire, in Edinburgh, 30 Dec 1795. [EMR][CM#11599][NAS.RD2.271.479][GM.66.80]

THOMSON, ROBERT, first son of Robert Thomson a farmer in the parish of Urr, Galloway, matriculated at Glasgow University in 1843, later studied theology at the United Secession Hall, then a catechist in Jamaica. [MAGU]

THOMSON, ROBERT CRAIG, of Sion House, Kingston, Jamaica, died in Manchester, Jamaica, 9 Feb 1854. [S.15.3.1854][EEC#22554]

THOMSON, WILLIAM, from Jamaica, died in Bath, 1817. [S.16]

THORBURN, ADAM WILSON, a planter in Clarendon, Jamaica, 1828. [NAS.CS17.1.47/242]

TIER, ANDREW, born 1815, with Rosanna born 1816, William born 1834, Andrew born 1836, and E;izabeth born 1840, arrived at Bluefields, Westmoreland, Jamaica,on 23 Jan 1841 aboard the William Pirie, from Stranraer. [NA.CO.140/33]

TINSLEY, GEORGE, born 1826, a laborer, arrived at Bluefields, Westmoreland, on 23 Jan 1841 aboard the William Pirie, Jamaica, from Stranraer. [NA.CO.140/33]

TOD, JOHN and CHARLES, merchants in Kingston, Jamaica, 1762. [NAS.AC.Decreet. Vol.50]

TODD, JOHN, educated in Edinburgh, a physician in Jamaica, FRCS Edinburgh 1753, MD from Marischal College, Aberdeen, 1792. [MCA]
TOD, OLIVER, sometime a merchant in Kingston, Jamaica, later a Captain of the Honorable East India Company. 1762. [NAS.AC.Decreets.50]
TOP, ADAM, late in Jamaica, died at 53 Constitution Street, Aberdeen, 26 Aug 1868. [S#7824]
TORRANCE, JAMES, merchant of the House of Torrance and McLeod, died in Kingston, Jamaica, 1817. [S.2.60]
TORRANCE, WILLIAM C., born 1822, assistant surgeon of the Royal Navy in Jamaica, eldest son of Collector Torrance in Greenock, died in the RN Hospital in Jamaica on 24 Oct 1848. [GrAd: 12.12.1848]
TOSHACH, WILLIAM, in St Thomas in the East, Jamaica, 1776. [DCA.H1620]
TRAN, ROBERT, a wright in Greenock, then in Jamaica, 1811. [NAS.CS38.2.57]
TRAVERS, HORACE, Asst. Commissary General, died in Jamaica, 26 June 1867. [S#7487]
TRENCH, WILLIAM, son of William Trench a merchant in Jamaica, at King's College, Aberdeen, 1824-1826. [KCA#2.454]
TROTTER, JOHN, a merchant in Kingston, Jamaica, 1755. [NAS.AC7.47.598]
TROUP, GEORGE, in Jamaica, 1788. [NAS.NRAS.1368/118]
TROUP, JAMES, a witness in Jamaica, 1780; late of Jamaica, 15 Mar1785. [NAS.RD2.234.1086; RS29.120]
TROUP, WILLIAM, born 1822, a clerk, emigrated from Aberdeen aboard the Rob Roy bound for Jamaica, arrived at Kingston on 11 May 1841. [NA.CO140/33]
TULLOCH, JAMES PRENDERGAST, clerk in Greencastle, St Mary's, Jamaica, a witness in Kingston, Jamaica, 1783. [NAS.RD2.236/2.612; RD3.246.892]
TULLOCH, Dr JAMES, late surgeon in Jamaica, father of Robert apprenticed in Edinburgh, 1799. [REA]
TULLOCH, JOHN, of Tulloch Castle, born 1769 in Ross-shire, died in St James's, Jamaica, 1837. [Kensington MI, Jamaica]
TURING, Sir INGLIS, born 4 Dec 1743, son of Reverend Alexander Turing and his wife Anna Brown in Foveran, Aberdeenshire, chaplain to the 52nd Foot and rector of St Thomas in the Vale, Jamaica, died there on 15 Nov 1791. [Gl.Cr.57][GM.61.1235][F.6.179]
TURNBULL, DAVID, son of David Turnbull [1720-1788] and Janet Whyte [1731-1784], died in Jamaica. [Dunfermline MI]
TURNBULL, JAMES, born 1805, son of William Turnbull and Jean Colquhoun, died in Jamaica, 29 Aug 1807. [St Ninian's MI]
TURNBULL, Mrs MARGARET, relict of Alexander Turnbull in Jamaica, died in Aberdeen, 20 Apr 1836. [AJ#4609]

TURNBULL, THOMAS, a Covenanter from Argyll, imprisoned in Edinburgh Tolbooth, who was transported from Leith to Jamaica in Aug 1685. [RPCS.XI.330]

TURNBULL, Rev. WALTER, born 30 Apr 1817 in Hawick, settled at Mt. Zion, St James's, Jamaica, 16 Aug 1849, died there 16 Mar 1850. [Mt. Zion MI, Jamaica]

TURNER, WILLIAM, Jamaica, MD Edinburgh University, 1819. [EMG#63]

TURNER, Mrs, relict of Mr Turner in Jamaica, died at Shakespeare Square, Edinburgh, 12 Jan 1799. [AJ#2664]

TYTLER, ALEXANDER, born Edinburgh, 20 June 1784, son of James Tytler of Woodhouselee and Elizabeth Carmichael, died at Fort Henderson, Jamaica, 14 May 1841. [Greyfriars MI, Edinburgh]

URQUHART, HECTOR, born 1816, with Margaret, born 1813, Daniel, born 1837, and Hector, aged 5 months, emigrated from Aberdeen aboard the Rob Roy bound for Jamaica, arrived at Kingston on 11 May 1841. [NA.CO140/33]

URQUHART, Mr., from Greenock aboard the brig Jane bound for Jamaica, arrived there in July 1794. [JRG:2.8.1794]

VALENTINE, HENRY, born 1819, arrived at Bluefields, Westmoreland, Jamaica, on 23 Jan 1841 aboard the William Pirie, from Stranraer. [NA.CO.140/33]

VEZEY, GEORGE, a book-keeper on Bellmont Estate, Jamaica, a witness, 1821. [NAS.RD5.239.54]

VINT, WILLIAM, in Jamaica, son of Thomas Vint in Craigflower, 1794. [NAS.RS.Fife.4031]

VIRTUE, DAVID, overseer, Paradise, Vere, Jamaica, a witness, 1811. [NAS.RD4.295.254]

VIRTUE, DANIEL, a planter in Jamaica, died 16 Nov 1823, inventory, 1836. [NAS.SC70.1.54; C1552]

WADDELL, JAMES, born 1753, a merchant in Jamaica, husband of Mary Dunbar, deeds, 1818, 1824, died in St Andrew's, Jamaica, 18 Nov 1825. [FH#203][EEC#18842][NAS.RD5.146.1; 278.381]; possibly father of James Waddell, born 1816, at Edinburgh Academy 1824-1828. [EAR]

WADDELL, Mrs, relict of James Waddell [1753-1825], died in Kingston, Jamaica, 18 Jan 1826. [AJ#4084][EEC#17878]

WADDELL, Mrs, relict of Matthew Waddell in Jamaica, died in Lanark, 1817. [S#18]

WALKER, ANN, relict of Dr James Walker, Jamaica, died 19 July 1836. [AJ#4620]

WALKER, DAVID, from Leith to Jamaica on the Roselle, arrived in Kingston in Apr 1793. [JRG:27.4.1793]

WALKER, DAVID, a saddler from Cupar, died in Jamaica, 2 Dec 1838. [FH.27.6.1839]

WALKER, DAVID, late of Westmoreland, Jamaica, died in Leslie, 26 July 1841. [AJ#4883]

WALKER, DONALD, a rebel and farmer from Otter, Argyll, imprisoned in Edinburgh Tolbooth, transported from Leith to Jamaica in Aug 1685. [ETR#373]

WALKER, DUNCAN, a rebel from Argyll who was transported from Leith to Jamaica in Aug 1685. [RPCS.XI.136]

WALKER, GEORGE P., born 1823, a book-keeper, emigrated from Aberdeen aboard the Rob Roy bound for Jamaica, arrived at Kingston on 11 May 1841. [NA.CO140/33]

WALKER, HUGH, of Carron Hall, died in Jamaica, 17 Aug 1820. [AJ#3801]

WALKER, ISOBEL, born 1771, daughter of Rev. William Walker and Margaret Manderston in Collessie, Fife, married Paul Samuels of Negril Spots, Jamaica, died at 15 Rutland Street, Edinburgh, 9 Feb 1853. [F.3.135][EEC#22393]

WALKER, JAMES, born 2 Oct 1791, second son of William Walker of Dempsterton and Allison Lyon, died in Jamaica, 1813. ['Lyons of Cossins and West Ogil', Edinburgh, 1901]

WALKER, JAMES, from Montrose, Angus, in Jamaica, inventory, 1826. [NAS.SC70.1.34]

WALKER, JAMES, in St Ann's, Jamaica, died 31 Oct 1827, inventory, 1829, Comm. Edinburgh. [NAS]

WALKER, JAMES, in Jamaica, testament, 10 Nov 1829. [NAS.CC8.152.195]

WALKER, JAMES, born 1784, son of William Walker and Isabella McIntyre, a planter in St Anne's, Jamaica, died in Dunoon, 16 Apr 1844. [Cardross MI]

WALKER, JOHN, born 1818, a servant, arrived at Bluefields, Westmoreland, Jamaica, on 23 Jan 1841 aboard the William Pirie, from Stranraer. [NA.CO.140/33]

WALKER, MARGARET, third daughter of Hugh Walker in Jamaica, married Dr James Stewart of Tulloch, in Edinburgh, 3 Aug 1840. [AJ#4831]

WALKER, ROBERT, in St James's, Jamaica, 1790. [NAS.RS61.263]

WALKER, WILLIAM, transported from Leith to Jamaica in Aug 1685. [RPCS.XI.136]

WALKER, WILLIAM, an indentured servant who absconded in Jamaica – *"a lusty well-set fellow, about five feet ten inches high, of a ruddy complexion, pretty much marked with the small pox ... two pistols reward"*. June 1754. [JC#254]

WALKER, WILLIAM, born 1768, son of Rev. William Walker and Margaret Manderston in Collessie, Fife, an attorney who died in Jamaica 1799. [F.3.135]

WALKER, WILLIAM, an overseer, Bellmont Estate, Jamaica, a witness, 1821. [NAS.RD5.239.54]

SCOTS IN JAMAICA, 1655-1855

WALKER, Mr., from Greenock aboard the Friends, Captain Dunlop, bound for Jamaica, arrived there in Oct 1794. [JRG:25.10.1794]

WALLACE, FRANCES, only daughter of Hugh Wallace of Ricony, Jamaica, married Alexander Home Renton, MD, in Madeira, 21 Apr 1836.[AJ#4614]

WALLACE, HUGH, son of Thomas Wallace of Cairnhill, in Westmoreland, Jamaica, 1764. [NAS.RS81.7.167]

WALLACE, HUGH, from Greenock, a planter-merchant at Biscany, Jamaica, 1820s. [NAS.CS239.W36/1; CS96.4515]

WALLACE, HUGH, born in Jamaica, first son of Hugh Wallace of Biscany, matriculated at Glasgow University in 1774. [MAGU]

WALLACE, HUGH RITCHIE, born in Glasgow, first son of Hugh Wallace formerly of Biscany, Jamaica, matriculated at Glasgow University in 1802. [MAGU#201]

WALLACE, JAMES, in Jamaica, a burgess of Edinburgh, 1749. [EBR]

WALLACE, JAMES, in Savanna-la-Mar, Jamaica, 1780. [NA.CO137.1-35]

WALLACE, JAMES, born 1789, son of John Wallace a teacher, died in Jamaica, 23 Jan 1820. [Blackfriars MI, Glasgow]

WALLACE, JAMES, in Kingston, Jamaica, married Anne Maria Brooks niece of John Smith, Salisbury Plain, St Andrew's, Jamaica, at Halfway Tree House, Jamaica, 12 Jan 1830. [PA#35]

WALLACE, JAMES, in Kingston, Jamaica, married Alison, second daughter of Robert Tullos late of Cupar, in Markinch, 14 July 1835. [AJ#4567]

WALLACE, Mrs JAMES, died in Kingston, Jamaica, 5 Jan 1834. [FJ.5.4.1834]

WALLACE, JANET, guilty of infanticide, imprisoned in Edinburgh Tolbooth, who was transported from Leith to Jamaica in Aug 1685. [RPCS.XI.330][ETR#369]

WALLACE, JOHN, late of Jamaica, now of Neilstonwell, husband of Janet, daughter of Richard Colquhoun in St Kitts, 1765. [NAS.NRAS.0623.T-MJ.424]

WALLACE, MARGARET, in Savanna-la-Mar, Jamaica, 1780. [NA.CO137.1-35]

WALLACE, PETER, born 1764, died 15 July 1782. [Kingston MI, Jamaica]

WALLACE, WILLIAM, a merchant in Jamaica, a burgess of Edinburgh, 1752. [EBR]

WALLACE, WILLIAM, born in Jamaica, third son of Hugh Wallace a settler there, matriculated at Glasgow University in 1775. [MAGU]

WALLEN, JOHN, son of Matthew Wallen in Jamaica, MA Marischal College, Aberdeen, 1773. [MCA.II.346]

WALLIS, JOHN, born 1717, a merchant in Kingston, Jamaica, died 7 Nov 1746. [Kingston MI, Jamaica]

WALSH, ELEANOR, in Jamaica, a deed, 7 June 1828. [NAS.RD5.365.312]

WALSH, JOHN, a merchant in Jamaica, 1789. [NAS.AC.Decreets.53]

WARREN, JOHN, a planter in Jamaica, 1776. [NLS.ms8794/5]

SCOTS IN JAMAICA, 1655-1855

WATERS, JOHN, in St Mary's, Jamaica, died Mar 1834, inventory, 1834. [NAS.SC70.1.51; C1125]

WATHERSTON, JOHN, formerly in Greenlaw, late of Jamaica, letters of administration, 1808. [NAS.GD2.384]

WATSON, ALEXANDER, a merchant burgess of Glasgow, to Jamaica 1668, died on Nevis. [NAS.Unextracted Processes, 1671]

WATSON, ALEXANDER, son of Dr David Watson in Jamaica, at King's College, Aberdeen, 1791. [KCA#2/373]

WATSON, ANDREW, son of John Watson in Jamaica, at Marischal College, Aberdeen, 1779-1783, later a schoolmaster in Aberdeenshire. [MCA.II.355]

WATSON, GEORGE, in Jamaica, died 3 Apr 1835, inventory, 1835. [NAS.SC70.1.53; C1369]

WATSON, GILBERT, steerage passenger from Greenock to Jamaica aboard the Mary of Glasgow in Nov 1773. [NAS.CE60]

WATSON, or CULLEN, Mrs ISABELLA, widow of John Cullen late of the Bengal Horse Artillery, died in Jamaica, 3 Apr 1834, inventory, 1854, Comm. Edinburgh. [NAS][AJ#4511]

WATSON, JAMES, in Port Royal, probate 25 May 1669, Jamaica.

WATSON, JAMES, in Jamaica, 1744. [NAS.NRAS.859.box 25, fr.2]

WATSON, JAMES, a merchant in Kingston, Jamaica, deeds, 1749. [NAS.RD2.167.216; 170.264]

WATSON, JAMES, from Berwickshire, a merchant in Jamaica, 1769. [NAS.RS18.15.353]

WATSON, Rev. JAMES, born in Johnstone 11 Feb 1799, pastor and missionary in Jamaica 1827-1868, died in Edinburgh, 17 May 1873. [Lucea MI, Jamaica] [St Andrew's Presbyterian Church MI][AUPC]

WATSON, JAMES, from Aberdour, graduated MA from King's College, Aberdeen, 1847, a minister in Jamaica. [KCA#296]

WATSON, JOHN, son of Captain Andrew Watson, a merchant in Jamaica, a burgess of Edinburgh, 1792. [EBR]

WATSON, JOHN, Jamaica, married Ann Baillie Wood, born 19 June 1782 in Rosemarkie, daughter of Rev. Alexander Wood and Janet Houston, in Jamaica, 1805. [F.7.23]

WATSON, THOMAS, a surgeon, son of William Watson in Glasgow, died at Black River, Jamaica, 31 July 1798. [AJ#2652]

WATSON, WILLIAM, a Covenanter from Islay, who was transported from Leith to Jamaica in Aug 1685. [RPCS.XI.136]

WATSON, WILLIAM, from Aberdeen, a merchant in Port Royal, 1689, executor to John McFarlane, probate 1690, Jamaica.

WATSON, WILLIAM, late of Jamaica, then in Fife, 1782. [NAS.GD7.2.23]

SCOTS IN JAMAICA, 1655-1855

WATSON, WILLIAM, late in Jamaica, died in Perth,1786. [GM.IX.420/21]
WATT, Mrs AGNES GLENNIE, from Inverurie, Aberdeenshire, died in St George's Plain Estate, Savanna-la-Mar, Jamaica, 8 Sep 1865. [AJ:4.11.1865]
WATT, ALEXANDER, son of Alexander Watt MD in Jamaica, at King's College, Aberdeen, 1796-1800. [KCA#2/380]
WATT, EDWARD LINDSAY, from Jamaica, MD Edinburgh University, 1818. [EMG#57]
WATT, ELIZA, born 1824, with Jane Watt born 1820, arrived at Bluefields, Westmoreland, Jamaica, on 23 Jan 1841 aboard the William Pirie, from Stranraer. [NA.CO.140/33]
WATT, JOHN, from Jamaica, MD Edinburgh University, 1809. [EMG#42]
WATT, PETER, husband of Agnes Glennie Watt, died in Jamaica, 12 Sep 1865. [AJ:4.11.1865]
WATT, R., from Kirkwall, a planter in St George's, Jamaica, 1778. [NAS.GD31.390]
WATT, ROBERT, son of Alexander Watt MD in Jamaica, at King's College, Aberdeen, 1796-1800, possibly MD Edinburgh University, 1803. [KCA#2/3810][EMG#34]
WATT, ROBERT, Member of Assembly for St Elizabeth, Jamaica, died at Montego Bay, 8 Mar 1841. [GSP.654]
WAUCHOPE, ANDREW, after 50 years in Jamaica, died at Cooper's Hill, Honore, Jamaica, 1803. [AJ#2930]
WAUCHOPE, MARY RIDDELL, late of Jamaica, died in Loanhead, 22 Oct 1839. [AJ#4780]
WAUGH, JOHN, born in Melrose 179-, '21 years in Jamaica', died in Melrose, 27 Dec 1832. [Melrose MI]
WAUGH, PATRICK, in Jamaica, 1811. [NAS.GD171.985]
WAUGH, PETER, son of Thomas Waugh a merchant in Leith, died in Jamaica, May 1807. [AJ#3107][DPCS#262]
WEBSTER, THOMAS, a servant, died in Jamaica, June 1749. [AJ#107]
WEBSTER, THOMAS, born 1818, arrived at Bluefields, Westmoreland, Jamaica, on 23 Jan 1841 aboard the William Pirie, from Stranraer. [NA.CO.140/33]
WEDDERBURN, ALEXANDER, born 1739, died in Westmoreland, Jamaica, 1764. [Blue Castle MI, Jamaica]
WEDDERBURN, ALEXANDER, born 1741, died in Westmoreland, Jamaica, 1771. [Blue Castle MI, Jamaica]
WEDDERBURN, JAMES, in Jamaica, son of Sir John Wedderburn of Blackness, deeds, 1764, 1774. [NAS.RD2.286.408; RD4.272.176]
WEDDERBURN, JAMES, born 1752, died in Westmoreland, Jamaica, 17 July 1797, probate, 1799, PCC. [Paradise MI, Jamaica][NAS.GD1.8.36.3]

SCOTS IN JAMAICA, 1655-1855

WEDDERBURN, JOHN, in Hanover, Jamaica, son of John Wedderburn of Blackness, was granted the lands of Idvies, 6 Aug 1766; 1772. [NAS.RGS.109.12; RS35.XV.104][DCA.H1931]

WEDDERBURN, JOHN, born 18 Aug 1776 in Inveresk, son of James Wedderburn, at Glasgow University 1789, to Jamaica 1794, died there 19 May 1799. [MAGU#157]

WEDDERBURN, PETER, born 1736, died in Westmoreland, Jamaica, 1773. [Blue Castle MI, Jamaica]

WEDDERSPOON, LAURENCE, born 1701, died 25 Apr 1788. [Tennant's Estate MI, Clarendon, Jamaica]

WEDDERSTON, JOHN, youngest son of the late John Wedderston a smith, a surgeon in Jamaica, 1773. [NAS.CS16.1.-]

WEIR, ALEXANDER, a physician in Jamaica, dead by 1808. [NAS.RD4.283.895]

WEIR, JAMES, a merchant in Charleston, South Carolina, 1771-1778, a Loyalist who settled in Jamaica, 1782. [NA.AO12.51.249]

WEIR, JOHN, a Covenanter who was transported from Leith to Jamaica in Aug 1685. [RPCS.XI.130]

WEIR, JOHN, graduated MD from King's College, Aberdeen, 8 Nov 1794, a surgeon in Jamaica. [KCA#140]

WEIR, JOHN, born 1766, son of John Weir and Jean Martin in Lesmahagow, died in Jamaica, 1796. [Lesmahagow, Lanarkshire, MI]

WEIR, ROBERT, Unity Estate, Portland, Jamaica, 1790. [NAS.CS16.1.173/416]

WEIR, THOMAS, a Covenanter in Lesmahagow, Lanarkshire, who was transported from Leith to Jamaica in Aug 1685, landed at Port Royal in Nov 1685. [RPCS.XI.329][LJ#225]

WEIR, THOMAS, a merchant in Jamaica, died in London, testament, 14 June 1740. [NAS.CC8.8.103]

WEIR, THOMAS, his wife Mary Yates, and children William and Margaret, in Port Royal, Jamaica, 1786. [NAS.RD2.264.402]

WEIR, Dr WILLIAM, born 1812, eldest son of Dr Weir in Roxburghshire, died at Montpelier, Clarendon, Jamaica, 17 Nov 1841. [AJ#4909]

WELCH, ..., son of Rev. John Welch, was born in Goshen, Jamaica, 10 Nov 1869. [S#8232]

WELSH, JAMES, in Kingston, Jamaica, a burgess of Arbroath, 1789. [ArBR]

WEST, JOHN, born 10 Apr 1756 in Logie, Fife, son of Rev. West and Margaret Mein, at St Andrews University, 1776, a minister, to Jamaica, 1785, died there 17 Oct 1817. [EMA#62][FPA.21/316]

WEST, MAURICE, a merchant in Kingston, Jamaica, co-owner of Glasgow ships, 1793-1803. [NAS.CE60.11.3/65,72; 5/21; G/1/67/106; 8/27]

WEST, STEWART, died in Kingston, Jamaica, 12 Nov 1830. [EEC#18603]

SCOTS IN JAMAICA, 1655-1855

WHITE, ANDREW, a plumber at Old Harbour, Jamaica, inventory, 1854. [NAS.SC70.1.82]

WHITE, DAVID, born 1730 in Ayrshire, resident in Jamaica later in Bristol, died 27 Nov 1797. [Bristol Cathedral MI]

WHITE, HUGH, second son of Samuel White lately a merchant in Jamaica, matriculated at Glasgow University in 1757. [MAGU]

WHITE, JAMES, a minister, son of Reverend George White in Maryculter, Aberdeenshire, emigrated to Kingston, Jamaica, before 1692. [APB.2.188]

WHITE, JAMES, a planter in Jamaica, later in Newmilns, testament, 10 Dec 1825, Comm. Dumfries. [NAS.CC5.4.141]

WHITE, JOHN, son of David White in Jamaica, at King's College, Aberdeen, 1806-1810, graduated MA. [KCA#2/400]

WHITE, JOHN, St Elizabeth's, Jamaica, 1811. [NAS.GD2.252]

WHITELAW, THOMAS, late in Jamaica, now in Glasgow, 1782; a witness in Kingston, Jamaica, 1784. [NAS.CS17.1.1/61, 123; RD4.255.417]

WHYTE, GORDON, a millwright in Jamaica, third son of Rev. Thomas Whyte in Libberton, a deed, 1790. [NAS.RD2.249.1059]

WHYTE, MALCOLM, a rebel from Argyll, transported from Leith to Jamaica in Aug 1685. [RPCS.XI.126]

WIGHT, ALEXANDER, a merchant in Jamaica, testament, 19 Sep1785. [NAS.CC8.8.127]

WIGHT, CHARLES, a merchant in Jamaica, 18 Apr 1833. [NAS.RS.Edinburgh.42/47]

WIGHT, MARION, daughter of Alexander Wight WS, wife of Dr Peter Daly Murray, died at Fort Auga, Jamaica, 15 Feb 1841. [EEC#20193]

WIGHT, ROBERT, in Jamaica, 1821. [NAS.CS17.1.40/292]

WIGHT, WILLIAM, late of Jamaica, died in Edinburgh, 28 Mar 1817. [S.I.1]

WILKIE, DAVID, from Glasgow, in Jamaica, died 12 Oct 1808, testament, 13 Apr 1809. [NAS.CC8.8.137]

WILKIE, THOMAS, a merchant in Glasgow, later in Kingston, Jamaica, died 1794, testament, 22 Nov 1794. [NAS.CC8.8.129]

WILKIN, JOHN, born 1798, son of James Wilkin, a farmer in Kirkblain, and Helen McMorine, died in Jamaica, 17 Oct 1815. [Caerlaverock MI]

WILKIN, WILLIAM, born 1789, son of James Wilkin, a farmer in Kirkblain, and Helen McMorine, died in Jamaica, 22 June 1827. [Caerlaverock MI]

WILL, ANDREW, a Lieutenant of the 92nd Highlanders, died in Jamaica, 7 Oct 1819. [Brechin Cathedral MI]

WILLIAMS, CHARLOTTE STEWART HISLOP, daughter of William Williams in Westmoreland, Jamaica, married Dr D. Dewar, 11 May 1857. [EEC#21027]

SCOTS IN JAMAICA, 1655-1855

WILLIAMSON, ALEXANDER, in Jamaica, 1780, later in Haughs of Edinglassie, testament, 23 Dec 1791, Comm. Aberdeen. [NAS. RD4.249.742]

WILLIAMSON, JAMES, son of John Williamson a writer in Annan, and Dorothea Wallace, settled in St Ann's, Jamaica, died 1793. [Annan MI]

WILLIAMSON, JOHN, a surgeon in St Thomas in the Vale, Jamaica, 1798 -1812.

WILLIAMSON, JOHN, born 1805, son of John Williamson and Jane Russell in Blackdam, died in Jamaica, 16 Nov 1850. [Dipple MI]

WILLIAMSON, ROBERT, born 23 Apr1780, son of Rev. John Williamson and Janet ....., a surgeon in St James, Jamaica. [F.2.298]

WILLIAMSON, ROBERT, husband of Catherine Campbell, to Jamaica, Captain of the 3rd West Indian Regiment, died in Jamaica, 1798. [NAS.CS26.911.10]

WILLIAMSON, SINCLAIR, a merchant at Ocho Rios Bay, Jamaica, died in Cuba, June 1809. [PC#34]

WILLIAMSON, THOMAS, in St Elizabeth's, Cornwall, Jamaica, 1822, 1823. [NAS.SC49.48.25.18/100; RD2.272.272]

WILLIAMSON, WILLIAM, educated at King's College, Aberdeen, an Anglican minister to Jamaica, 1793, later in St Thomas in the Vale. [FPA#136]

WILLIAMSON, WILLIAM, born 1787 in Elgin, settled at Mount Holstein, Portland, Jamaica, died 28 Nov 1855. [Cedar Valley MI, Jamaica]

WILLIAMSON, ..., from Greenock to Jamaica on the _Bell_, arrived in Kingston in Jan 1793. [JRG:19.1.1793]

WILLIS, GEORGE, a surgeon, died at Golden Grove, Trelawney, Jamaica, 30 Dec 1812. [AJ#3405]

WILLIS, GEORGE, a surgeon, son of Thomas Willis in Kirkcaldy, Fife, died in Bellemont, Jamaica, 16 Dec 1825. [AJ#4032]

WILLIS, THOMAS, of Annandale, MD, died in Annandale, St Ann's, Jamaica, 6 Sep 1841. [AJ#4898][EEC#20284]

WILSON, ADAM, son of John Wilson of Mountgrew, died at St Ann's Bay, Jamaica, 10 Nov 1850. [AJ#5374]

WILSON, ALEXANDER, son of John Wilson of Mountgrew, died in Jamaica, 1834. [AH#15.11.1834]

WILSON, ANN, born 1787, relict of James Colquhoun Grant, late of Jamaica, died in Glasgow, 21 Aug 1845. [W#602]

WILSON, CHARLES, a planter in Trelawney, Jamaica, died 25 Mar 1843, inventory, 1834. [NAS.SC70.1.66; E229]

WILSON, GEORGE, a mason at Roslyn Castle, Jamaica, died 9 Mar 1834, inventory, 1834. [NAS.SC70.1.51; D652]

WILSON, JAMES, in St James, Cornwall, Jamaica, a testament, 1814. [NAS.RD5.271.425]

WILSON, JAMES, born 1796, died in Jamaica, 27 July 1828. [Monigaff MI]

SCOTS IN JAMAICA, 1655-1855

WILSON, JAMES, born 1745, late of Jamaica, died in Macduff, 5 Oct 1829. [Macduff MI]

WILSON, JAMES, born 1815, 5th son of John Wilson in Banffshire, died in Smallwood, St Catherine's, Jamaica, 2 Mar 1840. [AJ#4820]

WILSON, JAMES, born 1811, emigrated from Aberdeen aboard the Rob Roy bound for Jamaica, arrived at Kingston on 11 May 1841. [NA.CO140/33]

WILSON, JOHN, a planter in St Elizabeth's, Jamaica, 1797. [NAS.NRAS.0623.TMJ.27/26]

WILSON, JOHN, son of John Wilson of Mountgrew, died at St Ann's Bay, Jamaica, Dec 1850. [AJ#5374]

WILSON, JOHN, born 1801, late of Keith, died at Draxhall, Jamaica, 5 Dec 1850. [W#1185][EEC#22071]

WILSON, JOHN, Postmaster General of Jamaica, inventory, 1851. [NAS.SC70.1.73]

WILSON, JOHN, died in Georgia, Jamaica, 12 July 1878. [EC#29317]

WILSON, MARY, born 1816, arrived at Bluefields, Westmoreland, Jamaica, on 23 Jan 1841 aboard the William Pirie, from Stranraer. [NA.CO.140/33]

WILSON, ROBERT, a planter in St Andrew's, Jamaica, 1754. [NA.CO137/28]

WILSON, ROBERT, in Kingston, Jamaica, May 1774. [Caribbeanna.6/23]

WILSON, ROBERT, born 26 Feb 1791 in Cluny, son of Nathaniel Wilson and Euphemia Angus at the Mill of Kincardine, died in Jamaica, 19 Dec 1814. [Aboyne, Aberdeenshire, MI]

WILSON, WILLIAM, son of Adam Wilson in Glasgow, at King's College, Aberdeen, 1820-1823, a merchant in Jamaica and in New South Wales. [KCA#2.441]

WILSON, ..., from Glasgow aboard the Mary bound for Jamaica, arrived in Kingston in May 1793. [JRG:18.5.1793]

WILSON, ..., daughter of F. W. G. Wilson, was born in Lucca, Jamaica, 4 Apr 1851. [AJ#5392]

WINCHESTER, WILLIAM, a planter in St Andrew's, Jamaica, 1754. [NA.CO137/28]

WINGATE, JOHN, a merchant in Trelawney, Jamaica, 1794. [NAS.RD4.255.660]

WOOD, JOHN, from Jamaica, married Isobel Philip in Edinburgh, 21 June 1761. [EMR]

WOOD, JOHN, born 28 June 1797, son of Rev. Charles Wood and Mary Gray in Wiston, died on Grange estate, Jamaica, 13 Jan 1819. [S.3.117][F.3.322]

WOOD, JOSEPH, born 29 July 1770 in Rosemarkie, son of Rev. John Wood and Sophia Irvine, to Jamaica, died 21 Feb 1811. [F.7.23]

WOOD, ROBERT, a physician-surgeon, HM Naval Base, Port Royal, Jamaica, will, 1786. [NAS.RD2.264.402]

SCOTS IN JAMAICA, 1655-1855

WOOD, SOPHIA, born 4 Oct 1775 in Rosemarkie, Ross and Cromarty, daughter of Rev. Alexander Wood and Janet Houston, married James Fowler of Grange, in Jamaica, 1792. [F.7.23]

WOOD, WILLIAM, late in Jamaica, died at Port Glasgow on 24 Oct 1806. [GrA: 31.10.1806][NAS.RD.Renfrew#8647; SC58.1.9]

WOOD, Mr., from Glasgow aboard the Betsy and Brothers bound for Jamaica, arrived in Kingston in May 1793. [JRG:25.5.1794]

WOODROW, ANDREW, born 1830, son of Andrew Woodrow and Janet Allen, died in Jamaica, June 1869. [Campsie MI]

WOODROW, JOHN, son of Andrew Woodrow and Janet Allen, died in Jamaica, Mar 1868. [Campsie MI]

WOODS, GEORGE, born 1812, arrived at Bluefields, Westmoreland, Jamaica, on 23 Jan 1841 aboard the William Pirie, from Stranraer. [NA.CO.140/33]

WORDIE, JAMES, born 1799, third son of Thomas Wordie a craftsman in Denny, at Glasgow University, 1809, a minister in Kingston, Jamaica, 1823-1843, then in Cupar, died 3 Aug 1862. [F.7.671][MAGU#241]

WRIGHT, BUCHAN WARREN, son of Robert Wright MD in Jamaica, at King's College, Aberdeen, 1824-1826, surgeon HEICS, MD Edinburgh, 1837. [MCA][KCA#2.455]

WRIGHT, JOHN, a merchant in Jamaica, a burgess and guildsbrother of Ayr, 4 Apr 1751. [AyrBR]

WRIGHT, NICOLA ELIZA, in Jamaica, died 20 May 1835, inventory, 1858. [NAS.SC70.1.96]

WRIGHT, Dr ROBERT BENSTEAD, MD Edinburgh University, 1803; husband of Nicola Watson from Edinburgh; in Southampton, Jamaica, deeds, 1808; in Kensworth, Jamaica, died at Snowden, Manchester, Jamaica, 19 Nov 1820. [EMG#40][EEC#17109][NAS.RD3.324.703; RD5.208.131]

WYSE, THOMAS, eldest son of David Wyse in Clermont, Jamaica, died in Hillbank, Dundee, 1816. [Laurencekirk MI]

YOUNG, Miss EDMONSTONE, from Glasgow, died in Kingston, Jamaica, 1817. [S#19]

YOUNG, EDWARD JAMES, of Mt. Stewart, Westmoreland, Jamaica, married Helen, second daughter of Thomas Grieve, Buccleugh Place, Edinburgh, in Glasgow, 1837. [DPCA#1841]; son of Rev. Young of Inverness Academy, died at Melrose Castle, Manchester, Jamaica, 22 Jan 1844. [W#5.42]

YOUNG, EDWARD JAMES, born 5 Oct 1838 in Shettlewood Pen, [SG#727]; eldest son of Edward James Young in Melrose, Manchester, Jamaica, died on the Kelvin off Calloa, Sep 1858. [CM#21780]

SCOTS IN JAMAICA, 1655-1855

YOUNG, GEORGE, a Covenanter from Teviotdale, Roxburghshire, who was transported from Leith to Jamaica in Aug 1685, landed in Port Royal during Nov 1685. [RPCS.XI.329][LJ#17]

YOUNG, JAMES, a Covenanter from Netherfield, Avondale, Lanarkshire, imprisoned in Edinburgh Tolbooth, who was transported from Leith to Jamaica in Aug 1685. [RPCS.XI.129][ETR#373]

YOUNG, JAMES, was banished by the High Court of the Justiciary and transported to Jamaica 13 Feb 1749. [EBR: Black Book, 1736-1755]

YOUNG, JAMES, a planter in St Andrew's, Jamaica, 1754. [NA.CO137/28]

YOUNG, JAMES, born 1742 in Uphall, '22 years a planter in Jamaica', died in Edinburgh, 10 Nov 1784. [Uphall MI, West Lothian]

YOUNG, JAMES, an overseer, St James, Jamaica, 1774. [BL.Add.MS22676/8]

YOUNG, JAMES, from Stonehaven, died in Kingston, Jamaica, 1805. [AJ#3033]

YOUNG, JAMES, in Pimento Grove, St Dorothy's, Jamaica, son of John Young in Glasgow, died in Jamaica, 12 Oct 1838. [SG#8/745]

YOUNG, JOHN, born 1728, son of John Young, a weaver, and Helen Brown in Milnathort, '12 years in Jamaica', died in Milnathort, 10 Jan 1774. [Milnathort, Kinross, MI]

YOUNG, JOHN, son of William Young a merchant in Glasgow, died in Trelawney, Jamaica, 26 Dec 1817. [AJ#3660][S.I.29]

YOUNG, JOHN, born 1824, arrived at Bluefields, Westmoreland, Jamaica, on 23 Jan 1841 aboard the William Pirie, from Stranraer. [NA.CO.140/33]

YOUNG, JOHN, first son of John Young in Jamaica, matriculated at Glasgow University in 1833. [MAGU]

YOUNG, ROBERT BERRY, an overseer on Papine Estate, Jamaica, son of Thomas Young a teacher in Edinburgh, died in Jamaica, 5 Jan 1809. [EA#4712]

YOUNG, THOMAS, second son of James Young a brewer in Leith, died in Jamaica, 24 Oct 1798. [AJ#2661]

YOUNG, THOMAS, born 18 May 1758 in Leslie, son of Rev. Robert Young and Jean Newton, died in Jamaica. [F.5.110]

YOUNG, WILLIAM, from Berwickshire, in Jamaica, 1773. [NAS.RS18.16.222]

YOUNG, WILLIAM, born 1748, a planter, via London to Jamaica on the Dawes, Dec 1775. [NA.T47.9/11]

YOUNG, WILLIAM, born in Uphall 1800, son of Alexander Young and Joan Quarrier, settled in Trelawney, Jamaica, letter/will, died 28 Mar 1815. [NAS.RH1/2.804/1][Uphall, West Lothian, MI]

YOUNGER, THOMAS, born 16 Aug 1747, son of Andrew Younger and Helen House, from Glasgow, then in Wilmington, North Carolina, died in Lucie, Jamaica, 1795. [GM.65.794]

YUILLE, ANDREW, in Jamaica, 1783. [NAS.CS96.647]

SCOTS IN JAMAICA, 1655-1855

SOME SHIPPING LINKS

Acadia, master John Marshall, from Greenock to Jamaica in Jan 1786. [NAS.E504.15.42]

Adam and Betty of Inverkeithing, master David Inglis, from Leith to Jamaica in Nov 1763. [NAS.E504.22.11]

Adventure, a snow, master .... Smith, from Glasgow to Jamaica in Aug 1749; master James Hamilton, arrived in Kingston, Jamaica, during June 1754 from Leith. [AJ#83][JC#295][NAS.AC7.47.598]

Alexander, master Raeside, from Greenock to Jamaica, Sept 1796. [NAS.E504.15.73]

Betty of Glasgow, a doggar, from Port Glasgow to Jamaica and return in 1729. [NAS.AC.Decreets.35.354]

Champion of Leith, 130 tons, master Robert Spiers, from Leith to Jamaica, in Oct 1775. [NAS.E504.22.20]

Charming Molly of Fort William, from Fort William with 66 passengers bound for Jamaica in June 1734, arrived at Port Royal in Sep 1734. [NLS.NRAS.1279]

Edinburgh, from Leith to Jamaica in 1789, shipwrecked on voyage. [NAS.AC.Decreets.52]

Elizabeth of Montrose, master David Gentleman, from Montrose to Jamaica in 1716. [NAS.AC.Decreets.23.100; 26.908]

Fortitude, master ...... Johnson, arrived in Kingston on 25 Aug 1781 from Glasgow. [CCGA]

Grandvale of Glasgow, master William Hamilton, from Greenock to Jamaica in Jan 1773. [NAS.E504.15.22]

Hope of Greenock, master John Hunter, from Greenock to Jamaica, Aug 1796. [NAS.E504.15.73]

Hume, master ... McLean, arrived in Kingston on 21 Dec 1776 from Glasgow. [CCGA]

Janet, from Greenock to Jamaica in Jan 1774. [NAS.CE60.1.7]

Jupiter of Aberdeen, master Arthur Gibbon, from Aberdeen to Jamaica, in Apr 1761. [NAS.E504.1.7]

Lady Forbes, master David Gourlay, from Leith to Falmouth, Montego Bay, and Lucea, 1809. *'millwrights, plumbers, and tradesmen, will meet with good encouragement'*. [EA.XCII.4786]

Lark, from Jamaica to Inverness, 1733. [NAS.AC.Decreets.40.276]

Lillie, from Greenock to Jamaica and return in 1729. [NAS.AC.Decreets.35.1065-1134]

Lincoln, master Joshua Richmond, from Leith to Morant Bay, Kingston, and Old Harbour, 1809. *'millwrights, plumbers, and tradesmen, will meet with good encouragement'*. [EA.XCII.4786]

Malvina of Greenock, master Hugh Hogart, from Greenock to Jamaica, Aug 1796. [NAS.E504.15.73]

Mary, master Andrew Mason, from Leith to Jamaica in Jan 1776. [NAS.E504.22.20]

Mary, master William Walkingshaw, from Greenock to Jamaica in Nov 1773, [NAS.CE60]; arrived in Montego Bay on 22 Feb 1777 from Glasgow. [CCGA]

Phoenix of Glasgow, master Alexander Houston, from Greenock to Jamaica, Sept 1796. [NAS.E504.15.73]

Rob Roy, arrived in Kingston on 11 May 1841 from Aberdeen. [NA.CO140/33]

Robert of Glasgow, master ....Hendry, from Greenock to Jamaica in Jan 1773. [NAS.E504.15.22]

Robert of Glasgow, master Alexander Murdoch, from Greenock to Jamaica in Feb 1778. [NAS.E504.15.29]

Rose, master Archibald Yuill, arrived in Greenock on 16 Oct 1728 from Jamaica. [EEC#559]

Ross of Glasgow, master John Cathcart, from Greenock to Jamaica in Jan 1773 and Nov 1773. [NAS.E504.15]

Royal Widow, master Alexander Ritchie, from Greenock to Jamaica, Apr 1755. [NAS.E504.15.7]

Royal Widow, Captain Hutcheson, from Greenock to Jamaica, Sept 1755. [NAS.E504.15.7]

Silvia of Liverpool, master James Clymens, from Scotland to Jamaica in 1718. [NAS.E508.12.6]

Swallow of Inverness, master David Nevoy, from Scotland to Jamaica in 1728; from Jamaica to Inverness, 1733. [NAS.E508.22.6; AC.Decreets.40.276]

William of Glasgow, master John Denniston, from Greenock to Jamaica in Feb 1773. [NAS.E504.15.22]

William Pirie, arrived at Bluefields, Westmoreland, Jamaica, 23 Jan 1841 from Stranraer. [NA.CO140/33]

Wilmington of Cape Fear, master Thomas Murray, from Jamaica to Leith in 1755; from Leith to Jamaica, Nov 1755. [NAS.AC.Decreets.48.595; E504.22.7]

Wolf, master ...... Marshall, arrived at Montego Bay on 10 May 1777 from Glasgow. [CCGA]

Woodstock, Captain Clark, from Greenock to Jamaica, Jan 1819. [EEC.16796]

www.ingramcontent.com/pod-product-compliance
Lightning Source LLC
Chambersburg PA
CBHW072135160426
43197CB00012B/2123